About the aut[

Jane Caro is an author, novelist, columnist, speaker, broadcaster, enthusiastic tweeter and award winning advertising writer. She is on the boards of Bell Shakespeare and the Public Education Foundation and is a timber grower and beef producer. She appears regularly on Channel 7's *Weekend Sunrise*, Channel 9 *Mornings*, ABC's *The Drum* and *Gruen Planet*. She never quite knows what she may be doing from one day to the next and likes it that way. Her husband and two daughters have learned to live with it.

Antony Loewenstein is an independent Australian journalist, photographer and blogger. He is the author of two bestselling books, *My Israel Question* and *The Blogging Revolution*, co-editor of *Left Turn* and *After Zionism* and has written for the *Guardian*, the *Nation*, *Huffington Post*, the *Sydney Morning Herald*, *Haaretz* and other prominent publications. He appears on the BBC, Al Jazeera English, ABC and many other media outlets. In 2013, he will be releasing a book, documentary and photo exhibition about disaster capitalism. His website is http://antonyloewenstein.com/

Simon Smart is a Director of the Centre for Public Christianity. A former English and History teacher, Simon studied theology at Regent College, Canada. He has years of experience writing and editing both academic curricula and popular books. He is the author of *Bright Lights Dark Nights – the enduring faith of 13 remarkable Australians* and was the editor of *A Spectator's Guide to World Views*. His writing has appeared in the *Sydney Morning Herald*, *The Australian*, *The Drum*, *The Punch* and *ABC Religion and Ethics*. Simon lives on Sydney's Northern Beaches with his wife and two children. He is an enthusiastic but inept surfer.

Rachel Woodlock, M.Islam.Std. (Melb), is an academic and writer specialising in Islam and Muslims in the West. She has worked at both the University of Melbourne and Monash University, as well as writing for *The Age* and the *ABC Religion & Ethics* website among others. Most recently, she contributed the 'Islam in Australia' section for *Oxford Bibliographies Online*, and guest edited a special edition of the State Library of Victoria's *La Trobe Journal* on the Muslim experience in Australia. When not buried under piles of books and manuscripts, she can be found cooing at cows and sheep in rural Ireland where she recently moved with husband, daughter and family cat. Her website is http://rachelwoodlock.com/

FOR GOD'S SAKE

Jane Caro, Antony Loewenstein,
Simon Smart & Rachel Woodlock

MACMILLAN
Pan Macmillan Australia

First published 2013 in Macmillan by Pan Macmillan Australia Pty Limited
1 Market Street, Sydney

National Library of Australia
Cataloguing-in-Publication data:

Caro, Jane.
For God's Sake

9781742612232 (pbk.)

Philosophy and religion.
Religious disputations.
Belief and doubt.

Other authors:
Loewenstein, Antony.
Smart, Simon.
Woodlock, Rachel.

210

Typeset in 11.5/15.5 pt Bembo by Midland Typesetters, Australia
Printed by McPherson's Printing Group

Papers used by Pan Macmillan Australia Pty Ltd are natural, recyclable products made from wood
grown in sustainable forests. The manufacturing processes conform to the environmental regulations
of the country of origin.

Contents

FIRST WORDS

FIRST WORDS

The idea for this book came originally from a publisher who approached Scott Stephens, editor of the ABC Religion & Ethics website, who in turn approached me about developing a book that would compare and contrast the views of a believer (Scott) with an unbeliever (me). For all sorts of reasons, that project didn't end up going anywhere, but I was hooked. I felt that the idea mattered because it was an opportunity to demonstrate that just because people see the world very differently doesn't mean they can't debate their views in a respectful and civil fashion. In an age of growing fundamentalism at both ends of the religious spectrum, I wanted to present a more nuanced view. (And it turned out my eventual fellow authors did, too.) Apart from that, I had already done some work, and if there's one thing I hate it's work that goes to waste!

Scott very kindly gave me permission to pursue the idea without him and it slowly evolved from a two-way debate into a four-way one. Once Antony, Simon and Rachel agreed to come on board, and the wonderful Ingrid Ohlsson from Pan Macmillan expressed interest in publishing the book, we thought we were off and running. We signed contracts and agreed to timings. Then cold, hard reality set in.

How were four different authors with very different world views, one of whom was based in Melbourne (and then Ireland), going to wrestle this beast of a book into shape?

Simon got the ball rolling by suggesting the list of big questions that have formed our chapters.[1] Then we got together (Rachel via Skype) and agreed that we would rotate which author began each chapter in alphabetical order, not of surname, but of world view – in other words atheist, Christian, (atheist) Jew, Muslim. This meant I began the first chapter, Simon the second, Antony the third and so on. This seemed fair because it gave each of us opportunities to set the tone, although, as you will see as you read on, we are all very good at taking the topic in the direction we want it to go, no matter where our contribution may sit. We didn't know if this simple, logical structure would work but decided the only way to find out was to get started and see.

Contrary to our expectations, it worked very well. It was easy to follow, but we didn't get rigid about it, either. If someone finished their piece early, they went ahead with the next one regardless. As time went on, we grew more relaxed and fluid about this, believing we could rearrange contributions if we needed to once it was all finished. We have not needed to. We were also open to the length of contributions each of us wanted to make. As you will see, some of us have had more to say on some questions than others, but this also felt right and reasonable.

We hope you find the structure as easy to follow as a reader as we have done as writers. We hope that, whatever your personal beliefs, you enjoy the different perspectives each of us brings to the big questions we have asked ourselves as much as we have enjoyed expressing them. We do not always agree (obviously), and each of us has been robust in making our differences clear. Respect and civility do not mean wishy-washy or timid.

We are, perhaps, an odd collection of authors but we think we have achieved a crazy kind of balance. We have two women, one a believer, one an atheist. We have two men, one a believer, one a (Jewish) atheist. We have two converts and two who have been brought up in their faith or lack thereof. We all strive to be open-minded and liberal in our approach to different perspectives. You will not find much fundamentalism here although we are all passionate believers in our different ways. It has been revealing for me personally to see just what we all agree on and where the differences in our world views seem irreconcilable.

I have learnt a great deal by writing this, and for that I thank the grace, humour, civility, flexibility and decency of my fellow authors.

Jane Caro

WHY I BELIEVE
WHAT I BELIEVE

Jane Caro

I'm an atheist for the same reason most believers are members of their particular faith: I was born into a family of unbelievers.

We are all products of our background, atheists and believers alike. At a speech by the (in my opinion) much-maligned Richard Dawkins, an audience member asked for his response to a questioner's passionate affirmation of his deep and profound personal belief in the Christian God. Dawkins respectfully pointed out to him that it was very likely his questioner would have felt just as deeply about Shiva had he been brought up a Hindu.

I think that those of us who have been raised in a particular culture and remained true to the values we were taught in childhood must, in all honesty, admit we are – in the main – products of our upbringing. Converts, like Antony and Rachel, have had a different journey.

So, at least in part, I'm an unbeliever because I was brought up that way. I have had flirtations with religious belief, however. I was a precocious reader and many of my favourite authors were profoundly religious Victorians (George Eliot, the Brontës, Mrs Gaskell). Heavily influenced by their spiritual – even quasi-pagan – world view, I used to try saying prayers secretly at night, waiting for some kind of momentous spiritual experience (I was also a horribly melodramatic and exceedingly morbid child). As far as revelations went, however, I experienced nothing, nada, zip, zero, and, as a result, grew bored with my own grandiosity and soon gave it up.

Many years later, as an unhappy young woman struggling with a mental illness, I sought solace in religion. I earnestly tried to believe there was some kind of higher power. (I was never much tempted by any particular brand of religion. A true child of the 1970s, I sought spirituality.) I even went to a local church once just to see what was on offer but fled in horror, never to return, when the minister announced a film night that would expose why Muslims followed a false god.

When, thanks to the skilled and compassionate help of a secular psychotherapist, I finally made the breakthrough that helped calm my irrational anxiety and dissipate my depression, I was filled with gratitude.

I wanted to place this sense of grace with someone or something bigger than myself or my therapist, and so I tried to believe in some kind of supernatural force that had helped me resolve my fears. I was never quite convinced, however. In fact, I had a second breakthrough listening to Richard Dawkins explain his theory that religious faith is a misfiring of the gratitude impulse. As he explains it, as herd animals, human beings are hardwired to feel gratitude and repay debts: reciprocity holds the herd together. But good things also happen for reasons outside human agency. After a week of rain, your wedding day dawns fine, warm and sunny. You feel immense relief and gratitude, but who should you thank? Who can you repay? A God, of course, that's who. After my own experience of gratitude, such an explanation made perfect sense to me.

I think that's the essence of my lack of belief, in fact: that it just makes sense. I come from a household of intellectuals. My parents migrated here from the United Kingdom, and both my father and grandfather were graduates of St John's College, Cambridge. I think the influence of that university on my family has been profound. Here's what Salman Rushdie had to say about his alma mater:

> At Cambridge University I was taught a laudable method of argument: you never personalise, but you have absolutely no respect for people's opinions. You are never rude to the person, but you can be savagely rude about what the person thinks. That seems to me a crucial distinction: people must be protected from discrimination by virtue of their race, but you cannot ring-fence their ideas. The moment you say that any idea system is sacred, whether it's a religious belief system or a secular ideology, the moment you declare a set of ideas to be immune from criticism, satire, derision, or contempt, freedom of thought becomes impossible.[2]

I was brought up in an atmosphere of passionate argument and discussion. No quarter was given around our dinner table to age or experience. If you put forward a proposition, you were expected to defend it. Our family get-togethers were (and still are) noisy, argumentative and intense. Lazy, illogical thinking earned you scorn and ridicule. Many of my Australian friends and boyfriends fled our dinner table in horror at the furious verbal exchanges that were so common there. Indeed, my sisters and I sometimes joked that we ended up marrying the only boyfriends who could withstand the onslaught. They proved their worth and courage by coming back for more. (Unlike many of my friends raised in more religious households, all three of us are still married to those same brave men.)

The arguments that earned respect were those that made sense. Belief alone didn't cut it, there needed to be some kind of evidence and proof. And while the arguments could be intensely passionate, there was much humour and honesty around our family dinner table. If someone thought you were saying something foolish, they said so; you were neither patronised nor protected.

And my parents didn't fit neatly into any particular box. My mother was a stay-at-home mum (at least while we were young) who was a passionate feminist and free-market capitalist. She was also unequivocally, scornfully atheist, having been brought up a Methodist. Her view was (and still is) that religion is all about blokes. I agree with her. My father's family was probably Jewish once upon a time, but there is literally no memory of that. His father Jack (John Everard) and grandfather Wilkinson, as their first names indicate, styled themselves as typical members of the British middle class, despite their exotic surname. My father was a very successful businessman, a lifelong Liberal in the English rather than the Australian tradition. He was (and still is) energetic, opinionated and funny. He has always claimed to be an agnostic. He treats everyone as an equal, even his children. We benefited immeasurably from this.

Little was disapproved of in our household, except dishonesty and lying. You could swear, lose your temper, drink, smoke and have sex. At eighteen, when I wanted to move in with my boyfriend (now my husband of thirty-seven years), my mother gave me – a full-time uni student with only a part-time job – an allowance so I wouldn't be financially dependent on him. My parents applied logic to their decisions, not tradition or fear of what other people might think. They valued independence, not just of behaviour, but also of thought.

I was brought up to be sceptical, particularly of the establishment and of entrenched power and privilege. I was brought up to fear certainty and celebrate doubt. I was taught to despise pretension, pomposity and self-importance. I was encouraged to see the gap between the rhetoric of the powerful and their actions, and to point it out. I was encouraged to ask the difficult questions.

I was brought up not to believe.

Rachel Woodlock

I love religion. If there's a religion gene, I have it in spades. I could happily spend my days surrounded by incense and chanting, stained-glass windows and prayer beads, books of theology and people in funny robes. I'm not fussy – Buddhist nuns, Jewish rabbis, and Sufi whirling dervishes are all fascinating to me. I spent many childhood weekends pilfering bedsheets from the linen closet to imitate Audrey Hepburn in *The Nun's Story*, and schooldays reading books with prominently bold religious titles, imagining that one of my unsuspecting and unbelieving school chums might wander by and ask, 'Oh, Rachel, what's that interesting book you're reading?' so that I might launch into earnest theological debate with them.

The religious gene must have skipped a generation to land on me, however, as both my parents are inoffensively only mildly believing. They were adventurous enough in the 1960s to join what was then a relatively unfamiliar new religious movement called the Baha'i Faith. Originally founded by a nineteenth-century Persian nobleman, the faith had more overtly Islamic aspects that were later moderated by his great-grandson, who tailored the Baha'i religion to suit its shift into the Western world.

The early Australian Baha'i community was an assortment of odd-bod hippies, progressives, seekers and a handful of Iranian missionaries. My parents were, like most of the early converts, happily persuaded by the Baha'i social message but resolutely Australian by culture. After 1979, waves of Iranian Baha'i refugees fleeing fundamentalist Shi'i Muslim persecution hit Australian shores, and the small communities of peaceniks and eccentrics were gradually submerged by the sea of Iranian expatriates. This coincided with a time of financial difficulties for my parents, and, not receiving the pastoral care they desperately needed, both Mum and Dad lapsed in the face of the new style of Baha'i community and religiosity.

As for me, I was beginning to explore the vast world of religion. My open-minded parents sent me to the state primary school's Christian religious instruction and later the Jewish version, the two options available at my school back then. I confused a Salvation Army volunteer by asking 'Why are all manifestations of God male?' and recited the Shema prayer along with Jewish girls preparing for their bat mitzvahs. As is customary, at fifteen I declared myself a Baha'i and among other things founded a small library, joined the local youth committee, and became skilled in what Persians have been famously good at for millennia: bureaucracy. I defy anyone to find another youth who so meticulously slaved over such punctilious agendas and minutes as I!

At twenty-one I had a profoundly life-altering, mystical experience. Being a stalwart Baha'i, I was no stranger to prayer. My favourite little prayer book with its padded grey cover was well thumbed and stuffed with handwritten devotions that had taken my fancy at one time or another. I often experienced that calming, meditative state known well by those familiar with the ritual of prayer, and I was quite happy to believe in God and recognise that he was a continuing source of comfort and guidance in my life.

But none of this prepared me for one night in a little outback town in Far North Queensland called Forsayth. I had been saying my nightly prayers as tiny insects buzzed around the lamp in my room. After a while I put down my prayer book and prayed the most unselfish prayer I knew from the bottom of my heart: 'God, I give my life to you.' At that moment I was flooded with the most beatific, loving sensation of an intensity I have never managed to describe adequately. It didn't feel like it was coming from within me; rather, it felt like I was enveloped, wrapped, nurtured by love, and it seemed as if time and space had melted away. When I emerged from this unutterably wonderful state of felicity, I hardly knew what to make of it. Over the years since, I have gone through many illnesses, frustrations, trials and difficulties, but the unshakable conviction that God is more real than anything – everything – else has never left me. Now, I know that the sensations I experienced, at least on an ordinary level, were produced by chemicals in my brain and body, but that's because the body is the tool we're given to experience reality while sojourning in this material universe.

I don't know why God gave me that taste of heavenly assurance then, and I've never experienced it since, but it held me in good stead through my leaving the Baha'i Faith and converting to its older parent religion, Islam, a few years later. It has also meant that I take seriously the Qur'anic statement:

> To each We have prescribed a law and a way of life. Had God willed, He would have made you a single community, but that He should test you in what has been given to you. So compete in doing good. To God, you all will return, and He will inform you about that in which you differed (Q5:48).[3]

While I'm Muslim because it is the religious music to which I respond most energetically, I have enough humility to recognise that God seems to enjoy diversity. He continues to create people of various colours, genders, cultures, languages – and yes, religions – all through this great pulsating evolutionary vehicle called life!

Antony Loewenstein

Birth is a beginning
And death a destination.

Rabbi Alvin Fine[4]

This poem has remained with me since childhood, when I remember hearing it recited at my family's liberal synagogue during Jewish New Year celebrations. It is moving, mysterious, revelatory and lyrical. I recall listening to it as a young boy and not understanding its power.

As I became older and distanced myself from the organised Jewish community, this poem, recited in English and not Hebrew – we were not, after all, Orthodox Jews – has stayed in my mind. Although it doesn't make me think fondly of Judaism itself, it's a reminder for me even today of the power of emotive words to conjure both melancholy and warmth.

I was born Jewish in 1974 in Melbourne. I'm an only child to Jeffrey and Violet, liberal Jews who were born in the same city, Melbourne, during the Second World War. Their parents had escaped Nazi Europe and arrived in Australia in 1939. Most of the rest had realised too late the threat posed by Hitler and perished in the death camps. Being Jewish back then, in the heart of supposedly cultured Germany and Austria, was a death sentence. It's not something I forget.

When I visited the sites of this Holocaust in the 1990s – from Dresden where my father's family resided to Auschwitz where many of them perished – my affection for Judaism was enhanced, though not with any desire to become more religious. It was a secular Judaism fuelled by resilience, a determination to survive and thrive after the greatest catastrophe to befall the Jewish people.

My interest in Judaism was both accidental and intellectual. I had no control over being Jewish, but Judaism continues to fascinate me, especially the various ways Jews can practise the religion and still proudly call themselves Jews.

Close friends in New York regularly attend a synagogue for Humanistic Judaism. Its website states, 'Judaism is much more than a set of religious beliefs and practices. It is the cumulative cultural and historical experience of the Jewish people.'[5] This is correct, but it then goes on to claim Israel is a key aspect of Jewish identity. When even the most liberal Jewish movements blindly praise Israel in this light, they ignore the country it has become: an occupier and a brute.

Zionism is not the answer. And this ideology has almost comprehensively forced me away from Judaism and into a Jewish atheism that feels more comforting but also incomplete. Most of my serious relationships have been with non-Jewish women and, although the failures of these relationships had nothing to do with my or their religious beliefs, I sometimes wonder what it would be like to be with a Jewish woman who truly understands why I've had to reject the organised Jewish community. She'd have to feel as proud as I do of pissing outside the tent rather than within it.

In my teens I started feeling uncomfortable with the casual racism towards Palestinians and Arabs I heard in the Jewish community, from Jewish friends and from my family around the Friday Sabbath table. At that age I wasn't fully across the reality of the Israeli occupation of Palestinian land but something felt wrong even then. It was a created victimhood born of a collective fear, both real and imagined. Jews, now largely successful members of Western society, were powerful and connected but many still clung on to the belief that we were weak and trapped in a ghetto, unwilling to hear criticisms of sacred issues. 'Don't air our dirty linen in public,' I was constantly told. This was shouted routinely in my direction by the time I published my first book, *My Israel Question*, in 2006.

It was a dangerous delusion that allowed perceived enemies – Muslims, Arabs, Palestinians or 'the other' – to threaten our newfound strength. It allowed Jews to claim that Israel, a superpower possessing nuclear arms, was vulnerable when in fact it was the dominant force in the Middle East. Despite this, however, insecurity was the country's middle name, a disease that has spread like cancer throughout the Jewish diaspora in the last few decades.

By the time I was in my early twenties, Judaism had become indistinguishable from Zionism and we parted company. My lapsed religiosity wasn't a great loss to the devout in the Melbourne community – I enjoyed bacon and sex and dabbled in drugs – but I felt the religion left me rather than me having to deliver the divorce papers. I didn't miss most Jewish rituals and almost enjoyed being the outsider critic of the community.

I had never been a regular synagogue attendee. My parents usually had to drag me to a Jewish event or holiday and I don't recall ever embracing prayer or Jewish spirituality. Although I attended a Jewish group called D&M (Deep and Meaningful) in my teenage years, led by a progressive rabbi, I wasn't like the others there. Israel was already in many of my friends' DNA, despite most of them never having been there.

In an age before the internet and easily accessible information that revealed the harshness of Jewish actions against Arabs, it was too easy to romanticise the Zionist state, especially since Melbourne had one of the highest percentages of Holocaust survivors in the world. The community lived in denial about the present and future, convinced that the best way to commemorate old losses was to deify a state that bloomed a few years after 1945. Israeli occupation was largely invisible, dismissed as Palestinian and anti-Semitic propaganda.

My disillusionment with Judaism may seem illogical or even irrational. After all, Judaism isn't Zionism. Or shouldn't be. But for the vast bulk of Jewish communities in the last decades, the two ideologies have become interchangeable. You can't be a Jew if you're not a Zionist. Being a non-Zionist Jew in any organised sense is virtually impossible in Australia, though nothing stops me, of course, from living my life as a cultural Jew on my own and with close friends.

Naturally, you can be a proud Zionist if you aren't Jewish, but this usually involves taking a hardline conservative position, embracing evangelical Christianity or standing as an Islamophobe after September 11, 2001. Loving Israel is no longer cool, if it ever was, when we're constantly bombarded with images of rampaging Jewish colonists shooting Palestinians; Israeli politicians talking proudly of ethnic cleansing of Arabs; and Knesset members finding ways to censor unpopular, anti-Zionist views. This is what modern, mainstream Judaism has largely become, a deformed beast that encourages debate on most issues except arguably the most important one, Israel. This is the opposite of what I believe a religion should be if it wants to prosper in the twenty-first century.

My Jewish atheism isn't settled. I feel open to exploring a truly secular religion that embraces diversity. I've felt deeply moved and proud to be Jewish when I've met members of the Jewish community in Cuba and Iran. They're resilient in the face of tough conditions. For them, regular prayer is salvation. For me, I felt connected to a global religion that had persevered.

When I hung out with Afghanistan's only known Jew in 2012 in Kabul, a grumpy, Orthodox man who chastised me for not practising Passover during my visit and showed me the country's only known synagogue near his basic, one-room apartment where a box of matzo sat on the table, I was surprised by my emotional response. I felt proud to be Jewish. Here was a solitary man, offered asylum in America and Israel, but dedicated to remaining proudly in Afghanistan, a man who had survived years under the Taliban and remained openly Jewish.

My reaction had nothing to do with Israel, Zionism or the Middle East. It was a visceral response that left me wondering if my Judaism was lying dormant and could be awakened by the sight of Jews living in a repressive regime. What did that say about my faith? Today, nearing forty, I wonder if my appreciation of the Jewish faith, one not besmirched by the state of Israel, leaves me vulnerable to reintegration into some kind of progressive, secular, cultural, anti-occupation, anti-Zionist Jewish community.

I'm still looking for that comfortable space.

Simon Smart

I don't find it easy to say 'why I believe what I believe', because my response is complex and multi-layered in a way that remains a bit of a mystery even to me. I'm sure my answer now, at forty-five years old, would be somewhat different from the one I would have given when I was, say, twenty-six. Ask me again in twenty years' time, and my response may have changed again. But there are definitely constants in my journey of faith, a journey that certainly hasn't ceased.

It's fair to say I was born into a very Christian home – my father was an Anglican minister in Tamworth, a large rural centre in north-west New South Wales, known, much to my dismay, as the home of country music. I notice that Jane says she's from at least three generations of atheists, so it turns out she and I are about as rebellious and original as each other!

Mercifully, when I was eight years old Dad became the head of a school and for most of my growing up he was known for that rather than for being the local pastor, a burden that I know was too much for some preachers' kids to bear. Nonetheless, in my early years I was happily raised on a diet of stories of a great and mighty God who created the world, who knew me and loved me and who had things under control.

That was all fine until I hit my teenage years. I wanted to be 'cool', and being Christian was decidedly uncool. As a young guy I was interested mostly in sport and music and hanging out with friends. I read my Bible most nights out of fear and guilt and what I now realise was superstition. But I learnt some things along the way.

At university I was free to live as I chose, and the choice I made was mostly not living as if God had any real place in my life. As all self-respecting university students do, I had the odd minor existential crisis here and there, but on the whole I was more interested in the next game of golf or holiday up the coast. Yet I could never shake the God question completely. In those days I would slink into the back row of a church without any real involvement in the community that accompanied it.

In my twenties, most of my friends were non-believers and I went out with some great girls who didn't share my faith. But slowly it dawned on me that I did believe and that I was a Christian. I never had the ecstatic spiritual experience many people describe. I didn't once feel the need to go to the front at evangelistic services and declare a newfound faith, and this bothered me for a time. It was more a case of gradually feeling that from the beginning I'd been introduced to the truth, and that there was nowhere else to go.

Over the years, my faith has become stronger and a much more central part of who I am. The biggest boost to this was a couple of years of studying theology in Vancouver, Canada, at Regent College, where I was given the freedom to ask the hardest, most honest questions of my faith and access to satisfying, if not exhaustive, answers. Coming to understand the way the Bible holds together coherently and that it has withstood the ruthless critique of some of the finest minds for more than twenty centuries is a significant reason I am still a believer. At Regent College I feel I came to know God in a much richer, more profound way.

What I have come to understand is that right from an early age, through my family, I was blessed by contact with people who seemed to embody something authentic, who had latched on to something that appeared real and true and larger than any individual or group. It's what, if you hang around Christian groups long enough, you will hear someone describe as the indefinable quality that initially drew them to the faith.

I hope I am not misunderstood. It wasn't that I was exposed to an unrelentingly fabulous array of individuals who oozed goodness and light from every pore. But there were enough people who could tell of the impact of God in their lives for it to be compelling. Anyone who has spent time in a church community will report that it's a mixed bag of people from the saintly to the ordinary to the truly nutty, much like other communities or clubs you could choose to be a part of. It may in fact be that churches have an over-representation of misfits.

But there are at least two brilliant things about that. One is that, at their best, churches bring together in one community people from all walks of life and ask (actually demand) that they love each other. Very few other places will insist on genuine and sometimes costly relationships involving meals in homes and weekends away and sharing a life together in which barristers mingle with baristas, plumbers with anaesthetists, dancers with dropouts, musicians with the mentally ill, refugees with professors. When it works, it is a captivating vision of community.

The second, and this was very important for me to understand, is that the Christian community involves a belief that God calls all to him no matter who they are and what they've done, and asks them to follow in the way of Jesus. That means there are plenty of people in the church who are no better and in some cases much worse than those who shun religion completely. But the key is – and I have seen this plenty of times and even in my own life – faith very often makes people a better version of themselves. And even when it doesn't, Christianity offers a vision of wholeness that remains immensely attractive even and especially when we fail to live up to it. It's some of that vision on which I hope to elaborate in this book.

I've always had a fascination with the world: travel and literature, music and poetry, film and sport – all the good stuff of life. There was a time, when I was younger, when I felt that those things were somehow in conflict with my faith or were at least an awkward fit. I've come to believe that isn't the case, and that all the world is God's world – that beauty and friendship and laughter and love and surfing and art and humour are all part of God's good creation. I'm very grateful for life as we fortunate ones in the West experience it. Psychologists tell us it's a good practice to develop habits of thankfulness. And I'm grateful to have someone to thank.

A common and understandable criticism of people of faith is that we are merely wishing for comfort in the face of the grim reality that life is hard and death is the end. The suggestion is that religion is a man-made safety blanket that only the truly clear-thinking and courageous can do without.

There's no doubt that my Christian faith *is* an enormous comfort to me, without which I would feel bereft. But I would find it hard to believe in it if I didn't think there was extremely good evidence (not proof) for my belief. While I wouldn't pretend to have been able to remove myself completely from my upbringing and experiences in order to test objectively all that I understand about the world (who can truly do that?), I have tried to consider the objections to my faith and to critique it.

Like all honest believers, and I hope honest non-believers, I have my moments of doubt along with unanswered questions. The issue of the immense human suffering we all know of even if we haven't experienced it ourselves, remains a formidable challenge to my belief in an all-powerful, good God (more on that later).

But one of the most appealing things about my Christian belief is the profound hope it has offered me even in some of the hardest times of my life. One of the things I love about this hope is that while it is in many ways about the future, it's also about now. By this I mean I have a sense that my life is part of a bigger story. This doesn't mean I think God will make my life okay and protect me from bad stuff. Instead, it's the sense that every aspect of life matters eternally. For me that's a really invigorating and exciting idea. Again, I want to elaborate on this later.

And finally, I'd have to say that the figure of Jesus is the most compelling reason for why I believe what I believe. I'm not, in truth, a particularly religious person. I'm not drawn to ritual and formality and what can sometimes be the overblown seriousness of how things are done. I'm naturally averse to being told where I have to be and how I am to behave. But I keep coming back to this mysterious, ancient story of God becoming a person – and then listening to that person and what he says and how he says it, and I find that I'm convinced by his claims in general and indeed his claim on my life.

And unlike my teenage self, I don't find this a life-suppressing thing but in fact the opposite. It now feels like a connection to a vision of a flourishing life – life to the full, which, of course, Jesus promised to anyone who would follow him.

Right in the middle of the Gospel of Mark, Jesus asks his disciples, 'Who do you say that I am?' It's the critical question of the whole story, and it became the critical question for me. I've found that in coming to believe Jesus is God I also believe I've been welcomed into the family of the creator of the universe.

QUESTIONS

WHAT IS THE NATURE OF THE UNIVERSE?

Jane Caro

I am lucky enough to own (with my cattle-breeder husband) a small property in a very remote corner of New South Wales, on the edge of the vast temperate rainforest that is Barrington Tops. We can see no other place of human habitation from our verandah, which means there's absolutely no light pollution. When the night is overcast and moonless, it's dark – very dark. The thick, velvety blackness is so close and dense it can feel almost suffocating, though the worst injury I usually sustain is a stubbed toe as I (foolishly) attempt to navigate my way to the bathroom without a torch.

When the night is clear, however, and the stars are out, I suspect the view of the universe from our garden is much as it would have looked to the original inhabitants, thousands of years ago. The universe – or our little bit of it anyway – is laid out for us to see. Sometimes we gaze at it for hours. As I stare, I feel utterly insignificant, minuscule in comparison to the spectacular vastness above. But it's not an unpleasant feeling, rather the opposite in fact. I feel strangely comforted. The glittering but indifferent universe soothes my anxiety by reminding me that my fears, problems and tragedies don't matter at all. In comparison to the universe I am the equivalent of a single cell in my own body, if that, of no importance at all. I find enormous peace in this thought.

I make no judgement about the nature of the universe (just as I suspect it makes no judgement about me). I feel no desire to anthropomorphise it. It is a mystery, vast and unknowable – at least by me – and I have no desire to change that. I have no idea how it works but, in the words of a poem I rather liked when young, do not doubt that the universe is unfolding as it should. I suspect there is both order and chaos, that – just as they do on our tiny blue planet – things happen for no reason and also for many reasons. I do not think the universe is either cruel or kind. Those are people-feelings. I doubt the universe has any feelings at all. It's neither moral, nor immoral; it's bigger than both those pipsqueak definitions of right and wrong.

I don't need the universe to have meaning or purpose. I'm happy for it just to be. If a meteor is hurtling towards earth as I write, no doubt I will be momentarily dismayed when I realise that the world and everything on it that I care about is about to be destroyed, but does that mean it matters? In the greater scheme of things, I doubt it. That's the thing about us atheists: far from the arrogance we are usually accused of (more about that later), ours is a fundamentally humble position – we do not believe that humanity is in any way special. For the atheist, there is no vertical structure to the universe, with a god at the top, men next, followed by women (more about that later, too), then all the animals, reptiles, fish and insects, with amoebae and bacteria at the bottom. For atheists, particularly when confronted with the vastness of the universe, amoebae are us.

Unlike Christianity, Islam, Buddhism, Judaism or any other of the world's great religions, atheism is quite content to remain in lower case – unless it appears at the beginning of a sentence. After all, atheism claims little for itself except the right to examine all theories and beliefs critically and only accept those that live up to the test of evidence and reason. Atheism is much more attached to questions, in the same way that religion is attached to answers. The religious fears doubt, the atheist celebrates it. So I feel no desire to answer the big question about the purpose or nature of the universe. I admire cosmologists and astronomers whose curiosity about the space that surrounds us drives them to explore, ask questions and posit hypotheses. When they discover something, I read with interest the stories about it in the media. But just as it took us millennia to discover every corner of our planet, I suspect, as far as knowing the universe is concerned, we're a little like a few tribal Neanderthals a couple of hundred thousand years ago setting off into an unknown ocean in a rickety canoe.

I think my lack of need to understand, explain or control the unknowable thing we call Universe, my comfort with its indifference to me and all my fellow creatures, stems from a very human experience – my introduction to parenthood. From being so anxious as a young person that I had a mental illness (Freud christened it 'obsessional neurosis'), I have become the opposite. I would not claim to have achieved serenity (I'm not really sure I want to), but my anxiety levels are much lower than they once were. I accept what comes and rarely anticipate much.

Anticipation, I suspect, is the source of most anxiety. I am no longer even afraid of flying. Paradoxically, it was my first real experience of deadly danger that soothed my neurotic fears. Let me tell you how.

My first child – a daughter – was born prematurely. For no reason anyone has ever been able to fathom, my fore-waters broke at thirty-four weeks and I was admitted to hospital and ordered to stay in bed in an attempt to maintain the pregnancy. After a week of this, I was told that my womb was no longer sterile due to the leak and that my baby would have to be induced at thirty-five weeks to prevent infection for both of us. I was also injected with steroids to accelerate the development of the baby's lungs. In a previous era, both my baby and I would have died slowly and agonisingly of infection. Thanks to science, today this is a relatively minor problem.

The birth itself was relatively uneventful (thank you, epidural) and Polly was delivered at 2.555 kilograms, a very healthy weight for a 35-week-old. Her Apgar score at birth was 8, then 9 when routinely rechecked five minutes later. As a result she was not put into a humidi-crib, but merely a special care nursery. This, I believe, is where she must have picked up the infection that very nearly killed her. We spent another week in hospital, during which she was put under the lights to treat jaundice (very common in premmie babies), but she appeared to be thriving, and we were discharged with every expectation that all would be well. The next day, however, I noticed thick white snot running from her nose and that night I could neither get her to feed nor settle.

It was a Sunday and all the doctors' surgeries and medical centres we drove to were closed. Feeling like a paranoid new mother, I insisted we drive to Camperdown Children's Hospital (this was twenty-five years ago, when it still existed) and have her checked out. She was admitted immediately with suspected RSV, a virus that causes bronchiolitis and remains the biggest killer of babies under one. It is particularly dangerous for premature babies.

Suffice to say that after a few days in the babies' ward, the worst happened: Polly stopped breathing and had to be resuscitated. It happened twice on the ward and a third time while she was being intubated in intensive care after having been assessed as the sickest baby in New South Wales and so given the last available intensive care paediatric bed in the state that night. I had been attempting to breast-feed her when she first gave up trying to breathe, and it remains the single most terrifying and dramatic moment of my life. I remember thinking that I'd only known her for thirteen days and yet, if she died, so would I.

The next morning a friend insisted I talk to a neonatologist at Camperdown who was also a grief counsellor. He had trained as a counsellor when he had lost a child of his own. He met me in the coffee shop. He wasted no time on the niceties, he just said the follow-ing, words I've never forgotten and that have formed my approach to parenting and to life (and, it seems, the universe) ever since.

'Terrible things can happen,' he said. 'They can happen to anyone. There's nothing special about you and nothing special about Polly. Danger is reality, safety is an illusion.'

Perhaps it reads brutally, put down bluntly on the page like that, but as he spoke metaphorical bricks fell from my shoulders. I gave up making secret bargains with a god I didn't believe in, casting supersti-tious magic spells about room numbers and days in hospital, and trying to pre-disaster everything by imagining the worst. Instead I accepted that what would be would be. I stopped seeking safety. And as I stopped seeking safety and certainty, as I gave up trying to control what might happen and just accepted the reality of what did, my anxiety fell away. Terrible things can happen, they can happen to anyone. We are all children of an indifferent (but not malevolent) universe. Of course, wonderful things can happen, too. Polly survived with no ill effects and is now a robust and productive 24-year-old.

I love my children. I love my family and friends. I love my country, my planet, my home. But I cannot save them, control them or make them safe. No one and nothing can protect me or them. Richard Dawkins said recently in a debate on the ABC's *Q&A*, 'I'm more interested in what's true than what I would like to be true.'[6] My sentiments exactly.

Physicist Lawrence Krauss told the audience at the 2012 Global Atheist Convention that scientists now understand the universe is 70 per cent empty space, 30 per cent dark matter, and that everything else we can see – stars, galaxies and so on – makes up less than 1 per cent. 'Cosmology has taught us you are far, far more insignificant than you thought,' he said.

The universe is the universe. There's no taming it.

Rachel Woodlock

Jane is incredibly fortunate to see the night sky unpolluted by the haze of the metropolis. Ordinarily I try to avoid places without working toilets, but I fondly remember a school camping trip high up on a mountain somewhere out Woop Woop and being dumbstruck at the overwhelming brilliance and colour of the myriad stars, galaxies, satellites and shooting stars, and the grand belt of misty white that is the Milky Way. The mind buckles at the strain of imagining what lies beyond this tiny life-sustaining ball of water and soil that is our home.

When Jane quotes Max Ehrmann's *Desiderata* – 'Do not doubt the universe is unfolding as it should' – and describes a numinous feeling of comfort in the face of its vastness, she is expressing exactly the right attitude according to Islamic theology. From one perspective, what theologians call *tanzih*, we are insignificant because we are evanescent and have no real independent existence in comparison to the true reality, God. But from an alternative perspective, called *tashbih*, we each partake in a grand creative flowering of divinely endowed life and love.

Mainstream Muslim theologians, particularly the largest group called Ash'aris, adopted the view that causation is ultimately attributable to God. The great eleventh-century theologian and mystic Imam Abu Hamid al-Ghazali (d. 1111) wrote:

> The connection between what is normally thought of as cause and effect is not necessary in our view ... If one aligns with the other it is because of holy God's prior decree, not because the connection is inherently necessary and indissoluble.[7]

In other words, when you jump out of a plane with a parachute strapped to your back, the phenomenon of gravity is what God uses to make you plummet towards the ground, but he could suspend you in midair like a cartoon character if he chose.

Because cause and effect are not inherently linked, God could turn the moon into cheese or randomly make the sun rise in the west, north or south. For sanity's sake, however, 'God has created in us the knowledge that he would not produce these possibilities.'[8] His constant habit is that the physical laws of the universe operate nearly always predictably. I say nearly always, because things seem to go a bit wacky when it comes to quantum mechanics and rare miracles. But, by and large, we can rely on things such as gravity operating as they should. Phew!

As God is the constant underlying cause of absolutely every single thing that happens in the universe, everything between the first moment of the Big Bang and the ending of space-time on the future day of judgement is known and willed to occur by his leave. That's why the universe is indeed 'unfolding as it should'.

Jane writes of giving up 'trying to control what might happen' and surrendering to reality. That's the very definition of the word *islam*, except that in Arabic this word for surrendering is drawn from the same root that gives us peace, safety and security. When Jane writes that the universe is 'indifferent' to us and 'danger is a reality, safety is an illusion', Muslims say the opposite: the universe is indeed benevolent, and every-thing that happens to us is for our benefit, even when it seems so unlikely – 'Indeed, with hardship is ease' (Q94:5–6).

I think this is the fundamental difference between materialist atheism and Islam. The former says that the universe is indifferent and even dangerous to us. Ebrahim Schuitema, a South African Sufi shaykh who belongs to the lineage known as the Shadhili-Darqawi order, argues that the chain of atheistic logic goes like this: there's little old me and there's the other – this massive universe that contains everything that's not me, both sentient and non-sentient beings and objects. At any moment the universe might accidentally or deliberately take me out, because I'm merely flotsam and jetsam. What can I do but take measures to protect myself against the universe? Logically, others are similarly trying to protect themselves against me, and ultimately there is only one person I can trust: myself.[9]

This lack of trust is what characterises the modern world, and increas-ingly our societies are populated with people who feel they're under constant threat from strangers; untrustworthy governments; belligerent foreign nations; global crises like climate change, disease pandemics, and terrorism; and even an asteroid strike that will do us in like the dinosaurs.

Alternatively, from an Islamic perspective we're not separate, isolated individuals, standing against the universe – we *are* the universe. We are fashioned from dust (Q30:20) and when we die our bodies return to the great vastness (Q50:1–4), until the folding up of space-time (Q81). At each moment, whether the tarnished mirror of my soul is being rubbed clean with tests and difficulties, or abundant blessings remind me of the benevolent creator who is kind and loving, I'm convinced it's all for my wellbeing. The entire universe is a personal communication from God to each of us, for the Qur'an says 'wherever you turn, there is the face of God' (Q2:115).[10]

Antony Loewenstein

Nobody understands a damn thing. We don't know why the universe was created or why earth is the only known planet that sustains life. We have no idea why some human beings grow up to do good deeds while others are seemingly destined to live lives consumed by violence.

But uncertainty doesn't matter. Or at least doesn't concern me. The world can be strange and ordered or calm and chaotic. There's no way to define a planet with such diversity. Placing a neat framework on our existence has always seemed to me a sign of a religion or group uncomfortable with the randomness of the universe. And not appreciating the beauty of it.

Any thinking person knows far less than they think. For me, as an atheist Jew, the complexity of life isn't easy to appreciate without imposing some kind of intellectual and spiritual guide. But that's personal and not ordained from a book, rabbi or god. When you don't believe in life after death, the inevitability of death becomes less scary and merely unavoidable. Perhaps I feel this as a relatively young man, and I don't doubt that age and sickness could invoke deep pessimism about the purpose of my tiny number of years on this earth, but none of this convinces me to reach for a text that offers supposed answers.

I've had countless conversations with religious believers across the world and they're mostly confused when I tell them I don't subscribe to a religion. How do I explain life and birth, death and sickness or happiness and depression? I struggle to know why the world is how it is but I don't feel empty for not relying on ancient words to explain it to me. Or a religious group to gain sustenance.

But I do share some of the beliefs expressed by Alain de Botton in his book *Religion for Atheists*, where he argues that the 'error of modern atheism has been to overlook how many aspects of the faiths remain relevant even after their central tenets have been dismissed'.[11] He writes that he wants to gain insights into areas that may be useful in secular lives, especially in relation to community issues and human suffering.[12]

When it comes to understanding the universe, physically and spiritually, de Botton challenges believers of all stripes to accept the undeniable power of religion over the centuries, arguing that they have changed society in far greater ways than any secular organisations.

He's right, of course, but only because secularism has been a main feature of modern, Western life since the second half of the twentieth century. The vice-like grip of the church consumed politicians and media alike, deeming what was allowed and how it was to be explained. The advent of modern science, and its ability to partially explain the history of the universe, added to this necessary decline – it takes a certain kind of mind today to truly believe that the world was created in seven days – and organised religion has never been the same since.

But too often in the West we ignore the facts in parts of the world where religion isn't just thriving, but growing. The countless countries still experiencing the effects of the Arab Spring prove that Islam is vital to the majority of the populations in the Middle East. It isn't just being a Muslim but living in a nation that's ruled by some form of Islamic law. Members of other religions, such as the Coptic Christians in Egypt, are rightly worried about what that means for their own viability.

Of course, none of this means that the true believers in Libya, Yemen or Syria have any better understanding of the universe than a secular soul in Sydney or London. But the lack of understanding between the devout and the rest is one of the great challenges of our age. It sometimes feels like there's little in common between a Christian fundamentalist and a militant atheist, that imagining a just world where they can both live freely, without harming the other, challenges the very essence of democracy. Where does free speech begin and end? Is racial vilification vile but necessary in a robust state? And what does democracy really mean when many citizens have views that suggest they have no interest in granting all peoples equal rights?

The universe isn't designed to be just. It isn't destined to be fair. I find Jane's moving description of her child's harrowing birth as almost the perfect definition of why a godless belief system is self-sustaining. Some would say that if she had God in her life she would have managed the trauma much better. That's possible, but an atheist spirit gave her enough strength to breathe life into her daughter. A devout woman would find this hard to understand.

What is the nature of the universe?

If the universe is ordered in a way that benefits some and disadvantages others it's enough to make a secularist like me confused. The major religions don't agree, as Rachel says, about 'divinely endowed life and love', and instead find major points of contention. I'm not a militant atheist who opposes individuals taking comfort in the simplistic explanations of a Bible, Qur'an or Torah but in a modern world it seems far too easy and comforting to subscribe to that.

I can't visit places like Afghanistan, Haiti or Palestine, and see the suffering and inherent brutality in their societies due to tradition, religion and outside forces, and simply blame God for it. The places are messy, confused and chaotic not because of a preordained plan but because of the very human and fallible actions of people who either created, contributed or mitigated it.

I celebrate the messiness of the universe because the alternative sounds eerily like authoritarianism.

Simon Smart

When I was a little kid I was fascinated with space travel. I would pore over books about the original Apollo missions and, not yet discouraged by my inability to grasp even simple maths equations, nor my terror of small, enclosed spaces, I dreamt of blasting out of the atmosphere and going to the moon.

Although harsh reality had long replaced those dreams by the time I was seventeen, my dad took me to hear an after-dinner speech by Jim Irwin, an astronaut who spent three days on the moon in 1971. Irwin's mission famously involved the use of the moon buggy for the first time.

During the address, Irwin described standing on the moon, and looking back at earth. Closing one eye, he could cover the *entire* earth with his thumb. He said it made him feel terrifyingly small.

Irwin, a Christian, reported that the experience deepened and enriched his faith, but said the same experience was always an earth-shattering one for astronauts, producing either adoration of a creator God or permanent existential angst at the immeasurable meaningless-ness of it all.

What is the nature of this universe we find ourselves in? This is a good topic to begin with because it's foundational to so many other beliefs and immediately sets up the distinctive perspectives of the four of us. Jane and Antony have given us their view that the universe is just there and it's a mystery and there's no way our tiny brains can ever comprehend it. This, apparently, doesn't bother them at all.

Jane's rural contemplations of the celestial realm leave her feeling the comfort that she is of no importance whatsoever and nor are any of us. We are all merely microscopic blips on an ocean of time and space, of no more significance than the proverbial grain of sand on the beach or that brain cell killed off with the last beer at Friday drinks.

But any meditation on the universe begs theological questions. Is there anything or anyone behind it all? How did it all begin? Where will it end? Is there a purpose to any of this? The famous biologist and atheist Richard Dawkins says it's silly to ask 'Why are we here?', but it happens to be the question virtually every person and civilisation has asked at one time or another. Professor Dawkins has his own answer, denying that there's any purpose to our existence and saying we have exactly what you'd expect if there were no God. 'There is at the bottom no design, no purpose, no evil and no good,' he writes, 'nothing but blind, pitiless indifference.'[13] That really sounds like a bleak view of life to me, despite the way it is embraced by some.

Dawkins may be right, of course, that somehow the universe burst into existence out of nothing and a tiny corner of it produced a planet perfectly and uniquely suited to the only kind of life that could have produced and sustained beings like us. There's just no way of proving it one way or the other.

What I find perplexing, though, is the (relatively recent) phenomenon of the non-believer somehow finding 'good news' in a godless and singularly material universe. The most accomplished atheists of previous centuries, such as Friedrich Nietzsche, Bertrand Russell and Jean-Paul Sartre, were at least clear-sighted enough to recognise the crushing implications of such a vision of the reality we find ourselves in – a comfortless, meaningless and value-less universe. The consequences of 'God's demise' are serious. As Peter Hitchens, younger brother of the famous atheist Christopher Hitchens, wrote in his riposte to his brother's book *God Is Not Great*, it would be ridiculous to pretend that it's a neutral act to tell a child that 'the heavens are empty, that the universe is founded on chaos rather than love, and that the child's grandparents, on dying, have ceased altogether to exist'.[14]

I'm tempted to say Antony is right, nobody knows 'a damn thing' about whether or not there's a God behind the universe. As a believer I'm not claiming any sort of proof for God. It's more like assessing life as we experience it and making a judgement about what looks most likely. I feel like there are hints of God's existence or, as Timothy Keller describes it, 'fingerprints of God' all around us.[15] And funnily enough, the more we know about the universe through our scientific knowledge, the more some of us are convinced that the most likely explanation is an immense force behind it all.

The famous physicist Professor Paul Davies, who is not a believer in any conventional sense, nonetheless finds the idea of timeless laws of nature, capable of bringing the physical universe into existence, compelling. 'Atheists claim that the laws exist reasonlessly and that the universe is ultimately absurd,' he writes;

> As a scientist I find this hard to accept. There must be an unchanging rational ground in which the logical, orderly nature of the universe is rooted. Is this ground like the timeless God of Augustine? Perhaps it is.[16]

Knowledge of the extraordinary detail of DNA was instrumental in the famous philosopher Antony Flew coming not to accept Judaism, Christianity or Islam, but to relinquish the atheism he had so long promoted and extolled. DNA research, he said, 'has shown, by the almost unbelievable complexity of the arrangements which are needed to produce life, that intelligence must have been involved'.[17]

Similarly, the idea of a Big Bang – that the universe is expanding explosively from a single point – fits comfortably with theism and may even point to it. Francis Collins, who led the Human Genome Project, suggests that the beginning of the universe 15 billion years ago from an infinitesimally small point implies there was nothing before this – creation out of nothing, or ex nihilo as the theologians describe it. 'I can't imagine how nature, in this case the universe, could have created itself,' writes Collins. 'And the very fact that the universe had a beginning implies that someone was able to begin it. And it seems to me that had to be outside of nature.'[18]

I sometimes hear cosmologists and other experts talk about the fine-tuning of the universe, arguing that it looks a lot like the whole thing was prepared with humans in mind. They roll out a litany of mindboggling facts about the fundamental regularities and constants of physics that are absolutely necessary for organic life to exist, and explain that they all fall within the most ridiculously narrow range for it all to work – the rate of expansion of the universe, the weak and strong nuclear force (whatever they are), the electromagnetic force, the speed of light, gravitational force, the mass density of the universe, and on and on it goes. Everything had to be just right, calibrated within the tiniest range, for life to develop like it did or the whole project would never have got off the ground. If the atmosphere were even a tiny bit thicker we'd all freeze to death and even slightly thinner and we'd fry. You get the picture. The more detail you get on this, the more extraordinary it is to understand how unlikely we were ever to exist. It's a compelling reason to consider whether there's a God behind it all.

Even if you looked at these amazing facts of the universe and were pushed in the direction of theism, that would still be some distance from the Christian God. According to Christianity the whole show is the work of an infinite, transcendent or totally *other* God who is personal (i.e. not the Force from *Star Wars*), and good. The writer of Genesis (the first book of the Bible) poetically tells us that God created the universe with humans in mind. In this account God speaks and it happens. He steps into the abyss of the formless and dark space and creates the extraordinary, ordered and balanced universe we all know and, importantly, declares it all to be 'very good'. It's an extravagant and immensely positive vision that provides a resounding affirmation of the material realities of life.

This is highly significant for both the Jewish and Christian faiths. Unlike other creation stories, where the physical world is an aberration or the result of conflict between the gods, unlike Greek culture that denigrated the physical realm and looked for true significance primarily in the spiritual, the Genesis account suggests enormous value in the material realities, the physical stuff of the created order. This resonates with those of us who enjoy the physical realities of our world. It tells us that playing in the mud, feeling the warmth of the sun on our back, swimming in the sea, climbing up or skiing down a mountain, all have meaning and are to be enjoyed. They're all part of engaging with and appreciating the world that God created.

Such a belief can add a rich dimension to the study of science, literature, history, geography and maths. It can deepen the meaning of our relationships and our physical work. The intention of the writer of Genesis was to indicate God's purposeful, intricately planned cosmos in which the pinnacle of his creation is humanity.

But of course none of us needs to be told that things don't appear to be the way they're supposed to be. Spend an evening watching *SBS News* and you'll know that the world can be a cruel place, a dangerous and brutal place. And even when we are protected from conspicuous horror, we all know that fear, loss, brokenness, dashed hopes, disappointment and death are part of the human experience. Christianity doesn't hide from this. It paints a picture that matches reality, speaking of a fallen and broken world we all inhabit, a place where things are cracked and precious things can't be mended. We are all in need of redemption. We long for something better, and there isn't a person who doesn't know something of that longing.

The whole Christian faith centres on the first-century carpenter Jesus as God's dramatic response to the mess we find ourselves in. His life, death and resurrection are the centrepieces of a large story of God finding a way to bring the redemption and healing we're incapable of producing ourselves.

This is a long way from the contented stoicism of Jane in the face of a meaningless universe, and from the shoulder-shrugging who-can-ever-know posture of Antony. It's not even the fatalistic, 'everything that happens to us is for our benefit', of Islam expressed here by Rachel. Rather, Christianity offers a defiant hope in the face of the crushing realities, as well as the joys, of the human experience (more on this in 'Where do we find hope?').

Scientists and theologians agree that the universe had a beginning and will have an end. Right at the end of the Bible in Chapter 21 of the book of Revelation, there is a vision presented of a time when God will draw all of history together and 'make everything new', where he will establish 'a new heaven and a new earth'. There is a tender image of God wiping away every tear from his people's eyes, and creating a situation where there will be 'no more death, or mourning, or crying or pain, for the old order of things has passed away'. You may not believe that to be true, but you'd have to admit that if it were, it'd be a beautiful picture of where the universe is heading. It's a vision that has inspired millions of believers for more than two millennia.

In his book *The Rage Against God*, Peter Hitchens makes the obvious point that arguments will rarely be decisive in changing anyone's heart on the question of a god-filled or godless universe. He writes of his older brother, Christopher:

> As [Christopher] has become more certain about the non-existence of God, I have become more certain that we cannot know such a thing in the way we know anything else, and so we must choose whether to believe or not. I think it is better by far to believe.[19]

I too see belief as something of a choice – not a baseless leap in the dark, but nonetheless a choice. And it's my firm view that it's better to believe. During the course of this book I hope to explain why.

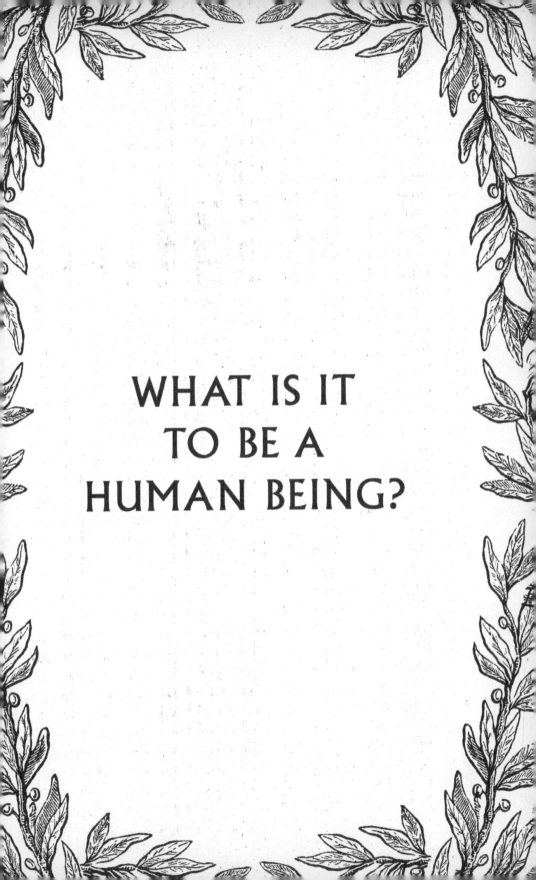

WHAT IS IT TO BE A HUMAN BEING?

Simon Smart

What is it to be human? This is a critical question with profound implications for how we view ourselves and other people, and therefore how we think we ought to live.

Shakespeare picks up on this in *Hamlet*:

What a piece of work is a man! How noble in reason, how infinite in faculty, in form and moving how express and admirable, in action how like an angel, in apprehension how like a god – the beauty of the world, the paragon of animals! And yet to me what is this quintessence of dust?[20]

Hamlet's insight captures the complexity of the human condition. Intricately made, we are capable of much that is godlike and yet at the same time we remain 'dusty', both fallible and mortal.[21]

We probably all agree with Hamlet's picture of the human condition, but it's also obvious that there are different and competing ways of understanding what it is to be human. An atheist pretty much has to think of a person as a singularly physical and material being. It follows from this that there can't be any soul or self, or anything we could describe as touching the transcendent. The only logical position for the non-believer is to regard humans as merely animals (albeit extremely complex ones), and to consider every aspect of existence in purely material terms.

The problem I have is I don't know anyone who lives like that is true.

In my own life, this question resonates most when I think about my experience as a parent. One recent Christmas I found myself sitting by the bedside of my ten-year-old daughter, getting ready for what was to be her third operation in a week, to remove a blockage in her bowel. Nobody knew how the operation would work out or what the surgeons would find. The feelings I experienced before she went into the operating theatre were intense. There were the memories I had of sitting next to her as a baby, a few hours old, in awe of what was before me – this little life that was and is so precious. There was the lurking fear that something would go wrong in the operation. And I also felt an almost overwhelming love and connectedness to her.

Any parent would feel the same, and of course, I don't mean to imply that you need religious belief to feel such a thing. But if I were to accept naturalism – i.e. that there is no God or gods or anything like God – I would have to think that as I sat in the hospital stroking my daughter's cheek, the sense I had of experiencing something beyond precious, beyond language, maybe even sacred, was, ultimately, just the function of chemistry resulting from the firing of millions of neurons in my brain (or something of that nature) – a physical reaction with some connection to our wider evolution as a species.

American philosopher Alvin Plantinga writes that if humans are merely highly advanced machines we might be left wondering if we are of any more significance than other physical things – such as a starfish or a rosebush or a horse. Most naturalists will point to our capacity for thought, speech, and moral reasoning to show that we are immensely valuable.[22] But you might notice that such value comes entirely from our utility – our capacity to perform important functions – and you'll be left wondering whether this value disappears once you have a stroke or a car crash and lose one or more of these functions.

Yet, in the West, following a few hundred years of challenges to theism, your average person might say a human is a particularly intelligent animal, and the result of accidental forces of evolution. In the face of this hard fact, humans may construct stories and rituals to ease the pain of life, but ultimately these are fictions. The best thing they can do is live as if life has meaning, knowing that the only meaning it truly has is what we can construct for ourselves. There is nothing beyond us that provides any preordained purpose. We are the sole authors of our lives, including the moral laws by which we live.[23]

Importantly, when death occurs, the naturalist has to conclude that it truly is 'game over' – the end of personality and individuality. The naturalist vision is one of complete extinction once the body stops working, and many would say we have to face this grim news and not hide in fantasies of an afterlife. Perhaps, but death remains an important and unavoidable question when considering human nature.

So it's worth taking a moment to compare that view with the Christian understanding of the human person that has been with us in the West for 2000 years. According to the biblical picture, right at the beginning, in the book of Genesis, humans are created in God's image. Humanity is the high point of the whole creative act of God. Given a unique place in the cosmos, humans are called upon to be God's special representatives on earth, to be God's 'children', reflecting his good character in the world.

In such a framework, on the scale of finitude and personality, we are closer to God than the animals.[24] Psalm 8, in the Old Testament, describes human beings as made 'a little lower than the heavenly beings'. The Genesis account poetically describes human beings as formed differently from the rest of creation – as God *breathed his spirit* into humans whereas he merely decreed life to the rest.

Christianity takes this concept of *imago Dei* from Judaism and turbocharges it with the incarnation – God himself becoming a person in Jesus Christ. If God did in fact become a person, as the Bible claims, then Jesus's life, death and resurrection declare in the most emphatic way imaginable that human beings are stamped with divine approval. Every human bears the image of God. As such, each and every person is of inestimable and eternal value.

There's no doubt that being human involves a fair dose of mystery. But from at least the time of Augustine – the great theologian of the fourth century – writers and artists have in various ways depicted a sense that human restlessness and longing in the face of our obvious vulnerability is like a magnet drawing us towards God, the source of all life.

The Christian notion of the nature of the human person is not all 'beer and skittles'. It's realistic and hard-edged, noting the paradox that humans are both astonishingly capable of great goodness, but at the same time broken, fallible and in need of redemption. On this, philosopher and theologian David Bentley Hart writes:

The Christian view of human nature is wise precisely because it is so very extreme: it sees humanity, at once, as an image of the divine, fashioned for infinite love and imperishable glory, and as an almost inexhaustible wellspring of vindictiveness, cupidity, and brutality.[25]

According to Christian teaching we are alienated from God, each other and everything else that has been created. Hope for a solution to this dilemma comes out of the central event of the Christian story – the cross and the resurrection.

In the West, the immense dignity and unimaginably exalted picture of the human person emerging from the Christian story in the first century brought truly revolutionary change, the reverberations of which are still felt today. It's important to note that not every culture has had such a lofty view of humanity – certainly not the culture that Christianity was born into in first-century Rome. The Graeco-Roman world – a place where babies could regularly be found on rubbish dumps outside city walls – simply could not conceive of such an understanding of human value that Christianity brought with it. It is demonstrably the case that Western culture has benefited from the legacy of this cultural shift, even when the reason for it has largely faded from collective memory.

David Hart believes it is this same idea of a bestowed human dignity (seen in the early Christians' treatment of orphans, widows, prisoners and the sick) that forged a revolutionary moral vision of the human person.[26] It is an idea that has haunted us ever since.

It remains to be seen how long we can hold on to that vision of human existence if the West is to finally and thoroughly reject the Christian revolution. Such a loss may be far greater than some critics appear to know or understand.

Jane Caro

We're shocking narcissists, we human beings, aren't we? If we can't be special, then somehow everything we do, think and feel must be meaningless. That's an either/or proposition I simply don't buy. We exist, as other living things exist. The difference for us is that we have consciousness whereas – to the best of our knowledge so far – no other living creature shares that particular characteristic. When chimpanzees – in particular Nim Chimpsky and Washoe – were taught to sign using the language of the deaf, there are various claims and counterclaims as to whether they were merely imitating their handlers or could respond spontaneously, using language to express their thoughts, indicating some level of consciousness. Some people ascribe great intelligence and abilities to creatures like dolphins and killer whales. They can certainly learn to do tricks. Does that mean they have consciousness? We don't know. If they did, would that mean they have the divine spark too?

In the absence of any evidence to the contrary, I'm perfectly content to think of myself as simply a mammal with an oversized brain. The fact that I'm in no way 'special' as a life form doesn't bother me at all, nor does it make me feel that if I can't be special then I must be worthless, or that if I have no soul I must therefore be just a 'highly advanced machine'. These two are not opposites. I know of no religion that would argue an elephant has a soul, but no one would describe it as a machine either.

Simon even argues that if human beings are merely animated by complex living processes, they can have no self. This seems absurd to me. Animals have selves. The cow being loaded on to a truck to be transported to the stockyard feels fear at the strangeness of its predicament. The cow left behind in the paddock feels nothing, because it has a separate self. Things can happen to it that do not happen to any other cow precisely because it is separate. It is an individual. It has a self. The fact that it cannot intellectualise or analyse fear, hunger or the feeling of the warmth of the sun on its back doesn't mean it has no self to experience them.

Like Simon, I have sat beside the hospital bed of a daughter and feared for her life. The terror I felt and the anguish I experienced would not have been belittled had I taken a moment to remember that my intense emotions were partly a product of my biological task to bequeath my DNA to the future and protect it at all costs, and partly empathy towards the suffering of our fellow creatures, particularly if they are helpless. As a farmer I have watched the intensity with which a mother cow will defend her calf if she thinks it's being threatened. I'm not arrogant enough to think that while her distress is merely 'mechanistic', to use Simon's word, mine is somehow divine. Nonsense – as mothers, regardless of species, our biological job is to protect our young, for perfectly obvious reasons, and we won't do it well unless we feel an intense connection. This doesn't make that connection worthless or less admirable. It remains just as gallant (and effective) no matter what the reason.

Perhaps our secret fear that we are not special is what fuels the taboos around reproduction, menstruation, female genitalia (after all, the last really shocking swear word in English describes them), even breastfeeding. Maybe it even fuels misogyny itself. Perhaps the way we are conceived, gestated, born and fed uncomfortably reminds us of our essential animal nature. Simone de Beauvoir, in the seminal feminist text *The Second Sex*, makes this point brilliantly. She also points out that we define civilisation as the distance we put between ourselves and our shit. The fact that we excrete just like other mammals may explain our taboos around this behaviour as well. After all, if we alone in the animal kingdom are really made in the image of the divine, does the divine shit, pee and menstruate too?

We're all aware of the biological trick nature plays on us to get us to reproduce when we first fall in love. The obsession with the loved person and the intense feelings of delight and despair that attach themselves to what eventually turns out to be just another perfectly ordinary human being, are still exhilarating, even though we know, in our few sane moments, that we're merely infatuated. Such intense love eventually peters out to be replaced, if we're lucky, with a more realistic and mature affection that can last a lifetime. Pain is still just as painful, even though we may understand it as the 'mechanistic' firing of nerves.

Orgasms are just as exquisite even though we know how the physiology of the clitoris and the penis create them.

Simon argues at length that our capacity for thought, speech and moral reasoning somehow proves that we are valuable. We are indeed valuable to ourselves and to one another. But why do we have to be valuable in some other way? Physicist Lawrence Krauss argues that we exist not because all the things necessary to our existence were created specifically so that we could, but because once gravity, time, space, the laws of physics and so on came into being it was then inevitable that we eventually would as well. It is no evidence of divine creation that the universe gives us precisely what we need to live; it is, in fact, evidence of the opposite. If the universe did not become precisely what it has become, we would simply never have existed. It's not there because of us, we're here because of it. Thought, speech and moral reasoning are of value to us because they help us survive and thrive. Why need there be more to it than that?

Scientist and communicator Dr Karl Kruszelnicki recently waxed lyrical to me about the fact that medical science would soon be able to keep us alive forever. I left him rather flummoxed when I reacted to this news with a groan. I'm a writer, I told him. I like deadlines, beginnings, middles and ends. We need to know our time is limited because it spurs us on to do things now, to make the most of the short time we have. One of my complaints about the promise of eternal life is that it has often been used to keep the powerless and the miserable in their place. Do as you are told now, say the fortunate to the servant, slave, chimney sweep or skivvy, and you'll receive your reward in heaven. How bloody convenient – for the privileged, I mean. It seems very much more moral to me to say, 'Rebel. This is the only life you have and you have just as much right to make the most of it as anyone else.'

The idea of eternal life, whether actual (Dr Karl-style) or spiritual, just makes me feel tired. I don't want to go on and on and on forever. I have no fear of death. (Plenty of fears about the manner of my dying, of course. I'd rather it was swift, painless and a long way off.) I've always felt quite content with the idea that what happens *after* my life will be very much the same as what happened *before* it, and I don't remember that being particularly unpleasant. I've also always found the concept of Christian heaven rather horrible, to be honest. Boring, endless and full of smug people. Give me oblivion any day.

Apparently, according to Christianity, we're all alienated not just from God, but from ourselves and one another, and our only way out is to believe the Christian God died for us and our sins. Some are going to find what I say next very disturbing, but, as an old ad woman, to me this smacks of the old create a problem no one ever knew existed and then tell people that only by buying your brand can they cure it. It's effective, but hardly divine.

As for Simon's point that our divine spark gives Christians their belief in the sanctity of life (all human life, apparently, except that of Jesus, whose death is celebrated), like many atheists, I have a more nuanced view, particularly when it comes to abortion and voluntary euthanasia, which I will explain at length in 'How do we know right from wrong?'. However, a quick glance at history will show that many of the religious must also have a nuanced view when it comes to the sanctity of life. It often appears to apply to only a privileged few, usually fellow believers. Killing blasphemers, stoning adulterers, slaughtering infidels, heretics and heathens are still seen among some religious groups as perfectly valid ways to buy a place in paradise. Supporters of state-sanctioned execution in the United States commonly describe themselves as good Christians. The right to be armed to the teeth is not just enshrined in the secular US constitution, but God-given, according to many of its exponents. And there's hardly been an army in the history of the world that hasn't marched into battle claiming its cause to be blessed by a god.

Rachel Woodlock

'Know, O beloved, that man was not created in jest or at random, but marvellously made and for some great end,' wrote al-Ghazali, in his book of distilled wisdom *The Alchemy of Happiness*.[27] He was speaking of teleology, a fancy word philosophers use to mean the idea that something has an end purpose, a reason for being. For example, the end purpose of a hammer is to whack something hard, such as your old computer before you leave it out on the nature strip for rubbish collection (handy tip for the security-conscious there). The end purpose of a book like this is to be read and its ideas digested. Now, you may incidentally use it to prop up a wobbly table, but that is not its *telos*.

Human teleology, the question of our nature and purpose, is expressed in the age-old question 'Why am I here?' People across the ages have been transfixed by this question, a fact that lends credence to its importance. Indeed, the science of psychology demonstrates how devastating nihilism can be to mental health. When people feel their lives are meaningless, that there's no future goal towards which they should strive, that there's no good answer to the question of 'Why am I here?', they become dreadfully dispirited. It's not narcissism to feel we must have a purpose; it's essential to the fabric of our human nature.

Without wishing to steal Antony's Jewish thunder, the great psychiatrist and Holocaust survivor Viktor Frankl had much to say on this topic. Frankl, who lost nearly his entire family to the Nazi death camps and who was himself imprisoned, found life meaningful even in the most desperate and horrific moments. He discovered that each life is a unique answer to the question of human teleology and found the answer in love, as have so many of the world's great saints and sages. 'I grasped the meaning of the greatest secret that human poetry and human thought and belief have to impart: *The salvation of man is through love and in love*' (his emphasis).[28]

Christianity, as I think Simon will agree, is particularly known for its theology of love. The Bible relates that Jesus taught us to love God with all our heart, soul, mind and strength, and love our neighbours as ourselves (Mark 12:28–34). More than any other, these are the greatest commandments, said Jesus. The Prophet Muhammad similarly taught us to love God and each other. He even made true belief conditional upon observing the golden rule: 'A servant does not attain the reality of faith until he loves for people that of the good which he loves for himself' (Sahih Hibban).[29]

To return to al-Ghazali and his alchemical prescription, love for God is the highest purpose and aim for the human being. 'Whatever we love in any one we love because it is a reflection of Him,' he wrote.[30] Eight centuries later, the modern Turkish theologian Bediuzzaman Said Nursi (d. 1960) taught that love is the animating essence of the entire cosmos.[31] He was perhaps echoing the Baha'i sage 'Abd al-Baha' (d.1921) who spent time in Istanbul and Edirne and taught and wrote in Ottoman Turkish – given the similarities in their teachings, I sometimes wonder if they ever crossed paths. 'Abd al-Baha' taught:

> Love is the most great law that ruleth this mighty and heavenly cycle, the unique power that bindeth together the diverse elements of this material world, the supreme magnetic force that directeth the movements of the spheres in the celestial realms. Love revealeth with unfailing and limitless power the mysteries latent in the universe.[32]

That is to say, all of creation is infused with love. It is turning away from love that causes decay, destruction and death.

Occasionally, when I feel myself getting too snarky, I use a mental discipline to snap myself out of my judgy-judgy state. I find a place where there are lots of strangers busy taking no notice of me – food courts in shopping centres are usually a good place – and I focus on each person that passes by, consciously reminding myself that God dearly loves and cares for them just as much as he does for me, 'for my Lord is indeed full of mercy and loving-kindness' (Q11:90). I try to remember that the person I'm looking at is a miracle that all the forces of the universe had to conspire to bring into being, from time immemorial. Part of this is to shift my perspective from my own perceived entitlement to the precious and unique specialness of the other, who reflects the divine to me and is part of the face of God to me.

*

I disagree with Simon that human beings are inherently 'alienated from God, from each other and everything else that has been created'. Western Christianity, following the interpretations of Augustine, Anselm and Calvin, among others, reads the Genesis story of Adam and Eve's fall to mean that human beings are tainted with the guilt of original sin. Although there are variations within the Catholic and Protestant interpretations, their essential point is that because our first parents disobeyed God by eating fruit from the tree of knowledge of good and evil, all humanity has inherited guilt from this first sin. Calvinist theology goes so far as to say that humans are actually incapable of doing good because of original sin. So according to the Western theory of the substitutionary atonement, Jesus took the punishment we all deserve by dying horribly on the cross. He is 'substituted' for us, and that's how God is able to forgive us and allow us into his presence. This version of the doctrine maintains that God requires somebody to be punished for sin, otherwise justice is not served. God *can't* just forgive us.

I was a bit of a firebrand in my youth, and I spent a good many hours in debate with Christian friends on how this idea is patently unfair. Evonne, my best friend in senior high school, copped it in particular. We clicked when we met and discovered we shared the same birthday and the same train line. She was also the daughter of a Reformed Church minister and quite passionate about her Christian faith. Hurtling past Blackburn, Box Hill, Camberwell and Richmond on our way in to Flinders Street Station in the city, I would point out that if a judge punishes an innocent person for another's crime, no one considers justice to have been done. Imagine that Adolf Hitler was brought up before the International Criminal Court and sentenced to death for murdering millions of Jews. We'd find it reprehensible if the judge electrocuted Mother Teresa instead so that Hitler could get off scot-free to walk around and enjoy his life. However, it seems I wasn't a very good proselytiser, because Evonne never converted from Christianity – in fact, today she's training to become an Anglican priest – but I've never changed my mind on the injustice of the substitutionary atonement.

So I was quite surprised to learn that Eastern, or Orthodox, Christians don't hold to original sin and Jesus's death as penal justification. They emphasise communion with God and healing from the effects of sin instead. In their eyes, Catholics became the original 'Protestants' by splitting from the other four ancient patriarchates and developing a much more legalistic theology.

Eastern Christianity's concept of human nature is much closer to Islamic theology. Mind you, given that Islam spread across much of the same geography as the ancient Eastern church, it's not much of a stretch to suggest there was cross-fertilisation of ideas between early Christian thinkers and their Muslim counterparts, not to mention Jews, Zoroastrians and other scholars attracted to the cosmopolitan centres of learning.

Like both Eastern Christians and Jews, Muslims do not have original sin in their doctrinal knapsack. Although the story of Adam appears in the Qur'an, it is subtly different from the biblical story – not the least of which is, Eve doesn't get the blame. Adam represents both humanity collectively and each of us individually. God creates Adam knowing that humanity will muck things up but tells the protesting angels he knows better:

> And when your Lord said to the angels: 'Verily, I am placing a vicegerent on the earth,' they said: 'Will you place on it such a one who will spread corruption and shed blood, and yet we glorify you with praise and sanctify you?' He said: 'Verily, I know what you know not' (Q2:30).

So what is God's good reason for creating such motley, stumbling, foolish, blundering beings and putting them in charge of things? I mean, as any boss or parent knows, mistakes come with the job description – some of them whoppers. In my own life, I'm not looking to be a supermum; frankly, I just hope my daughter survives her childhood well enough not to need expensive psychotherapy later on.

Anyhow, the twelfth-century scholar Ahmad Sam'ani (d.1140) has a particularly interesting interpretation of human nature. He focuses on Adam as the locus for God's names of love, mercy and forgiveness. Because this physical world is one of contrasts, we know justice because of injustice, we know truth because of falsehood, and we know love and mercy because of severity and wrath. For Sam'ani, God planned the human expulsion from paradise down to earth, so that we would fully yearn to return to God.[33] On this theme, the modern poet Muhammad Iqbal (d.1938) wrote:

I am a sinner, O Lord, banished from Thy sight,
But the angels could never make habitable that wasteland of yours.
That stark wilderness, that insubstantial world of Yours gratefully
    remembers my love of hardship.
An adventurous spirit is ill at ease in a garden where no hunter lies
    in ambush.
The station of love is beyond the reach of Your angels,
Only those of dauntless courage are up to it.[34]

As the Qur'anic account goes, as soon as our primordial parents realised they'd been tricked by wily Satan into eating the forbidden wheat (yes ... *wheat*), they asked for forgiveness from God and were granted it. Unlike the perfect angels who obey God and praise and glorify him constantly, fallible humans have need to say, 'Whoops, sorry, won't do *that* again.' Because the whole point of creation is to manifest the divine names, humanity is uniquely placed to bear witness to God as 'the oft-forgiving'.

We all come from the same source, the original soul, and are born undifferentiated from the universe (Q4:1, 7:172). As we grow out of infancy we become separated by developing personalities, a sense of being different and unique, of having concrete boundaries that define what is 'me' and what is 'not me'. The only way to overcome the potential terror this realisation holds, is through love and the remembrance of God (Q73:8–9, 13:28).

Yes, we struggle to become vehicles of divine love in this life, but that doesn't mean pleasure, happiness, and divine bliss are withheld as if they were a carrot torturously dangled in front of a slaving donkey.

God's felicity can be experienced now by those who embrace it, precisely because human beings are a bridge between the physical and spiritual realms.[35]

Antony Loewenstein

During the Israeli onslaught against Gaza in late 2012, prominent Rabbi Yaakov Yosef gave a sermon in the occupied West Bank town of Hebron and called for the murder of Arabs. 'The IDF [Israeli Defence Forces] must learn from the Syrians how to slaughter the enemy,' he said.

The comment was reported by the Electronic Intifada website but ignored by a Western press that's far happier covering the rantings of bigoted and incendiary Arab leaders or militants. With thanks to George Orwell in *Animal Farm*, all human beings are equal, but some human beings are more equal than others.

The simple act of living, breathing, procreating, sharing and loving is done by the vast majority of humans on planet earth. But what separates a good person from a callous, selfish or hateful one is how we live our lives and how we treat others.

I see myself as a considerate person. I know I've made mistakes in life and hurt friends, former partners and my parents due to my insensitivity and anger. But compared to a racist rabbi in Palestine, my attitudes are positively enlightened. I cannot understand how a fellow human being can spew such bile and still call himself human, let alone Jewish.

We are a tribal species, drawn to those who are similar to us. Although most Western democracies are multicultural societies, with various degrees of success, many ethnic communities still predominantly hang around with people like them. This is because of an innate urge to share ideas, thoughts, food and values with like-minded souls. We aren't machines pre-programmed to behave in a certain way; we're indoctrinated by our parents from the day of our birth. The vast majority of mothers and fathers want their children to grow up proudly, independently and fiercely. The values they try to transmit to their offspring have evolved over the centuries but the basic essence remains the same: be a good human being.

The nature and nurture debate — how much we as sentient beings are created by those around us from birth or inherently built a certain way — is not likely to be resolved any time soon. Believers in a higher being, such as Simon and Rachel, see something divine about human life and its spirit. I share their wonder at the incredible diversity of human beings and our inability ever to fully understand every nuance of the human mind, but this doesn't mean for me that a deity or God had any hand in my creation. I don't need an explanation for the inexplicable. I share Jane's sentiments: 'In the absence of any evidence to the contrary, I am perfectly content to think of myself as simply a mammal with an over-sized brain.'

The challenge for all of us is to make our communities as just as possible and to give our fellow beings the best opportunities possible, especially those less fortunate than us.

But humans aren't simply machines that need feeding and tending. During the 2011 visit to Australia by the famed American linguist and political activist Noam Chomsky to receive the Sydney Peace Prize, he reminded an audience at the Sydney Opera House that for French philosopher René Descartes:

> it was critical to distinguish creatures with souls or minds from those who didn't have them. The ones who didn't have souls and minds were machines . . . How would you determine whether some creature has a mind? . . . By testing their language abilities . . . It's the ability which all humans share.[36]

Chomsky himself explained that:

> There's no known difference among remote tribes in Papua that haven't had other human contact for tens of thousands of years and children who grow up here. And if you interchange them at infancy they'll grow into their own society without any problem.

This is the universality of humanity. We may have vastly different backgrounds, culture, language and surroundings but we have the ability to adapt and evolve in a variety of environments. We're not heartless machines. But neither are we divinely designed, programmed to act in a certain way towards others or an imaginary God.

There are philosophical questions about the purpose of us being on this planet. We're more than sheep who need shelter, affection, food and water. We're conscious creatures who strive for a higher purpose than just living, breathing and dying. My Judaism doesn't give me any answers or comfort. I wonder, if I'm ever struck down with a deadly disease or face the loss of a close relative, whether I'd take comfort from a religious figure or text. I'm open to the possibility that in a moment of desperation or sadness I'd look for whatever gave me warmth or spiritual nourishment. That may be a form of Judaism.

American philosopher Alex Rosenberg, writer of *The Atheist's Guide to Reality*, explained to an editor at *Harper's Magazine* in 2012 that:

> When people disbelieve in God and see no alternative, they often find themselves wishing they could believe, since now they have an itch and no way to scratch it.[37]

I have that itch but I'm content to keep scratching until the day I die. I don't need to know why humans are the most incredible creatures on planet earth. I don't want to understand every nuance behind rational and irrational behaviour. To be human is to thrive on uncertainty, pain, pleasure and hope. That's enough for me at this age.

Medical geneticist Harry Ostrer released a book in 2012 called *Legacy: A Genetic History of the Jewish People*. He argues that Jews are a homogenous group and can be described as a 'race'. There is, Ostrer states, a 'biological basis of Jewishness' and 'Jewish genetics'.[38] Human identity in the age of DNA is fundamentally shifting, and what was once settled, where we belong and with which group, is starting to change. The thought of Jewish wandering being central to our being remains alive and well. Ostrer sees our isolation due to cultural practices, religion and geography as undeniable, but the modern world has seen a dilution of the Jewish bloodline due to greater intermarriage and globalisation.

This talk can seem unsightly or even racist. I'm not suggesting Jews are superior in any way, far from it, just that the human identity is complex and becoming increasingly so. While I feel connected to a religion that stretches back thousands of years I'm far less enamoured of the tribalism towards Israel that is far too common in the Jewish community today. Zionism has replaced independent thought for far too many Jews. The robotic monotony of Jewish support for Israel, regardless of the crimes it commits against the Palestinians, is akin to a machine.

We can do much better.

WHAT IS A
GOOD LIFE?

Antony Loewenstein

Many centuries ago in Europe, killing a fellow human being would almost guarantee the death penalty for a lower class person. The same situation exists today in the United States, especially if you're black and poor. A report sponsored by the American Bar Association in 2007 found that only one-third of African-American death row inmates in Philadelphia would have received life sentences had they not been African-American. America has the world's highest incarceration rate and holds roughly one-quarter of the world's prison population.

Remembering these facts is important because America is both the world's most powerful nation and a proudly Christian state. It's inconceivable that a US presidential candidate would be an atheist, of the routine or militant kind, or a Muslim. The leader must constantly explain their embrace of religion, love of God and America's God-given place to lead the world. When Barack Obama ran for president in 2008 and again in 2012, critics deliberately created a public impression that he might be Muslim and therefore untrustworthy.

Can a truly good person endorse the death penalty and use Jesus or Allah as their alibi? Yes. In their minds. The Muslim world is filled with nations where the death penalty is common, and consistent polling and my experiences in these countries prove that a sizeable percentage of populations back killing individuals for a range of real and perceived crimes. Can we say that millions of Muslims are therefore barbaric because they believe their religion sanctions the ultimate punishment?

It's a humbling experience spending time in the Islamic world and listening to even the most liberal men and women endorse state-sanctioned murder. I've heard it in Afghanistan, Pakistan, Gaza, Saudi Arabia, Egypt. It can be justified, defended, even praised. This is not to suggest that every Muslim is bloodthirsty – the years since September 11 have seen a very public and brutal war fought between Al-Qaeda and its affiliates, with often helpless Muslims claiming the radicals have hijacked their religion – but the definition of being a good person and leading a good life is undoubtedly different in Riyadh and Sydney.

Putting aside the obvious human traits, desires and commonalities between virtually all cultures and races – shelter, love, family and peace – to even begin discussing goodness in life requires an understanding of basic values. Leading a good life is clearly very different for me than for any number of devout Hindus who can't understand how a person wouldn't want to live without a spiritually rich and God-filled existence. I recall arriving in Saudi Arabia and ticking the box on the arrival form as 'Christian' because atheist and Jew would confuse the immigration official and cause an incident. There's a time and a place for shouting loudly about atheism and Saudi Arabia wasn't one of them.

I would argue that we're all capable of being good human beings without much effort and yet as a species we're constantly asking if we could do better. Religion isn't central to living positively. In a largely secular West, however, becoming better people rarely involves greater belief in faith of the devout kind but a materialism that can never be satiated. The newest iPhone and biggest flat-screen television may not make us a better person, but we often tell ourselves that if we have them we'll be more content and therefore nicer to be around. Consume, procreate, enjoy, die.

There's a great Radiohead song, 'Fitter Happier', that perfectly captures the constant Western need for supposed perfection. In the process of achieving an unobtainable goal we lose ourselves.[39] Radiohead conjures a dystopian yet recognisable world where values are bought and traded and our desire to be good human beings is as simple as going regularly to the gym. It's a vision that would appal even the most devout person and yet commercialism has pervaded unexpected places. Nowhere is safe.

A massive, Western-style shopping mall recently opened in Papua New Guinea's capital, Port Moresby. It's clean, well air-conditioned and contains a supermarket with goods the 99 per cent simply can't afford. But it's an aspiration of many locals, I was told while there in 2012, to earn a higher salary and buy the goods on offer. In a deeply poor Christian nation, the lure of bright lights and shiny toys isn't just the prospect of living a more comfortable life but of lifting life beyond a monotonous daily grind your children may not escape.

It's impossible to resent Papua New Guineans who crave a washing machine or laptop computer even if we in the West patronisingly worry that traditional culture may be threatened in the process. When the lure of the dollar is a new Western religion – and I argue this not because I miss the days of Sunday churchgoing by the majority of citizens – we have no right to lecture developing nations not to follow our lead and discover good lives through the wallet. However, opposing rampant consumerism is a valid concern to be shared with anybody who'll listen.

Of course the erosion of traditional culture is a real worry, a view expressed by many community elders in Papua New Guinea, but it's far more complicated than blaming ubiquitous mobile phone usage among the population.

Many religious people argue that living a good life means abiding by key tenets of the Bible. Do not kill. Do not steal. Be kind to your neighbour. None of these principles, however, requires religious belief. They've become secular and basic human ambitions, codified in law. Western legal and social traditions are undoubtedly religious in nature, but teaching children not to kill can occur without Jesus, Muhammad or the Messiah entering the debate. Killing is (mostly) wrong because it's wrong. Full stop.

I often think about what being a good person means. Why do I believe what I believe and are my thoughts about being a good person at all influenced by my Jewish background? It's impossible to say they're not since I grew up in a liberal Jewish home where light adherence to the Torah was encouraged. I had a bar mitzvah and officially became a man in the eyes of my Jewish peers, despite my voice still embarrassingly being in the process of breaking on my big day. I never knew who God was or what he intended for the world or me but he seemed benevolent enough.

That was then. Today I see goodness as far less spiritual and far more achievable. In my professional life this means giving voice to the silenced in our world, whether this is the Palestinians or occupied Afghans. I do this because I feel the only legitimate response to injustice is challenging accepted wisdom.

This sense of outrage emerged from a troubled relationship with my father in my teenage years, when he was intolerant of me finding my own voice due to his conservative, Germanic-style upbringing. He has since apologised for this behaviour and today we're very close, but during those long, difficult years I was forced to articulate my beliefs and stand up for myself against a domineering father.

Our struggles back then weren't because of our Jewish faith but I often felt alone because of the narrowness of what I heard in the synagogue. Even at this most liberal of institutions, there was a clear distinction between human beings who deserved respect and the Palestinians who were suspect before they'd even opened their mouths. This was the opposite of goodness. It was tribalism without a soul.

Judaism, like every religion, has various shades and cannot be easily defined. It may therefore seem unfair to criticise the entire religion because of a leading Jewish synagogue in Melbourne. That's not what I'm arguing here. The important point is whether such people, alleged defenders of the Jewish faith, are in any moral position to be talking about what a good life could or should entail when their ability to see all human beings as essentially equal has failed. It's for this reason that I have trouble relying on traditional Jewish beliefs.

I feel culturally Jewish and happily pick and choose a range of lessons from Jewish history that I like. I believe this makes me a better person. But I'm equally open to appropriating aspects of Islam, Christianity, Hinduism and atheism in my daily life. I feel blessed that I live in a country where religion isn't rammed down our throats and adherence to a non-faithful existence is accepted if not praised in progressive circles. A good life that includes daily prayer or belief in a higher being seems incongruous in a secular life in a largely secular country. I fully accept that living a good life is entirely possible as a devout Muslim, Christian, Jew or Baha'i, but we don't need these religions for us to be content, caring, productive, loving individuals on planet earth.

As an only child, it would perhaps be normal for me to have issues with sharing. I don't believe I do but a former girlfriend taught me to think far less about myself and more about what others wanted and needed. It wasn't rocket science but her interventions affected me deeply. They transformed what doing good and being good meant for me. I started thinking how my actions, especially as an outspoken critic of Israel, would affect those closest to me. I didn't stop speaking out, but I quickly realised that I'd pay a personal price for being so committed.

The perceived lack of goodness in the world isn't due to a deficit of religion. I've long believed and experienced that most people are essentially good and kind. Most people don't murder. Most people don't steal. All of us have told lies, some necessary and some malicious. I've hurt girlfriends and been made distraught by them. I've witnessed horrible suffering at the hands of occupiers and invaders. I refuse to accept that I'd cope better with pain if I were religious or that the people who wronged me should embrace faith to become better human beings.

Religion can be as relevant or as distant for us all. I've chosen to try to live a good and fulfilling life without the aid of God or the power of organised faith. I have as many unanswered questions as my religious colleagues. Although I reject the militant atheist perspective that 'religion poisons everything' – such a comment from the late Christopher Hitchens was ironic considering his love of the United States' Christian-inspired violence against the Muslim world after September 11 – I'm susceptible to the argument that fervent religious belief closes the mind to alternative world views.

Leading a good life should be easy to define.

Simon Smart

I'd have to say at the outset that there are obviously almost as many versions of the worthwhile life as there are people. But I think the question must at some level involve the search for meaning that, to me, is such an essential part of the human experience. Viktor Frankl, a psychiatrist and neurologist who spent three years in Auschwitz, believed that, 'the striving to find meaning in one's life is the primary motivational force in man'.[40] Frankl thought his experience in the death camps taught him that the ones most likely to survive were those who 'knew there was a task waiting for them to fulfil'. Frankl also believed that the psychological health of individuals 'depends on the degree to which they are able to discover the pattern of meaning . . . of their experience'.[41]

Meaning and purpose. These are both critical for our health and I think essential for living a fulfilled life, and yet many commentators talk today about a deep inner emptiness and sense of ultimate meaninglessness pervading much of modern culture. Untargeted desire and an unsatisfied hunger for the transcendent appear to be hallmarks of contemporary existence. When life is thought of as purely comprised of physical matter, it results in a fragmentation that necessarily carries a loss of meaning.

I know Antony feels no need for God in his life, and I don't doubt his sincerity, but I would argue that the loss of God for so many in the West has had serious implications. I think it actually matters if God is dead. A lot.

Many of the great atheists have recognised this. The existentialist writers of last century faced up to the consequences of their atheism, acknowledging that when God is dead everything else dies with him – ideals, purpose, meaning and a sound base for ethics. In a godless world, while I exist, there is nothing that gives my existence any meaning or significance. Albert Camus, in *The Myth of Sisyphus*, wrote about 'the absurd' being the product of humanity's endless longing for the world to make sense in the face of its refusal to do so. He wrote of 'the unyielding evidence of a life without consolation'.[42]

If that doesn't sound morbid enough, let's not forget Jean-Paul Sartre, who wrote:

> Everything is indeed permitted if God does not exist, and man is in consequence forlorn, for he cannot find anything to depend upon either within or outside himself . . . We are left alone, without excuse. That is what I mean when I say that man is condemned to be free.[43]

Where does that leave the good life? It was Sartre's view that once we have lost God as the infinite reference point, we have nothing eternal to measure our journey by, and it thus becomes hard to know if we're doing anything meaningful at all. Cast adrift in the universe, where can we have confidence that our lives have any purpose at all?

Too often today, people talk about non-belief in a manner that doesn't appear to acknowledge the implications of such thinking. Theologian David Bentley Hart says that in the West to be truly modern is to have a fundamental and radical faith in what he calls *the nothing*. We place our trust in the fact that there are no substantial criteria by which to judge our choices – no underlying reality and therefore no inhibition to our will to make of ourselves whatever we choose. Everything therefore sits under the unquestioned good of free choice itself. All judgement, then, in some sense infringes on our freedom, even if that happens to be the judgement of the divine. Such an ethos is ultimately nihilism, says Hart, in the sense that it is a rejection of total or eternal truth beyond the world.[44]

For many of us, writes Hart, the highest good imaginable is that the will is obedient to nothing other than itself. Guided by such beliefs, society must therefore rid itself of any transcendent standard that has any claim on our desires. Hart says this potent and persuasive model of freedom isn't easy to criticise and is not all bad, since it emerges from a desire to grant dignity to each life. Yet to be true to the spirit of the age is to place ourselves not at the disposal of God or gods but 'before an abyss, over which presides the empty power of our isolated wills, whose decisions are their own moral index'.[45] Faced with such a chasm we may well ask what incentive there is to worry about meaning or significance or even concepts like 'the good'.

Don't get me wrong. Many non-believers respond with a determination to work nonetheless towards the brave, ethical life. Christopher Hitchens, in the memoir he completed not long before he was diagnosed with the cancer that would eventually claim his life, wrote that he didn't need the supernatural to find purpose in the universe, but saw a worthwhile life as one 'that partakes even in a little friendship, love, irony, humour, parenthood, literature, and music, and the chance to take part in battles for the liberation of others'.[46] I can say amen to all of that, and I don't doubt that Christopher Hitchens was able to pack plenty of all those things into his sixty-two years.

But in my view a vital ingredient is missing from this assessment of the good life and, unsurprisingly, that ingredient I believe to be a relationship with the creator of all these good things. 'You shall love the Lord your God with all your heart, and with all your soul, and with all your strength, and with all your mind; and your neighbour as yourself,' said Jesus (Luke 10:27). This he saw as the key to life.

Many people have found that Jesus is able to fulfil our need for meaning and coherence, giving us a sense of personal significance by telling us who we are. Picking up on the notion of each person being made in the image of God, Jesus taught, and especially showed with his actions, that every person is of incalculable value. He lived out a message of great love and compassion for every human life – women, children, those who thought they were righteous and those who knew they weren't. He sat down to eat meals with prostitutes and priests, despised tax collectors and the elite. He talked about being the good shepherd who would risk danger and death to find just one sheep. He healed the sick and the lame and railed against the powerful oppressing the weak. He spoke about the power and importance of forgiveness, even of our enemies. His death represented the most emphatic measure of the value of each person, because he believed he died in every person's place.[47] That makes sense of course only if he was who he claimed to be – God on a cross.

In the opening of Mark's gospel, the first words we hear from Jesus are, 'The time has come, the Kingdom of God is near, repent and believe the good news.' Luke's Gospel adds Jesus announcing:

> The Spirit of the Lord is on me,
> because he has anointed me
> to proclaim good news to the poor.
> He has sent me to proclaim freedom for the prisoners
> and recovery of sight for the blind,
> to set the oppressed free,
> to proclaim the year of the Lord's favour (Luke 4:18–19).

Here Jesus is quoting an Old Testament passage that adds, 'to bind up the broken-hearted . . . to comfort all who mourn . . . to bestow on them a crown of beauty instead of ashes . . . a garment of praise instead of a spirit of despair' (Isaiah 61).

Everyone would find that an attractive vision, and in Jesus's life we see him living that out – the works of what he called the new 'Kingdom'. The gospels record him healing the sick, opposing oppressive religion, offering forgiveness, introducing truth, bestowing mercy, driving out evil and raising the dead. This is what he meant when he talked about the Kingdom of God, saying that in him, it had arrived. His death, according to those who wrote the gospels, was a crucial act in overcoming a barrier between humanity and God. It's a life-giving message; living water in a desert as he described it.[48]

What Jesus seems to be saying, offers American writer Frederick Buechner, is that the Kingdom of God is the time, or the time beyond time, when it will no longer be humans in all their failings in charge of the world but God in his mercy. 'It's the time above all else for wild rejoicing – like getting out of jail, like being cured of cancer, like finally, at long last, coming home,'[49] he writes.

There's a mysterious sense in which this Kingdom announced by Jesus is both present now and yet remains a future hope. The call of Christ is to get in on the redemptive action of what God is doing in the world now. The Christian understanding of this is to, perhaps counterintuitively, lose your life in order to find it – locating the greatest meaning by laying down our lives for the sake of others. I wouldn't claim to have been able to do this very successfully, but I have been inspired by plenty of people who have, and their lives appear to be full of joy.

Our impulse, in our best moments, to act out of compassion, justice and care for the vulnerable is a vital part of being human – which makes sense if, as the Bible claims, we are all made in the image of God. I happen to believe that the sort of work Antony does in speaking up for those who are powerless, advocating for victims of injustice, and writing against systems of corruption and exploitation are in some sense a reflection of this God-ordained nature, even if Antony doesn't accept this himself.

There's great interest and research in the subject of happiness these days. I've been to the annual Happiness and Its Causes conference in Sydney a couple of times and there is broad agreement among the myriad of social researchers, psychologists, scientists and authors there that adopting an outward focus, living for others and concentrating on relationships and community are ingredients of a fulfilling life. This is ancient wisdom in which a relationship with God was once a crucial part of the equation. And in my mind, the idea of forgoing your own interests for the sake of others makes the most sense and gains the highest meaning when it is seen as partaking in God's action in the world.

Within such a framework of belief there's a unique role for each individual in finding a way to add to the truth, love and joy of the world in whatever way God has wired them for such a task. It gives a purpose and place to each person and even mundane interactions and activities. In many ways, this is the sense of *vocation* or 'calling', a Christian concept our culture has imbibed, one that's very attractive and motivating. If you truly believe you were made with a unique purpose, then meaning flows naturally from that belief.

Old Testament scholar Bruce Waltke believes that crucial to our personal identity is the ability to situate our lives within a story:

'Who am I?' is the fundamental question of our existence. Our self-identity is the window through which we perceive and engage the world; it determines all that we do . . . This identity . . . is formed by two factors: memory and destiny.[50]

Perhaps it's the sense of memory and destiny – where we have come from and where we are going – that is missing for so many of us today. Philosopher Leon Kass believes that modern life is redolent of such a lack, and alludes to the loss of God as central to the dilemma of contemporary life:

As the curtain begins to descend on the twentieth century, we who find ourselves still on the stage are, truth to tell, more than a little befuddled about how to act and what to think. To be sure, we seem to speak our lines and play our parts no less than did our ancestors. But we barely remember the name of the drama, much less its meaning or purpose. The playwright is apparently dead and cannot be consulted as to his original intention. Cultural memory still holds gingerly a tattered script, but many of its pages are missing and the guidance it provides us is barely audible and, even then, delivered in what appears to us to be a foreign tongue. Armed with newfangled, electronically delivered images and phrases, we are never at a loss for words. But we are at a loss for meaning.[51]

Jane Caro

Social researcher and author Hugh Mackay, in his book *What Makes Us Tick*, talks about the desires that need to be met – over and above the basics such as food, water, shelter, and so on – before we can live a good and satisfying life.[52] He lists ten and says that nine of them are in no particular order – things like the desire for 'my place', for something to believe in, to connect, be useful, belong, for more, for control, for something to happen and the desire for love. Interestingly, the desire he lists as the most fundamental – above love, belonging, connection or even belief – is the desire to be taken seriously.

Mackay's analysis clarified something important for me. To live a good life we have to feel that we matter, that our existence, perceptions and experiences are valid and respected by others. My kids sometimes use a slang term, saying that someone has 'dissed' them. What they mean is that they've been disrespected. When you respect someone you take them seriously, when you don't you dismiss them.

These days, I feel I live a very good life. I feel extraordinarily blessed (if the real believers here will excuse the expression). I think I tick just about every one of Mackay's desires. I certainly have a sense of place, personally, professionally and physically. I believe in many things – nothing supernatural, of course; I think my faith is in the fundamental goodness of human beings. I believe that most people, most of the time, try to do the right thing. I feel deeply connected with family, friends, neighbours, colleagues, peers – even the people I meet and chat with on Twitter. I think I'm useful. I share the responsibility with my husband of earning an income and I try, whenever I can, to make the people I meet feel better about themselves. I try to be an energy-giver rather than an energy-taker. I have a deep sense of belonging to my culture, my family, my society and my peer group. I do want more – not financially perhaps, but I want to know more, read more, write more books, meet more people, travel to more places, have some grandchildren, have more experiences. And while I don't feel I can control what happens – lack of such control is at the very core of my philosophy – I believe I can control my reactions and responses, and that belief gives me some courage. My life is rich and eventful. I never know what the next phone call or email will bring and I love it that way. And thanks in large part to my husband, I feel very loved. Much of this could change tomorrow. I could be diagnosed with a deadly disease, or someone I love or I could get run over by a bus or have a debilitating stroke. As I have mentioned before, a meteor could slam into this planet I occupy and end everything. So what? I'm happy today and today is really all we ever have.

I've reached this very contented place gradually. I wasn't always so sanguine. Indeed, as I've already mentioned, my early adult life was filled with neurosis, depression and anxiety. I feared almost everything, especially going mad. I was living an outwardly good life then – good job, great partner (still the same wonderful man), friends, good prospects, loving family – but inside I was shaky and very unhappy. That doesn't make for a good life.

Looking back from the calm harbour I now find myself in, however, I'm grateful for my struggle with mental illness. It taught me a very great deal, all of which I now see as essential to living a good life.

My obsessive neurosis was all about fear of losing control. I drove past pedestrians, convinced that only by dint of great effort had I defeated the impulse to run them down and that next time – the mental anguish of this thought always nauseated me – I might not be so lucky. I hated edges. Edges of train platforms, cliffs, open windows on upper floors. Staying in a hotel in Rome on an upper floor, I could only crawl past a long, low window on my stomach. I never knew if I had the mental strength to resist the twin urges that overwhelmed me whenever I came to an edge – especially unexpectedly – to either push someone else over or plunge over myself.

So many things nauseated me – sharp knives, little children, boiling water. I became convinced I carried a monster around inside me, a monster I had to control. Had I been a member of some religious faiths – even today, I might have believed I was possessed by a demon and perhaps undergone the horrible (and ultimately useless) experience of exorcism.

But I was already casting magic spells with fate, trying to make a bargain with gods I didn't actually believe in. I felt that I could (had to?) control my monsters by anticipating them and remaining on high alert. But what I really feared was an exaggerated idea of my own power. Slowly, I've come to understand that I have neither the power to defeat danger by imagining it in advance or, worse, make it happen by simply conjuring it up in my own mind.

I'm no longer trapped in the vicious circle of worrying about things. I now know it was egotistical, my belief in my own importance and power – my imaginary dangerousness. In the end, I believe it was humility that defeated the fear.

But my anxiety taught me much. It taught me not to rush to judgement, ever. To understand what struggling with mental anguish and the demons in the depths of your own mind is like. I cannot condemn the murderer, the evildoer, even the paedophile as others seem able to do. I thought I was a monster; I felt overwhelmed by terrifying, dark thoughts. I know their power and their terror. Who am I to judge? To live a good life is to be compassionate rather than judgemental, to empathise rather than blame. My anxiety taught me that.

My mental anguish made me a writer. Novelists, in particular, must be able to understand and value all their characters, even the worst of them. We must be able to fully occupy their inner world to make them real to our readers, to make them live. For me, being a good writer is essential to my ability to live a good life. Communicating with others is as necessary to me as breathing. Suffering informed my imagination, broadened it, honed it, softened it.

My interior misery forced me to seek help. Now I understand that my anxiety was the healthiest part of me at that time. It wouldn't let me go until I'd dealt with the patterns of thinking that were no longer working for me. I had to face my fears and they wouldn't leave me until I did. It was desperation that forced me to reach out to psychologists, psychiatrists and finally, most successfully, a counsellor. All of them taught me many things about being alive and what it is to be human. They couldn't cure me – in the end, I had to do that for myself – but they gave me the tools, the information, the common sense and the wisdom that – when I was finally ready – I picked up and used. I use them all still. And I remain happy to seek help when I need it, knowing

I'll find it. I've passed on many of the skills and wisdom I learnt, particularly to my daughters, neither of whom seem to suffer with the anxiety that so bedevilled my own youth.

My terror made me feel alive — painfully so — but very aware of myself, the world and my place in it. I struggled and I grew. Sometimes I miss that. I'm happier now but also more complacent and a little less present. Even self-confidence has its price.

For me, the first requirement before you can live a good life is to understand and make peace with yourself — to take yourself and your motivations seriously, if you like. Before you do good you must fully understand why you do it, otherwise you may have the very best of intentions but risk doing great harm. The word 'therapist' can be divided into 'the rapist'. If you use others, particularly those who are desperate or vulnerable — however benevolently — to work out your own unconscious fears, dramas and unresolved issues, you risk psychically raping them. This is why all reputable members of the therapeutic professions regularly undergo what's called supervision. Supervision under the guidance of another, disinterested therapist helps them separate their own issues from those of their patients and so avoid unconsciously doing harm.

This is not an argument for not doing what good you can in the world, however. Donating to the needy, volunteering, advocating causes, giving back in some way, done freely and with no strings attached (the true meaning of the word 'generosity', perhaps), enhances both the giver and the receiver.

It's common in religious teachings to tell us to put others before ourselves. I disagree. I believe it's far better and more responsible to get your own house in some kind of order (we'll all continue to have our dark, unresolved places all our lives) before we presume to go around telling others how to live. If you don't nurture yourself, what use can you ever be to anyone else? The essence of living a good life, it seems to me, is humility. We all struggle, suffer, fail and fall short of our own expectations and thank whatever deity we believe in for that. It's our weaknesses that make us human.

Rachel Woodlock

I'm tempted to answer 'What is a good life?' with 'Lindt Balls, a non-snoring spouse, and possession of the remote control', but a properly religious answer would be 'Everything God puts before a person if they respond appropriately'. In my defence, the latter doesn't necessarily exclude chocolate, sleep and chick flicks, it's just that they don't feature very much in the holy books, so I may be on shaky ground there.

The Arabic word for 'the good' is *al-khayr*, which means the desirable, the profitable, the useful, the beneficial. There are absolute goods, such as truth and justice, and there are subjective goods, like a Collingwood grand final win – great for Eddie McGuire and my one-eyed Pies-supporting husband, not so much for everyone else with a full set of teeth.

The Qur'an instructs us to do good – to live a good life – but doesn't go into pernickety detail, apart from some broad-brush outlines. It largely expects we should know what good is, even if we sometimes delude ourselves about it.

> Worship God and associate no partners with him. And do good to parents, and relatives, and orphans, and the needy, and near neighbours, and neighbours who are strangers, and to companions, and to travellers, and to your bondservants. Verily, God does not love the one who is proud and boastful (Q4:36).

Unfortunately, we can be temporarily blinded by tinsel and glitter instead of that which is really good. In our day, it's the disease of consumerism that Antony talks about. It's not that we're supposed to be mournful ascetics (although some early Sufis took that route), it's just that we have to remember that we're accountable for all the temporary material things God has given us to enjoy. 'We have made that which is on the earth its adornment so that we may test which of them is best in conduct' (Q18:7).

A good life is not necessarily comfortable; after all, surgery that removes a cancerous tumour-ridden organ can be terribly stressful and painful, but is good for saving the patient's life. It's the same with the pursuit of moral excellence. Standing up for the oppressed can take much bravery, as Antony describes in his battle to give 'voice to the silenced in our world'. Being willing to risk the censure of family and fellow community members is no small undertaking. Jane writes of an earlier period in her life when she had outward success but battled inner turmoil. It's a credit to her that she has surfaced from that period with such grace and equanimity. Simon recalls that most essential of Christian teachings, to lay down your life for a friend, as the ultimate good. So, living the good life is not necessarily a path of ease and luxury. It is, in Islamic terminology, a jihad (struggle).

A jihad to live a good life is like the process of becoming an athlete. Olympic sprinters do not merely wake up in a comfortable bed, yawn, stretch their arms, and think, 'Today I'll win gold.' They have to practise for many years, exercise their muscles with resistance, and compulsively return to the track, even after losing races time and again. But the good news is, because of the principle of psychological habituation, once you start doing good it becomes easier to keep doing good. The bad news is, once you start being naughty, it becomes increasingly easy to take that path, too.

In addressing its original audience of pagans in Mecca, the Qur'an presumes 'that a common ethical language is being used, understood clearly and in the same way by the speaker and the addressed parties', as the Christian scholar George Hourani wrote in his book on Islamic ethics.[53] That's why I think Antony is correct when he writes we don't need religious beliefs to know it's wrong to kill or steal and that we should be kind to others. However, it's one thing to know it's bad to lie, cheat, backbite and so on, it's another to actually refrain from fudging your tax returns or spreading gossip about the odd co-worker, and pretending to your spouse that you didn't drop a packet on the races.

As well as the problem of nihilistic emptiness Simon describes, I think the other great problem we face is the misconception we have as moderns, namely that the great religious and philosophical traditions are merely outdated myths that have little to teach us today. I commonly hear and read the accusation that Judaism, Christianity, and particularly

Islam, are relics with outdated moral codes inappropriate for us progressive, twenty-first-century people. While I cannot speak on behalf of Jews and Christians, we Muslims do have a certain mea culpa to proclaim in this regard.

The shari'a was designed to be a living system, evolving with various times and societies but based on a central, unchanging, ethical core: to believe in God and do good. The purpose of the shari'a was always to provide the societal support for each person to pursue a good life, not to make people's lives miserable like the Saudi religious police seem to believe. Instead, a process of crystallisation and stagnation occurred, particularly with the rise of nation-states that attempted to codify law into static written canons. Amira Sonbol makes this point in her criticism of how the particular patriarchal mores of the nineteenth century were mistakenly enshrined in the process of Westernising state law:

> Shari'ah in practice today has very little to do with the one practiced in Shari'ah courts before the reform of the law. After all, under the old laws, women worked and invested in businesses and they had access to divorce through the courts without the need for their husband's permission.[54]

Sonbol explains that when modern nation-states codified their laws, 'common practices, at the heart of a system which had been organically linked to the society it served, were replaced by particular laws suitable to nineteenth-century Nation-State patriarchal hegemony', which worked against more vulnerable members of society. Thus, insofar as we Muslims fail to appropriately adapt interpretations of shari'a to the contexts we find ourselves in, Islam will continue to be seen as outdated and even oppressive.

But to reject religion entirely is hubris. There's much value in the great world traditions because extraordinary minds have provided certain answers to the question 'What is a good life?' and that advice has been honed over the ages. We cast the traditions away from us at our peril, precisely because the good of their wisdom has stood the test of time, whereas contemporary thinking is still new, untested and suffers from being blind to its own assumptions.

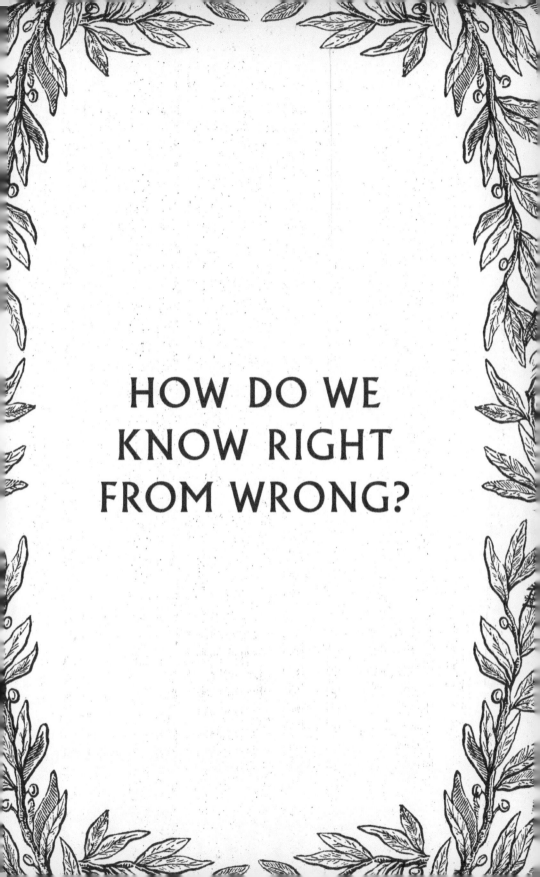

HOW DO WE KNOW RIGHT FROM WRONG?

Rachel Woodlock

She stared at me with big brown eyes. Both her and the small child on her hip looked wispy, their clothes threadbare, both living on the margins of existence. That's how I'll always remember them, be haunted by them. It was my last day in Yemen before returning to Australia. Maria, a fellow language student, and I were wandering through the local markets searching for gifts for friends back home. I think the Yemeni woman had seen us at the moneychangers. The fifty dollars we converted into riyals must have seemed like obscene riches to a poverty-stricken woman in one of the world's poorest countries. What was worse is that we were spending that money so quickly and so easily on trinkets.

I noticed her following from a distance, waiting for an opportunity to approach and ask if we might bestow some generosity on her. Finally, she came close and gingerly put out her hand to us. Maria shook her head firmly, and steered me away commenting, 'You should never give to beggars, it just encourages them.' I was embarrassed to challenge Maria, feeling foolish to seem so gullible. The woman stepped away but still followed us in the background. I'll never forget the look on her face – a mixture of sadness, disgust, hopelessness and curiosity that with all our money to fritter away, we had no heart to give her even a few token riyals. I'll spend the rest of my days haunted by her face, and from time to time I remember to pray for her.

Situations like these seem designed to test a person's flaws. They're like water to a clay pot, revealing where each otherwise unobservable crack is hidden. Often in such circumstances it's not intellectual consistency with a moral philosophy that's revealed, but some startlingly base behaviour: submission to authority, self-interest, and weakness to peer pressure. This is what Yale psychologist Stanley Milgram found in his famous experiment where people were ordered to administer (fake) electric shocks to a person in distress. Milgram and his team set up a scenario where unwitting subjects were asked to 'teach' a simple language task to a learner who was really an actor in a different room. Whenever the learner apparently made a mistake, the subject was instructed to shock the learner. The experimenters were actually playing pre-recorded distress noises, and the levels were increased to the point where the subjects were made to believe something dire had happened to the learner in the other room. Milgram wished to observe how bad things would have to get before ordinary people would buck against orders and do the right thing.

It turns out most of us will obey authority even when it so obviously conflicts with the commandment to avoid giving people electric shocks. This is why, taught Prophet Muhammad, the jihad (struggle) to live a moral life is greater than fighting in any military war. Battling to choose the good over self-interest takes a lifetime of training, according to the spiritual adepts.

On morality, the Qur'an takes a sort of Google 'don't be evil' approach (Q7:56). It presumes we can recognise what is good but warns us not to let selfish desires get in the way (Q3:57, 5:100, 16:128). We instinctively know it's bad to hurt others, say with electric shocks, but we must work hard to resist the pressure from external authority, self-interest and habit to do wrong – even when they seem religious. Generally the Qur'an doesn't speak kindly about people who use God as an excuse for wrongdoing (Q7:28, 2:224, 5:77).

While to the vast majority of us, acts of great evil – Nazis committing genocide against the Jews, Soviets starving political prisoners in communist gulags, paedophile priests assaulting children, Al-Qaeda suicide bombers targeting innocents – are clearly wrong, but more ambiguous moral conundrums require some introspection. Is it wrong to tell your friend she looks fabulous when she proudly shows off her mullet dress? Is downloading the new season of *Game of Thrones* so bad when the episodes are withheld from Australian television for an unreasonably long time? Why won't God let me eat bacon?

Historically, Muslim theologians and philosophers debated whether it's possible to distinguish right from wrong rationally, or whether we're dependent on divine revelation for morality. The three positions different groups took were these:

• Philosophers, heavily dependent on Greek philosophical premises, held that the good can be known rationally, independent of scripture.

- Mu'tazili theologians held that some things can be discovered using reason alone, but others require revelation.
- Ash'ari theologians taught that we're completely dependent on revelation to know right from wrong.

A lot of the debate centred around the question of whether acts are intrinsically good or bad, or whether they're arbitrarily named so by God. The Mu'tazilis argued that good and bad exist objectively, i.e. that killing and lying are inherently and obviously wrong, and these are things we can discover using our noggins. The Ash'aris, in what would become mainstream Sunni theology, taught that good and evil have no objective reality, but acts are decreed as such by God. For some things there may appear to be no rational basis to their prohibition but God simply decrees them unlawful (bacon springs to mind).

Although the Mu'tazili position seems more in line with common sense, the Ash'aris pointed out that in some rare cases it's right to kill and lie. The Aramoana massacre of 1990 was New Zealand's worst mass-murder shooting spree. David Gray shot and killed thirteen people, including a responding policeman, Sergeant Stewart Guthrie. After a police hunt, Gray was found the next day. When a counterterrorist unit, the Special Tactics Group, attempted to flush Gray out of a house with stun grenades, he emerged shooting indiscriminately. In response, as per orders, he was shot and killed, a death most of us would recognise as sadly necessary given the extraordinary circumstances.[55]

Or, take the case of the Muslims during the 1994 Rwandan genocide who saved many Tutsi lives based on a lie. In 2009, Jason Klocek interviewed the head mufti[56] of Rwanda, Sheikh Saleh Habimana, asking him how Muslims were able to shelter Tutsis, given the danger to their own lives, to which the Sheikh replied: 'We Muslims had an advantage.' He explained:

For many years Hutus had been taught to fear Muslims. They were scared of our mosques, so we could hide Tutsis there without fear of Hutus entering. Hutus had been taught that our mosques were houses of the devil. They were taught that the devil lived in Muslim homes, too.[57]

From one perspective, the lie that mosques are full of devils was harmful because it contributed to the prejudice that Rwandan Muslims had suffered for many years. Yet the same lie proved so useful in saving many innocent lives. So for the Ash'aris, if in some rare cases it's right to kill and lie, then goodness or badness cannot belong to the act itself, but rather our perception of it. 'There is nothing either good or bad, but thinking makes it so,' says Shakespeare's Hamlet.

The mainstream Ash'aris also argued that humans are motivated either by the pursuit of benefit or harm-avoidance. It was this simple binary of pleasure and pain that Ash'ari theologians like Imam al-Ghazali (d. 1111) and Fakhr al-Din al-Razi (d. 1209) saw as the basis for God dividing acts into those that promote benefit for us or cause harm. Some things are obligatory (e.g. saving someone's life, praying, giving charity); others are forbidden (e.g. murder, stealing, lying). Between these extremes, some things are recommended (e.g. hospitality to guests, caring for the sick, being respectful) and others are disliked (e.g. wasting water, causing inconvenience to others). The rest are neutral, merely depending on preference (e.g. eating watermelon, living in Canberra).

Although we can rationalise what we like and dislike here in the material world, the ultimate end of human pleasure is gaining paradise and avoiding hellfire. The kicker is, we can only know about this supernatural realm via divine revelation. But the theologians were in a bit of a pickle, because to imply that we *earn* paradise through good works, means God is compelled to do something – in this case reward us for things we've done. They weren't too keen on such a mechanistic view of the deity, especially as the Prophet had counselled 'Do good deeds properly, sincerely and moderately but know that it is not your deeds that will cause you to enter Paradise' (Sahih Bukhari). The theologians argued God could not even be compelled to inform us what we should do to live a good life and go to paradise. Rather, they argued, it's through his grace and mercy that he gives us instructions on how best to live. These are given to Muslims through the Qur'an and the lived example of Prophet Muhammad:

He commands [his followers] to do right and forbids them to do wrong. He permits them wholesome things, and prohibits for them bad things. He relieves them of their burdens, and the fetters that were upon them. So those who believe in him, honour him, help him, and follow the light sent down with him – they are the successful ones (Q7:157).

One class of Muslim scholars, the jurists, spilt much ink interpreting the shari'a, and developed all sorts of complex methodologies for deriving rulings. Actually, they're still at it, debating the morality of such things as embryonic stem cell research and instant divorce via text messaging. But for some Muslims, such as the saintly Rabi'a al-'Adawiyya (d. 801), this carrot-and-stick, pleasure-versus-pain morality was not good enough. In one of her most famous prayers she exclaimed:

O my Lord, if I worship Thee from fear of Hell, burn me therein, and if I worship Thee in hope of Paradise, exclude me thence, but if I worship Thee for Thine own sake, then withhold not from me Thine Eternal Beauty.[58]

Al-Ghazali was a little more generous to the vast swathes of common people stuck at the most basic level of morality. He taught that external acts of obedience to the shari'a are necessary as the first step on the path to happiness. However, if you want a real-deal connection with God, you have to cultivate inner virtue as well. The way to achieve supreme felicity is through the science of Islamic spirituality known to the West as Sufism.

I'll lay my cards on the table and admit I think Islam without Sufism is like footy without the grand final, coffee without the caffeine, sex without the orgasm: not much fun. Most of the great Muslims down the centuries were Sufis of one flavour or another, and it's only in relatively recent times that Muslim fundamentalists have attempted to de-Sufi the religion.

Islamic spirituality has been handed down over the centuries through lineages of great saints, men and women who had done the hard yakka and figured out the secrets of the path. Unlike the modern view of history, in which human beings gradually progress, getting better and better with each generation, casting off the myths of old, traditional spirituality says that the pre-moderns possessed well-tested knowledge that is still useful for us today. Not everything old is good, of course – the ancients were also known for slavery, terrible misogyny, and no internet. However, genuine wisdom stands the test of time and can be found across humanity's great religious and philosophical traditions. The Sufis emphasise individuals finding shaykhs; sort of like coaches for the soul. It's too easy, they say, to skip over the metaphorical flabby muscles and bad habits without one.

Sufi Shaykh Ebrahim Schuitema's basic thesis is: what's right is to do what's in the best interests of the other, in each and every situation. The degree to which we're confused about what this is indicates how much our selfish needs are still in the way. Knowing right from wrong is a matter of shifting from an egocentric view – 'What can I get from the other?' – to humility and surrender – 'What can I give to the other?' As Prophet Muhammad taught, we must be best companions and best neighbours to each other.

When we operate on the basis of trying to get something from others, they have power over us because they can deny us the things we want. The magic secret of true freedom is that when we truly and unselfishly act on the basis of giving, nothing has power over us. If we want nothing, nothing can be denied us.

There's quite a difference, then, between obeying rules because an external authority compels you with the threat of force – whether it's the government who might lock you up in prison or a deity who might throw you into hellfire – and being able to intuit what's the right thing to do and selflessly move and operate without fear, in awe and wonder at the majesty and beauty of all existence.

There's a postscript to my story of the Yemeni woman. Although I'll never know who she was or what happened to her, the shame of my weakness taught me that as I was unable to travel back in time and give her some riyals, at the very least I could be generous to others in need from that moment on. So when an old Yemeni friend reached out and asked for help, I knew immediately what the right thing to do was. The 2012 food crisis had hit him and his family hard, with the lack of work due to political turmoil affecting soaring food prices. With some generous and compassionate friends, including a number of Twitter mates, I got together enough funds to help his family repay some food debts and buy enough stocks for several months. I hope it makes up for my shame just a little.[59]

Antony Loewenstein

I was standing in a refugee camp in Port au Prince, the capital of Haiti. It was September 2012, more than two and a half years after the devastating earthquake that ravaged the impoverished country and killed up to 250,000 people. It was a steamy hot day and a sea of human beings – men, women and children – were living in squalor. Many had been there for years, failed by the UN, NGOs, the US government and other foreign powers. The smell of faeces filled the air as the day came to a close. The sun shone on the men playing dominos while many women stood around chastising their dirty children.

Words failed me. I asked questions of men who were keen to express their frustration to a Western journalist, but I felt impotent, an imposter, useless. All my questions seemed trivial. 'Why has the world forgotten us?' was a constant refrain. Giving a response seemed worse than saying nothing at all, so I simply expressed sympathy and solidarity with their plight, promising to report fairly what I saw. I'd rarely felt more aware of the inadequacy of journalism as a tool for positive change.

What I witnessed was wrong and cruel. It's hard to imagine anybody challenging that assessment. I didn't need God, spirituality, my Judaism or faith to understand that claiming to assist a place such as Haiti, and pledging billions of dollars to do so, is radically different from ensuring the money actually reaches the people who most desperately need it.

Talking about doing good is irrelevant when people are still suffering. It's a Western indulgence to think we're helping to bring any sense of true dignity to the Haitian people just by donating money to a favoured charity or believing our governments when they say they're doing all they can. We make a moral call, as I did when seeing the reality up close in all its grimness, that it's right to do more than simply express hurt and impotence. It's called being human.

Perhaps this is too simplistic. Rachel talks about witnessing poverty in Yemen and her Muslim faith giving her strength to pray for such people's predicament. But does this bring comfort to her or to those affected? I would argue the former. This is not to belittle Rachel's actions but to question the true effectiveness of prayer as a form of resistance. Of course, nothing stops a woman such as Rachel both praying and trying to better understand Yemen and its status as a US-backed client state wracked by violence.

There are undoubtedly many views about how a place like Yemen could become more developed and less marginalised. Since religious extremism has been fuelled and funded by Western powers for years in Yemen, the right response is surely to reduce tensions, and that means not resorting to militancy to subdue legitimate grievances that exist throughout the nation. In an age of heightened fears over Islamist terror, it's ironic in the extreme that many Westerners express shock that some Yemenis may want to attack America and Europe after suffering for years under the barrage of indiscriminate drone attacks. We can inflict violence but they cannot. We can claim to be good and right by fighting *jihadis* but Muslims who equally claim to be defending their country or home are deemed terrorists.

★

Like every conscious human being I have lied and cheated. I have wished ill on people. I have done wrong many times and will inevitably do so again for as long as I live. The older I become the less sure I am about the certainties of my youth. I don't believe my values have fundamentally shifted but I've become sometimes more tolerant of intolerance. Or maybe a better way to put it is that I'm far more interested in understanding where somebody who's acting correctly has come from, what in their past has made them do right. Equally, when a woman advocates the murder of a lover, brother or friend, it's far more important to understand why she does so than simply claim it's human nature.

I'm very much in the 'nurture not nature' school of thought. You aren't born good nor are you born a Nazi. The values we inherit from family, friends, media, religion, travelling or partners develop over a lifetime. But these values aren't universally shared. Sadly, in some Muslim communities, rape is defended and even encouraged. In some Jewish circles, the killing of Palestinians is classed as an unavoidable reality. In many Catholic communities, abortions are denied even in cases of incest. Some prominent atheists, such as American Sam Harris, can praise Israel as a bastion of civilisation in the Middle East because the Jewish state is 'genuinely worried about killing innocent people' (as he told *Tablet* magazine in May 2012).[60] Perhaps somebody should remind Harris of the tens of thousands of Arabs murdered by Israel in the last decades, in Lebanon, Gaza, the West Bank and beyond.

Faith can be distorted. Faith can bring renewal. Faith can be life-affirming. Faith can make people do good and give a moral framework within which to build a life. I don't think I'm being equivocal by arguing against the demonisation of religious faith in an age of reason. There are untold millions of people globally who give their time and money to various causes principally because they believe they're doing good in the eyes of Muhammad or Jesus. None of this means it's necessarily unthinking charity or pressure from an imam.

When there's no one definition of goodness and evil in the world – things that were seen as an abomination by the vast majority of citizens in the West a few decades ago, such as gay sex, are now popularised through mainstream Hollywood, situated in one of the most conservative Christian nations on earth – it's inevitable that most of us will be able to agree only on the bare minimum of what's wrong in our society. Don't murder (unless in self-defence and unless your husband or wife has been abusive for years or decades and your actions could be understood in the context of having no other choice). Don't covet your neighbour's wife (unless, of course, the woman is deeply unhappy in her marriage and is recently separated from her husband and simply looking for happiness with a man who just happens to be her neighbour). Don't steal (unless you're destitute and it's a matter of life and death for you to take that piece of bread or you're a believer in 'dumpster diving', the act of taking perfectly good food that's been wasted and discarded by supermarkets or restaurants).

As our values shift, so does our understanding of what's right and wrong, divorced from the ages-old decisions on such matters from the religious establishment. The secular, post-Enlightenment age in the West is one of the greatest liberating forces in the history of humankind, and represents a desire to no longer allow outside, unelected forces, such as a church leader, to dictate the way we live our lives.

How do we know right from wrong?

I'm not a postmodernist, arguing that everything is comparable and it's therefore impossible to say what's right and wrong. But I think it's a dangerous delusion, and presumptuous, for us in the West to dictate to the rest that our values and ideas should be theirs. Stoning adulterers is wrong in any language. Murdering civilians can never be good or just. Learning the value of life, goodness and what should be avoided in life can easily happen without a religious upbringing. We exaggerate allegedly noble Judaeo-Christian 'values' when many of them are inherently racist, homophobic and intolerant. Building a just society requires progressing beyond the tired arguments of past decades, when believers would instruct non-believers they would go to hell because they didn't feel the love of an omnipotent being. We learn what's right and wrong from experience and these can and should change throughout our lives.

It's incumbent on us all to remember that nobody has a monopoly on goodness or evil, right or wrong. We're all capable, no matter our background, of being a bit of both, and liking it.

Jane Caro

I love Twitter and took it upon myself to tweet throughout the presentations at the 2012 Global Atheist Convention. I was not alone. Atheists, apparently, are dead keen tweeters, and the 4000-odd delegates filled Twitter streams with quotes, comments and jokes during the two-day event – #atheistcon trended almost continually.

Indeed, one of my followers was so cross about my relentless tweeting that he/she grumpily told me they'd have to unfollow me for the duration of the conference. As I gained about 300 new followers as a direct result of those very same tweets, I confess I was not very fussed.

The first session after lunch on the second day of the conference was a (very moving) tribute to Christopher Hitchens. Originally scheduled to speak, he had died of cancer only a few weeks before. Instinctively, I decided not to tweet during the tribute. It just felt disrespectful, the wrong thing to do. I closed my iPad and concentrated on the stage. Later, when chatting to other delegates I learnt that everyone I talked to had done the same thing. We had all spontaneously decided to close our iPads and iPhones and stop the Twitter stream. Someone said they'd been told there were no tweets during the tribute at all. I have no way of verifying this – checking the times of tweets doesn't work because the wi-fi in the theatre was so poor and tweets could take up to fifteen minutes to appear – but, anecdotally at least, a large number of delegates independently decided it was wrong to tweet.

Why? No one said anything. There was no announcement from the stage or appeal from the organisers. Instead, a bunch of godless atheists just followed their instincts and closed their devices. If they had continued tweeting, there would have been no punishment or consequence for doing so. There was also no reward for stopping. It was simply a very human and normal instinct to mark the passing of a man we all admired with silence and respect. Indeed, this small but very decent response confirms my only fundamental faith: my faith in the basic decency, humanity and instincts of most human beings.

I do not believe that children are born in sin, or born sinners. I do not believe that people are only able to be good if they're bribed with promises of heavenly reward or threatened with eternal damnation. Actually, I believe the exact opposite, that people are intrinsically good and likely to do the right thing unless they're warped and damaged – particularly in childhood – and so have lost that innate capacity to treat others as they'd like to be treated. Do as you would be done by (immortalised for me as a child by Mrs Doasyouwouldbedoneby in Charles Kingsley's *The Water Babies*) is the much-disputed golden rule. The religious like to claim it as their own; the non-religious argue that it predates religion. I neither know nor care, but I do know you don't have to believe in a god to understand it or, more importantly, to live by the common sense and decency of such an injunction.

My own moral compass is fundamentally based on the golden rule. I find it fairly simple. If I wouldn't like something done to me, then I assume other people wouldn't like it done to them. Such a simple ethical framework, and yet it neatly covers murder, torture, stealing, cheating, lying, hitting, hurting, kidnapping, threatening, bullying, intimidation, slavery and a thousand and one other crimes both great and small. For me, it also means I cannot countenance racism, sexism or homophobia.

I also use another moral philosophy to help me decide right and wrong, and that's the right of everyone to live as they wish, as long as it doesn't hurt anyone else: the classic live-and-let-live moral position of the small-'l' liberal. It is also my interpretation of the positive side of the golden rule. My greatest desire is for the liberty and freedom to do what I freely choose to do without answering to others. To be granted the respect that I am capable of making my own decisions and strong enough to live with the consequences, be they good or bad, is how I wish to be 'done by'. As a liberal, I try to grant that same respect to others.

Also, as a liberal, I'm simply not interested in other people's sex lives. As long as all the activities involved are between consenting adults, I have no moral problem with multiple sex partners, use of any or all orifices, positions, combinations or even fetish behaviour, including freely consented-to sadomasochism. I regard such private activities as none of my business and neither moral nor immoral. How other people give and receive physical pleasure is not for me to approve or disapprove, and I actively object to attempts to restrict such behaviour. I have many more moral qualms about old-fashioned marriage – particularly when it included conjugal rights – for example, than I have about the honest, transparent, economic transactions involved in legal, well-regulated prostitution.

Which brings me to some more complex moral dilemmas. The first of these, of course, is the right to safe, legal abortion. Not only am I a firm believer in a woman's right to choose, I have had an abortion myself and feel no moral regrets or qualms about it whatsoever (I don't intend to go into my personal decision or circumstances here, but my own morality demands that I also do not act the hypocrite). In cases like abortion I'm guided by a pragmatic belief in choosing what I regard as the lesser of two evils. Because I don't believe in a soul, I have no hesitation in putting the rights, hopes, dreams and liberty of the sentient human being (the woman) ahead of the potential human being (her foetus). As a parent, I'm very much aware of the commitment and effort required, particularly from mothers, to bring up children well. I believe it's vitally important that such a demanding relationship always be entered into voluntarily and never due to compulsion. I would also argue that this is an entirely moral decision. I'm perfectly willing to accept (and to respect) that others make a different moral decision about abortion based on their own deeply held beliefs.

However, my moral beliefs about the world are also the reason I fiercely oppose the desire of others to restrict my access and that of other women to safe, legal termination services. It's also why I believe in the right of the terminally ill to access voluntary euthanasia, and yet am implacably opposed to capital punishment. To me, there's nothing contradictory about these beliefs because they are all about fundamentally respecting each individual's right to decide the shape and circumstances of their own life and death. To kill another sentient being – whatever they may have done – is against my moral code. To choose to be euthanised and so decide to take your own life, or to end a potential life because you don't believe you can adequately parent the child it will become, may be regrettable – even sometimes tragic (just as the sick and suffering person would no doubt prefer never to have become ill, the woman would have preferred not to fall pregnant) – but not immoral.

To be frank, I often find the use of shame by religions – particularly as a weapon to prevent adults enjoying the full delight of human sexuality – morally repugnant. To me, it's simply wrong to have made so many people feel so miserable and guilty about what's not only entirely human and natural behaviour but also the source of so much joy.

There's much I agree with in Rachel's opening to this chapter, particularly the intrinsic superficiality of only being good in hope of reward or not being bad to avoid punishment. Such morality has always struck me as infantile. Where I part company with her, and with many of the religious, is in the idea of both saintliness and selflessness. I'm deeply suspicious of both. I prefer enlightened self-interest, because I believe it's achievable for us common, garden-variety human beings. To me, always putting the other ahead of oneself smacks of masochism and – in its worst incarnations – manipulation. Because most of us find such self-abnegation impossible, the expectation of selflessness becomes another burden, another guilty inadequacy, another stick to beat ourselves with. I don't understand why seeking pleasure and reward for yourself, as long as it doesn't prevent others from doing the same, is a bad thing. The pursuit of happiness – inherently selfish, perhaps – seems to me an entirely reasonable life goal. I prefer the brisk, upfront honesty of the negotiation between what I want and what someone else wants, expressed candidly, to the sickly-sweet self-effacement of selflessness. Sometimes it's generous to take and allow others to give, in fact. And I'll never forget what a wise counsellor once said to me about the accusation of selfishness: 'What's someone really saying when they tell you not to be selfish? They're really saying, "Don't you be selfish, let me be selfish."' For me, true morality lies in being self-responsible.

In my view, right and wrong are not black and white. I recognise that to be human is often confusing, complex and hard but, as an atheist, I don't want to simplify such moral dilemmas. Instead, I prefer to allow them to inform my compassion and remind me never to rush to judgement. I believe it's always important to remember that there, but for the grace of whatever deity I do or don't believe in, go I.

Simon Smart

Very often the difference between right and wrong is complex and far from obvious. There are times when the answers to ethical puzzles involve choosing between the lesser of two evils. But from where do we source our wisdom for such choices?

On these sorts of questions, the West once relied on a world view that was thoroughly soaked in the Bible and its depiction of what is true and real. These days our culture adheres instead to what Dale Kuehne calls the three commandments:

1 Do whatever you want as long as it doesn't hurt anyone.
2 Do whatever you want with someone else as long as it's consensual.
3 Don't tell anyone else his or her choices are wrong or you will very quickly find yourself condemned.[61]

These are tenets of what we could call a Western fundamentalism in that these beliefs are seen as foundational and utterly inflexible. Jane's chapter perfectly captures them and what she calls her 'moral philosophy'. My problem with this philosophy is that while it sounds nice enough, it leaves out huge slabs of the human experience and in the end is too small and limited.

Jane makes a common error of confusing the silver rule, 'Don't do to others what you wouldn't want done to you', with the golden rule, 'Do unto others what you would have them do to you'. The difference is enormous. The more positive formulation involves actively seeking 'the good' for someone else and not merely avoiding doing them harm. It is, as a friend of mine likes to put it, like the difference between me deciding not to punch you in the head and me choosing to build a hospital to take care of you. The mind and heart are in very different places for these two things. The sort of choice Jesus urges people towards is about fostering a positive richness in people's lives. This is about a lot more than just common decency, which is what I think Jane is mostly talking about.

But Jane, or Antony for that matter, is certainly not alone on this one. There has been an enormous shift in the last forty years or so, as people have abandoned the idea of God (or something transcendent outside of ourselves) as the source for understanding right from wrong. For centuries in the Western world ethics were based on the character of God, who was thought to be good and who had revealed a sense of that goodness to humanity. Even as modernity took shape and a strong current of thought came to regard ethics as based on human reason, a massive system of moral values and practices based on Christ's teaching continued to exert influence in terms of what was considered good and right.

Since then, large and relatively sudden cultural shifts have delivered us to the point where the ultimate reference point for establishing right practice in the social realm appears to run no deeper than human desire and will. Desiring something is seen as a good enough reason for doing it. We want to be free and we want to feel good,[62] and as those two things become the dominant but flimsy basis on which to act, the notion of the common good suffers accordingly.

Of course you don't necessarily need faith to lead a good life. It's obvious that plenty of people who have rejected the idea of God or religion can and do make heroic contributions to society and lead thoroughly ethical lives. There are also plenty who live mundane and unspectacular lives who are nonetheless admirable and worthy of honour. But time will tell whether it will matter a great deal that a foundation for ethics eludes a godless universe. If you're a naturalist (in the philosophical sense of the word – you believe there's no God or gods), you have to think that there is no absolute standard to appeal to because the world and all of reality is simply *there*. It came into existence through chance and uncontrolled processes and simply *is*. Ethics, though, is all about what *ought* to be.[63] But what ought to be becomes philosophically nonsensical when you reside in a completely material universe.

Without an outside influence, ethics becomes about whatever we can construct for ourselves, or whatever stories our society tells itself. That could mean a society that chooses solidarity, kindness and compassion just as easily as one that chooses fascism and the building of death camps. Those who object have no higher authority to appeal to, and so, as atheist philosopher Richard Rorty admits, the 'good' under such circumstances becomes whatever those in power decide it to be.[64]

Having lost the transcendent, the ground on which ethics rests becomes decidedly unsteady. An example of this is the question of human rights – an important one today, and something most agree ought to be a core element of a civilised society. But on what do we base those human rights and decide, as the Universal Declaration of Human Rights states, that all men and women are equally valuable with an inherent dignity such that we should act towards them in a spirit of brotherhood?

Nicholas Wolterstorff, professor of philosophical theology at Yale University, wrote about this in his book *Justice: Rights and Wrongs*. According to him, the attempt to ground rights – or find a basis for them – apart from a theistic framework is bound to fail, whereas the notion of intrinsic worth bestowed by the creator establishes a firm foundation for rights in a way nothing else can. He argues that the 'image of God' status of each individual that emerges from the Judaeo-Christian framework (see 'What is it to be a human being?') provides the only stable basis for the notion of inalienable human rights.[65]

According to Wolterstorff, the only sure ground of human rights is the status of each and every person being made in the image of God and therefore loved by God. Our individual worth is conferred on us by God, and establishes a dignity and value to all men and women regardless of capacity, utility, race or creed.

Some would argue that human rights are just a social fact of a civilised society and it isn't much use trying to get 'beneath' rights in order to examine their basis. But Wolterstorff successfully shows that rights established according to such thinking are feeble at best and defenceless before powerful opposition, whereas taking the image-of-God status as a basis for rights brings with it a sense of the distinctiveness and preciousness of our neighbours and demands the sort of costly love for them that we see in a fully formed doctrine of human rights. Wolterstorff claims, and I agree with him, that human rights are widely accepted as a standard by which to measure a society only because we live in the wake of the Christian understanding of the value of each person.

Without that stable ground, things can become decidedly murky – something that's reflected in Antony's statements at the end of his chapter. To say that it's a dangerous delusion to presume to tell others how to live, and then follow that up with 'Stoning adulterers is wrong in any language' is an obvious contradiction, because unfortunately stoning adulterers fits perfectly with some people's idea of right and wrong, and most of us are not happy to let that go unchallenged. It's true that where Christians have held power, they have sometimes imposed their views on others in a damaging fashion. But I'm inclined to think that Antony's well-developed sense of justice and fairness owes more to the Judaeo-Christian heritage he has imbibed than he is willing to acknowledge. Instead, he is happy to largely dismiss that heritage as racist, intolerant and homophobic.

Today we must never tell anyone else his or her choices are wrong (unless they happen to be religious choices). This feigns tolerance and avoids being judgemental and so it's easy to see why people find that attractive. Lurking beneath this litmus test of enlightened thinking is our determinedly individualistic culture, which resists imposition and restriction and champions the autonomous self above all else. But surely we need wisdom to know how best to live. I know I do.

It's a fiction to claim that things done in private have no public implications. By way of illustration, imagine a family where the parents allow the kids to eat delivery pizza and drink cola while watching television or playing video games all day, every day and deep into the night. Suppose the children of the same family are taught to hate anyone different from them, to believe that women are weak and stupid and that education is pointless and teachers not to be trusted. The parents are free to do this. It's their choice. But wouldn't there be implications for those children and for those they grow up interacting with? Would it truly be an imposition to help those people see the value of regular sleep, good food, exercise, reading, kindness and snow peas? Might that involve pointing out to someone that his or her choices are simply wrong?

Freedom is obviously a good thing, but these days in the West freedom is thought of as endless choice. There is poverty in this definition and it has a bearing on our ideas of right and wrong.

In the ancient world, the concept of freedom was more about finding the person you were meant to be in order to flourish. Freedom had to do with shedding the things that prevented us from being who we truly are, including our own foolish choices. Being free, then, entails not just choosing but choosing well and continuing to do so. This is a much more elevated and enlivening concept than being defined by a vast horizon of unlimited options. And of course, the sort of freedom we can talk about in a godless universe is, as Peter Hitchens puts it, 'as available to monsters and power-seekers as it is to advanced intellectuals in comfortable suburbs'.[66]

The key ethic according to Christianity is found in love for God and neighbour, including care for the weak and oppressed. Jane and Rachel both find objectionable the concept of doing good merely to avoid punishment or find reward, and I agree. The sort of Sufism that Rachel speaks of – 'If you want nothing, nothing can be denied you' – sounds more like Buddhism than traditional Islam, which involves interaction between human and divine that is essentially legislative, with God as the lawgiver and humans the servants. This is very different from Christianity, where God is a personal father as well as King or Lord. In this dynamic love is primary. Just as in a family certain expectations make loving relationships possible, love is not the absence of self-interest or desire, but a desire to embrace the deeply relational nature of reality – a desire to love and be loved.

I suspect that Jane's resistance to the idea of living self-sacrificially might stem from her fear that women especially are likely to be disadvantaged by such thinking, and fair enough. But in Christianity, what Jane calls 'sickly-sweet self-effacement' is in fact not about being a willing subject of manipulation and other people's selfishness, but being drawn into a vision of reality that offers the mutual cultivation of human life and love. Putting ethical questions before the 'test of love' as the measure of how to act is a crucial part of this.[67] It's the sort of motivation for action that leads so many of the aid and charitable agencies to treat with dignity and care those on the scrapheap of urban poverty and homelessness; to pour resources into the developing world to ease crises and contribute to long-term change for those unlucky enough to have been born in the wrong place; to provide protection and dignity to the aged and people with dementia. It's what has for centuries impelled people to sacrifice comfort, time and wealth to alleviate suffering and work ceaselessly on behalf of powerless and vulnerable people. Can you get that from 'enlightened self-interest'?

Jesus talked about 'losing your life in order to find it', which, interestingly, is a paradox that all the current 'happiness' researchers say we need to understand – the centrality and priority of relationships, the benefit of 'other-person-centredness', and the personal satisfaction and benefit that comes from putting your interests aside to serve others.

My point is not that people of faith are the only ones doing this, but that they have a powerful reason to do it that is grounded in and consistent with their view of the world and all of reality. Our culture has been so shaped by the Christian story that even in cases where we have rejected or forgotten the story itself, its influence forms much of the ground on which we stand, shaping our view of each other and ourselves. That influence is undoubtedly waning, but what will replace it is hard to see. Perhaps we'll find ways to live well together and foster a culture of fairness, justice and love, but I suspect it will take something a heck of a lot more profound than polite civility, faith in human goodness and collecting your neighbour's mail when they're away on holidays.

HOW DO WE ACCOUNT FOR CONSCIENCE, BEAUTY, LOVE?

Simon Smart

In the mid-1990s, when I was backpacking around the world, I found myself lining up in the snow outside the Vienna State Opera House wearing jeans, boots and a skiing jacket, hoping to see Placido Domingo sing in Massenet's *Hérodiade*. In those days you could, for about two dollars, buy a spot standing in the rafters to see the show. I knew nothing about opera but understood that this was a big deal. I got in and, while leaning on a railing high above where the action would take place, waiting for the show to start, a woman approached me and, to my astonishment, offered me a place in a private box. The ticket was spare, she said. 'Come down if you like.'

So I did. This involved politely pushing past men in tuxedos and women in elaborate ball gowns and furs to get, not just into the box, but to the front seat. It was amazing – sitting in that stunning theatre, out of place. I was swept up into the colour, and the drama, and the exquisite, soaring beauty of the music. It was breathtaking and unforgettable.

Opera might not be your thing, but you'll have your own version of what I'm talking about. For you it might have been Guns N' Roses at Eastern Creek Raceway, a string quartet in Prague Castle, Ben Harper at Byron Bay Bluesfest or maybe Status Quo opening Live Aid at Wembley. Many of us have had our moments when, through the beauty of music, we've sensed that we're touching something much bigger, more elegant and important than our own shabby lives or, for that matter, those of the musicians or composers themselves. Music can make us feel like we're participating in something grand that transcends our own limited circumstances.

I tell the story here because it seems relevant to the question before us, 'How do we account for conscience, beauty, love?' This is a very large question and I couldn't possibly deal with it all here, but in a sense it is really the question: how can we explain the existence of things that are the non-material but obviously vitally important, aspects of human life, the things we can't measure or touch but that make life worth living? Do any of these things make sense outside of a theistic framework? Can we account for them if we are purely physical, material beings?

And what's going on for us at moments like my operatic encounter? We could choose any number of aspects of human life to illustrate the point but music seems like a good one because it's a universal experience and it can be so emotionally powerful.

For me, beauty of the sort we can sometimes experience in music, but also in plenty of other ways, such as engaging with art or the natural world, is like an echo of something beyond our material existence. It touches our imagination and introduces us to longings that evoke a sense of something beyond us.

Australian songwriter Nick Cave says of his music and the love song in particular, that it is a way to 'fill, with language, the silence between ourselves and God, to decrease the distance between the temporal and the divine'.[68] He says his art has been his attempt to articulate the deep sense of loss he has felt since the death of his father. Cave believes that writing allowed him 'direct access to my imagination, to inspiration and ultimately to God. I found through the use of language, that I wrote God into existence ... The love song is perhaps the truest and most distinctive human gift for recognising God ...'[69]

On this theme, the writer of the Narnia series, C. S. Lewis, argues that experiences of beauty awaken in us a desire for what he calls 'our own far-off country'. Through exposure to beauty we feel a longing for something that cannot be had in this world. So while Nick Cave believes that he conjures up God in his art to articulate the longing he feels (and perhaps he means this only as a metaphor), Lewis would say that God is calling Nick Cave through the music that he writes.

Lewis argues that if we find within ourselves a desire that no experience in this world can satisfy, the most likely explanation is that we were made for something or someone else – he would say for God. Each of us experiences a 'longing for home' – the place where we fully belong, where we are truly known, where we can rest and where we can be free. In Lewis's mind that longing for home, or for completion, animates our experiences of beauty, and stirs within us, bringing an ache into our soul at the sight and sound of beauty – whether that's first laying eyes on Monet's *Water Garden* or hearing Bach's *Goldberg Variations* or The Velvet Underground's 'Sweet Jane'.

Of course there are plenty of people – evolutionary psychologists, for instance – who are willing to explain distinctive human traits like our art, our humour, our love and sexual behaviour, our poetry and love songs, our music, morality and religion in Darwinian terms, claiming that these things contribute to reproductive fitness and adaptiveness.[70] Philosopher Alvin Plantinga describes this enterprise as a 'tall order'. How would our love of walking in the mountains or swimming at the beach or marvelling at the intricacies of a rose be an adaptive behaviour of our hunter-gatherer ancestors, he asks.[71] Where would our appreciation of Mozart or Bach or AC/DC fit into such a thing? Can a human activity only be important if it plays a prominent role in evolution and the ability to adapt or survive? It's hard to see the evolutionary significance of physics or mathematics or philosophy.

I would argue that there is much about the human experience that presents a challenge to those who want to cling to the notion of humans being only complex physical machines. Most of us resist being spoken of in such reductionist terms. Take eating, for example. Philosopher Leon Kass writes in *The Hungry Soul* that eating reveals something about our innermost desires, appetites and longings, shedding light on what is 'universally, permanently, and profoundly true about the human animal and its deepest hungerings'.[72]

Kass argues that humans certainly feed as animals do, this feeding being the most urgent matter of survival for a human being. Think Maccas drive-through on a trip up the coast.

But we also *eat* in a way that's different from other species, and we see this in the many customs, traditions and social interaction associated with eating. And as we move towards something more refined and sophisticated we can *dine* and even *feast*, activities that can involve beauty, art, wit, friendship, conversation and community. They incorporate grace, generosity, good taste and refined hospitality. And sometimes we are drawn to consider the mystery of where all this comes from and to give thanks for the source of such goodness.

When eating progresses in such a way it suggests something of the transcendent, the mysterious, that we are animals but something more than that. Think about a dinner party of old friends. Several courses appear over hours of dining, drinking and conversing. There's a scientific way of analysing all that takes place at this dinner – plenty that the biochemists, anatomists, physiologists and neuroscientists could accurately describe regarding chemical processes in various parts of the body and brain that are astonishing in their complexity and intricate detail.[73]

But of course, such a description wouldn't even come close to telling us all that's going on. One guest can't quite manage to lose the anxious feeling in his stomach as he tries and fails to forget just how precarious is the state of his career. Another diner, always the centre of her own attention, fails to notice the glazed look in the eyes of her fellow diners. The host, enlivened by the wine, smiles at his wife across the table. She smiles back, trying to hide the guilt she feels after last week's late return home from a work party. And another guest, at the first mouthful of her favourite dessert, is lost in thought as she nostalgically recalls the restaurant her Dad used to take her to as a child.

Can all of this interaction of memory and emotion be explained in purely physical, material terms? Some believe so, and that all that we can really say about what we feel at these profoundly significant human moments is that our brain chemistry is messing with our heads.

For example, atheist philosopher A. C. Grayling acknowledges that 'the hard problem' of consciousness is yet to be solved, and yet he allows no 'wriggle room' for those who see life in more than material terms.[74] While Grayling has no fear this difficulty will one day be solved by the scientific method, his view of the world leaves many unanswered questions. Where does consciousness come from if we are only the sum of our physical selves? Or what is the source of any moral requirement if naturalism is true? What about love or heartbreak or our anger at injustice? How do we account for evil and goodness? Because surely we can't truly account for such things if reality consists only of what we can see, touch and measure.

Leon Kass suggests there is a huge gap between the ethically sterile nature as it is studied by science and the morally freighted, passionate life lived by all human beings. When we start talking about meaning, and what's good, true and beautiful, our science comes to an abrupt end.

Perhaps it is the capacity of human beings to experience wonder, appreciate beauty and contemplate our existence that provides the strongest indication that we are more than physical bodies, and are unique among living creatures. Only humans have the ability to speak, plan, create, contemplate and judge.[75] Humans are alone in being able to imagine and articulate a future goal and use that imagination to bring that goal into being. Only the human being can think about the whole, and marvel at its splendour and feel a sense of awe and mystery.[76]

It's obvious that, as we ponder questions around beauty and love and so on, that they in no way provide proof of God's existence. But they might, on occasion, cause us to pause and wonder, not only about the source of such beauty but of our capacity to appreciate it. I find this highly suggestive of a mind behind the universe of immense and unfathomable creativity that is somehow, amazingly, reflected in human life and experience. Certainly it's been the case through the centuries that people ranging from the great artists, poets and writers through to everyday people going about their business have reason, in the face of breathtaking beauty of various kinds, to feel drawn to the idea of an ultimate being – perhaps God – behind it all.

But openness to the idea does require a certain disposition. In one of the Narnia stories from C. S. Lewis, at the appearance of the much-loved lion Aslan, Lucy exclaims her joy:

'I have been here all the time,' said [Aslan], 'but you have just made me visible.'

'Aslan,' said Lucy almost a little reproachfully. 'Don't make fun of me. As if anything I could do could make you visible.'

'It did,' said Aslan. 'Do you think I wouldn't obey my own rules?'[77]

Philosopher Peter Vardy cites this passage and reiterates that while Lucy didn't create Aslan, she made him visible. In the same way humans don't create truth but, if we are open to its existence and willing to pursue it, it might appear. Some might be driven to the idea of God through despair and meaninglessness, while others may be drawn to him through the lure and attraction of beauty in all its forms.[78] Either way, this is something that, to quote a song from Irish band U2, has to be believed to be seen.

Jane Caro

We know why flowers exist, why they're so colourful and varied and, yes, beautiful. We know why many of them emit delicious perfumes, and a few the odour of rotting meat. Whether we experience their appearance or smell as pleasant or not, the reason they exist is the same and it's sexual. Every living creature's purpose, it seems, is to bequeath its DNA to the future: to reproduce.

Birds of paradise display their extravagant plumes to attract a mate. Satin bowerbirds collect blue objects to decorate their elaborate bowers for just the same reason. We had one in the garden at our farm a few years ago. The blue objects arranged within steep grass walls of the bower made a fascinating and eclectic collection – feathers, flowers, weeds, blue milk bottle tops, twists of shiny blue paper. It was stuff that in any other context I would have seen as scraps of worthless junk, but it took on a whole new significance because we knew it had been gathered by a bird to attract a mate. Believers may see this as proof of a god, but I see it as something even more wonderful: proof of the absolute logic of our universe.

But it reveals something else, too. Beauty doesn't stand alone. Like everything else, it exists within a context. Beauty, really, is in the eye of the beholder. Biologists have recently discovered that a mathematical equation we've known about for centuries controls our perception of human beauty. This equation is called the 'golden ratio', and the closer someone's features conform to that equation, the more beautiful we perceive their face to be, and this is true across all cultures, remarkably. But our perception of human beauty also coincides with our fertility. The symmetry of the face apparently indicates the genetic health of the individual and therefore their suitability as a potential parent of our offspring. Perhaps that's why even the most symmetrical faces lose their appeal as they age. Once their fertility wanes, so does our perception of their beauty.

If the need to attract a mate is a satisfactory explanation for the often quite elaborate and complex display rituals across the animal (and plant) kingdom, why can't we be satisfied with it as an explanation for our own need to show off? One thing thirty years in advertising has taught me is that there are only a few real motivators for any of our behaviours and they are rarely, if ever, divinely inspired. As herd animals, we're extremely concerned about status because the higher our status, the more attractive we are to potential mates and the more chances we have to pass on our genes. Just as there is a firm pecking order in a group of horses or cows (we can always instantly recognise the herd member we call the deputy principal among our own farm animals; never the leader themselves, they are the perfect 2IC, doing all the dirty work for the leader, nagging the others and nipping at them to make sure they stay in line), so there is in human society, too. Anyone who has ever turned left when they enter a plane (I've done it twice) will be familiar with the wash of superiority that floods over you as you leave your less privileged fellow passengers behind. No matter how democratic and egalitarian you think you are, there's no escaping that particular, very human, pleasure.

If your parents have not bestowed upon you a face that conforms to the golden ratio, then you'd better hope they've conferred some other kind of status, either through money, aristocratic lineage or power. An ugly rich girl or boy has a much better chance at finding love, quite frankly, than an ugly poor one. Indeed, while wealth and status in themselves don't guarantee happiness (Christina Onassis, anyone?) they certainly help soften the blows. Advertisers well understand that the most powerful fear-based motivator is the threat of humiliation, which is really all about a loss of status (we sometimes literally refer to it as loss of face). The fear of social embarrassment is much more potent than fear of either death or injury, and has sold oceans of deodorant, breath freshener and anti-dandruff shampoos. However much we want to elevate human beauty and love above gritty, self-interested reality, it seems pretty clear that we use social-status markers – fashionable clothes, expensive accessories, being seen in the right places with the right people – to help us win and hold on to the most desirable mate possible. If we're programmed to pass on our DNA, it makes sense that we'd want to do so via the best genetic specimen we can find.

Now the romantics among you may be horrified by what I've written, but not only have I entirely missed the 'god' gene (if there is such a thing) I've also missed the romantic one. A friend once asked me how I'd managed to maintain such a long relationship (my husband and I have been happily together for thirty-seven years) and was shocked at my answer: 'I haven't a romantic bone in my body.' What I meant by that is I like to face things as they are and not romanticise them. It doesn't bother me in the least that human love probably only exists for two very prosaic reasons: to trick us into having sex and reproducing; and to force us to protect our herd, our partner, our relatives and – in particular – our offspring. The golden rule (like the golden ratio), as discussed in the chapter 'How do we know right from wrong?', is really about reciprocal survival. If I do to you as I would have you do to me, we're both more likely to survive long enough to fulfil our biological purpose and pass on our genes.

All the other things we claim to love – beauty, art, music, literature – are really about joy and pleasure, and I'm absolutely in favour of as much of both of those as possible. That's why I hate the attitude to 'the yarts' – as Les Patterson calls them – that has a slightly medicinal quality. You know, the take-two-operas-a-year-and-confirm-your-membership-of-the-intellectual-middle-class kind. That to me harks straight back to status markers rather than real, honest enjoyment. But make no mistake about it, great art both reminds us of what it is to be human (rarely divine) and is a marker of class. Most things are both good and bad.

And then there's conscience. My eldest daughter (yes, the one who nearly died) had one of those adolescences that parents fear. At thirteen, fourteen and fifteen she was angry, truculent and rebellious. It didn't help that she looked twenty and was so beautiful she was headhunted by a modelling agency. For a while there, my husband and I were seriously worried about her. Then, on a walk in the country one day, she said something that made me feel much more confident she'd be okay. 'You know, Mum,' she said, 'I was thinking the other day that if you wouldn't like what you were thinking of doing splashed all over the newspapers, then that was probably a good reason not to do it.'

In other words, is conscience another version of shame? Sometimes I think it is. But conscience and guilt are tricky things. If we tell a deliberate lie that works to our own advantage, many of us will have a troubled conscience about it – we'll feel ashamed of ourselves and fear being caught out and exposed. But if we tell a white lie – to save someone else's feelings, or to make a good story a little better – we may feel blithely unconcerned, even pleased with ourselves. If we nick a pen from the stationery cupboard at work, or fail to return a library book, most of us can live with the guilt, probably because if someone borrows a book of ours and fails to return it or absentmindedly pockets our pen, we're not very bothered about it ourselves. Do as you would be done by, again, it seems. But if we deceive or betray someone we love, by being unfaithful or keeping money or serious debt secret, we may feel quite guilty and ashamed, perhaps because we know we'd hate it if they did the same thing to us.

And sometimes conscience can be used quite unconscionably, often by religion. Why should anyone have a guilty conscience about masturbating, for example? And yet people did – for centuries. In the past, some very young children had their hands tied to the bed when they slept to prevent them touching themselves in a way that was then seen as sinful. The cruelty of this is hard to imagine. Yet those who bound the children's hands didn't feel any pangs of conscience; instead, they hoped the children did. Even today, we know rape and sexual assault victims are reluctant to report the crime because – weirdly – they feel ashamed, even though they've done nothing wrong. People burnt heretics with no sense of guilt whatsoever. Today, they crash fully loaded planes into skyscrapers to kill infidels with equal lack of conscience. And it's hard to imagine that the crowd who bayed for the blood of the eleven-year-old Pakistani girl with Down syndrome suspected of blasphemy against the Qur'an felt anything but righteous. The Sydney Anglicans feel no guilt at resisting women's ordination or asking women to 'submit' to their husbands in their wedding vows. And the religious police who forced fourteen-year-old school girls back into their burning school dormitory to perish because they were not properly covered probably still feel entirely justified. Do the Catholics who lied to vulnerable Africans about the permeability of condoms to the HIV virus feel any pricks in their conscience? Sadly, I doubt it.

In fact, does a belief in a god, far from enhancing our ability to use our conscience as a sensible guide to our actions, actually distort it? My daughter, the same one who used to be a rebel, is now a high school English teacher. She was musing the other day about how difficult her students find it to ask the 'why' questions – which is the one indicative of higher order thinking. They can ask the 'what', 'how' and 'who' questions about a text quite easily, but look blankly at her when she probes as to why an author may have chosen to do what he or she has done. Her hypothesis is that for a lot of people the 'why' question is not one they ever ask in their own life, because it's usually automatically answered by the word 'god'. Why did Grandma die? Why must mum wait until everyone else has eaten to eat? Why must I do the dishes while my brothers watch television? Why is it bad to be gay? 'Because God says so' as an answer actually negates the need to use your conscience at all.

Antony Loewenstein

The hours I climbed Mount Sinai in Egypt haunt me to this day. It's 2007 and I arrive at the base of the mountain around 3.00 am. It's pitch black apart from a few stray spotlights darting through the air. I begin the ascent with a group of Westerners and local guides. It's cold and the walk is steep along a rocky path. Egyptians sell water and snacks along the way. I'm aiming to arrive at the summit before sunrise to watch the day's beginning.

The mountain is situated on the Sinai Peninsula at 2285 metres above sea level, and the air thins as I approach the peak. As the first shards of light illuminate the sky, I hear soft chanting from Christian pilgrims a short distance away. It's repetitive and hypnotic and adds to the eerie mood of the moment. The sun appears in the distance, first hesitating to rise above the horizon before fully accepting its inevitable path, and the rocks around me glisten in the morning light.

It's an intensely spiritual moment. My mind is both calm and racing to understand why I'm so moved. The pilgrims continue their singing, in German, in the place according to Islamic, Jewish and Christian tradition where Moses received the Ten Commandments. I don't feel any noticeable connection to my Judaism but I deeply appreciate the beauty of where I am. I have tears in my eyes and I don't know why. I'm not upset by this, quite the opposite, so I simply let the minutes wash over me.

Seeing true believers in a holy place – and I've been fortunate to witness this in the Vatican, Saudi Arabia, Palestine and Israel – elicits a sense of wonder and even awe. Wouldn't it be so satisfying to see a site or deity and feel an immediate association with a religion and become even more committed to its beliefs and teachings? Perhaps, but in the Sinai the spiritual core of that moment for me allowed a kind of inner peace, respecting the pilgrims' journey beside me while being separate from it. The dozens of people huddled under jumpers and sleeping bags as the sun rose on a clear and spectacular morning were all there for a different reason. They all saw beauty. They were all affected by it. But I didn't need a holy book or religious text simply to see the natural order of things progress as it has done ever since the Big Bang. I couldn't fully explain it. I didn't want to.

Love can't be defined and neither can beauty. Love can be between a man and a woman, two women, two men or a young boy and his pet goat. It isn't for anybody to define it. Consenting adults can behave as they want as long as it doesn't hurt anybody else. All major religions spend obsessive amounts of time telling their followers who to love, who not to fall for, why only certain relationships are acceptable and what will be tolerated by God. It's wholly unsurprising that an increasingly secular West is rejecting the staid definitions of love offered by mostly male leaders and creating new relationships that suit the times.

During the Jewish New Year celebration of Rosh Hashanah in 2012, an event at the Jewish Museum in Florida highlighted the ways an ancient religion is trying to remain relevant in a modern age. A rabbi asked the participants, men and women in their twenties and thirties, to text what they were thinking, so they could be 'fully present', and the messages appeared on a screen in the room. Various thoughts emerged, according to a New York Times report in September 2012: 'Be a better friend', 'Procrastinate less', 'Worry less, enjoy life more.'[79]

The atmosphere was warm and friendly, and the rabbi admitted that getting young Jews involved was no easy task in the twenty-first century. 'We can no longer assume that young people will join the Jewish community,' Rabbi Gary A. Glickstein said. A young woman from New York, Sarah Silver, appreciated the event. 'It felt like a community . . . It was great to share. I am not a super-strict practicing Jew, and it was nice to feel like other people are human, too.' Only a few decades ago, liberal Judaism, or 'reform' as they call it in America, would have found the idea of asking Jews their opinions about life anathema. Surely this is progress.

Community. That's what it's all about. When it comes to appreciating how we define love, beauty and conscience, it's a complex mix of upbringing, parents, school, popular culture, friends and partners. It doesn't stay static, and nor should it. The greatest fear of organised religion is that potential practitioners will no longer find it relevant or appropriate its belief system to define their lives.

A devout Muslim living in Kandahar may well find a naked woman appealing – I remember hearing Afghan men in Afghanistan talk about secretly swapping pornography on flash sticks because doing so publicly was impossible in a religiously conservative country – but his ability to define it openly is forbidden, *haram*. The key point is that the societal and cultural definition of beauty in Central Asia is a world away from bikini girls in the pages of *People* magazine.

I routinely hear when travelling in religious countries that Westerners objectify women in a crude and degrading fashion in movies, advertising and pop music. Undoubtedly there are countless ways in which this is true, with girls being subjected to societal beauty pressures that don't exist in more repressive states, though let's not idealise the reality for women in places where it's equally important to not be seen or heard.

The image of a thin, healthy girl is ubiquitous in the Western mainstream media and clearly contributes to eating disorders and other body-image problems. But a religiously enforced definition of what human beings should think and feel is the norm in vast swathes of the world. Are we in the West, with a gradual reduction in reliance on clerics, rabbis and priests, more enlightened, more open-minded, more accepting and more in touch with what real beauty may look like? I'm not convinced. A striking sunset or a newborn baby can be appreciated equally by an atheist or a devout Christian.

In her essay, Jane explains the 'logic of the universe' as all living creatures being innately programmed to reproduce. Science tells us this and so does common sense. But love isn't simply a chemical equation that sparks between some people and not others. It's inexplicable and all the more special because of it. Two individuals may look perfect on paper but remain ill-matched.

In my own life, I've been drawn to friends and partners because they're both similar to me but also challenging to my own ideas. As I get older, however, I don't think I could be in a serious relationship with a woman who was deeply religious and took the word of God, through its earthly messengers, at face value. I could respect her, depending on what she advocated, but human beings are linked by a sense of wanting to understand the universe, if only their own patch. I gladly admit that I understand far less than I knew in my younger years. I welcome this.

Accounting for beauty, love and conscience is a task no sensible human being will want ever to complete. Any faith that attempts to explain why a young child dies, or says that gay relationships are wrong or marriage is the best outcome for couples and conflict can be soothed by prayer doesn't deserve to be taken entirely seriously. You can have opinions as to why something is wrong, you can argue a particular point and claim it's because its reasoning exists in the Bible or Qur'an, but nobody has a monopoly on the truth.

Rachel Woodlock

According to a famous tradition of the Prophet, Islam has three dimensions, the highest of which is *ihsan*, 'to beautify'. The Qur'an declares 'To God belong the most beautiful names ' (Q7:180), and when human beings actualise divine qualities, such as love, truth, mercy, justice, they are engaged in *ihsan*. It's through this process that we move away from our base nature and become more exalted than angels, who by nature are stationary. 'Indeed, we created the human being in the best mould, then we reduced him to the lowest of the low, except those who believe and work righteousness' (Q95:4–6). Beauty, then, is a hallmark of good religion.

Whenever someone attempts to strip a culture of its beauty, art, music and dance, in my mind's eye I see a big, flashing neon sign saying, 'WARNING: FUNDALOONIES ON THE RAMPAGE.' This is nowhere more evident than in the pernicious influence of Saudi Arabia's Wahhabi-Salafism. This puritanical, iconoclastic sect developed in the eighteenth-century from the teachings of Muhammad ibn 'Abd al-Wahhab (d.1792) with political backing by the founder of the Saudi dynasty, Muhammad ibn Sa'ud (d.1765). Although claiming to return to the original teachings of the Prophet Muhammad and his earliest followers, Wahhabi-Salafism displays many characteristics of modern fundamentalism with selective retrieval of past doctrines, an emphasis on literalism, a dualistic black-and-white world view, rejection of flourishing cultural diversity, and opposition to concepts such as secular governance, democracy, pluralism, religious tolerance, individual freedom, and free speech.[80]

It's described particularly well in a short essay that floated around on the internet a few years after I became Muslim. Called 'The Wahhabi Who Loved Beauty' by Kerim Fenari, it described the tragic spiritual poisoning of Fenari's friend 'Jalal'. Gradually, Jalal shifted from the open-minded, joyful personality of his early Muslim years to the dark, depressive harshness of a Wahhabi-Salafi neophyte until he eventually apostatised, leaving Islam altogether.

His confidence that the sacred could be discerned in nature, in saints and in beauty began to waver, a process that clearly agonised him. At times, when we spoke, he would return for a while to his old self, and talk enthusiastically about architecture, of textiles, of the sacred geography of Muslim cities. But then a cloud would come over his face, and he would almost shudder, as his programming once again took him over, and he parroted the shallow slogans of Wahhabism.[81]

But this mutilated, disfigured, ugly version of Islam is far removed from the one that proclaims 'God is beautiful and he loves beauty' or that produced the majestic blue Imam Mosque in Isfahan; the astoundingly intricate calligraphic designs on handwoven prayer rugs; the poetic brilliance of Omar Khayyam's *Rubaiyat*; the mystical dance of Rumi's Whirling Dervishes; and the melodies of the Darqawi sung prayers.

The iconoclastic impulse is there in the new atheist movement that reduces love, beauty, art and music to the mere evolutionary purpose of propagating the species. Jane writes that human motivations are largely about gaining and preserving status because we are 'herd animals'. Perhaps a good many of us are stuck at this lowest level of human potential, but I'd go so far as to say that the whole purpose of the spiritual path is to allow us to transcend our most base impulses – we were made for so much more than merely passing on our genes.

It's precisely through developing spiritual virtues that we become free from the fear of loss of status. It no longer matters what others think of us, only what God thinks of us. Early on in Islamic history, a group of Muslims called the Malamatis took this to a rather odd extreme. They deliberately acted so as to draw public censure, so they could avoid spiritual pride. Now, to be fair, most other Muslims thought they were raving loonies who'd missed the whole point, but the Islamic principle of transcending egotistical pride is a very important one. This is so much the case that many spiritual practices involve deliberately performing menial tasks to serve others. There's simply no better medicine for the soul.

WHERE DO WE FIND HOPE?

Antony Loewenstein

I've never wanted to kill myself.

There have been times in my life when I've felt empty. Depressed. Unsure how to move forward, unable to see a path ahead that isn't paved with dark thoughts. After a terrible relationship break-up. When my heart was broken. A particularly nasty public attack because of my position on Palestine. A death threat against a girlfriend due to my work on the Middle East.

But I never completely lost hope. I've never taken antidepressants. There's no history in my family of depression, as far as I know, so I didn't grow up with a dour aunty or parent.

Hope wasn't something born of any religious belief or spirituality. The strongest emotion, a seemingly unstoppable drive, is to live – for my sake and my family and friends. Growing up in a Jewish family in Melbourne, I don't recall adherence to traditional ideas or God giving me particular advantage over an atheist friend. Weirdly, I have no recollection of any atheist mates in my youth and I wonder if this is simply a faulty memory, a lack of diverse school colleagues or an inability to understand a non-believer when I was a reluctant Jew myself.

Hope isn't the absence of despair but something far more important and difficult to define. I don't dismiss religious believers taking comfort from a scripture, sense of community or thrill of God's word, but they've never provided the necessary answers or direction I've craved in life.

It's easy to find examples in the religious world of hope being extinguished in the name of fundamentalism. Saudi Arabia's grand mufti, while in Kuwait in March 2012, said that it was 'necessary to destroy all churches in the Arabian Peninsula'. The top three Saudi clerics have more than a million Twitter followers combined, and one of them, Mohamed al-Arefe, gave a sermon in 2010 where he said, 'The desire to shed blood, to smash skulls, and to sever limbs for the sake of Allah and in defence of his religion, is undoubtedly an honour for the believer.' This is the flagrant abuse of religious power to incite hatred and violence. Hope is killed in an instant.

Or how about the example of an American United Methodist pastor, Teresa MacBain, who started questioning her faith and belief in hope years after dedicating her life to the church? MacBain began to express concerns and by 2012 told National Public Radio in the United States: 'I found that religion had so many holes in it, that I just progressed through stages where I couldn't believe it.'

At the American Atheists Convention in March 2012, she told the assembled 1500 people that she could no longer live a lie. 'My name is Teresa,' she started. 'I'm a pastor currently serving a Methodist church – at least up to this point. And I'm an atheist.' The audience cheered and warmly embraced her.

But that's where the hope ended. Her community largely shunned her, as did the church. Job interviews were cancelled. She missed the regularity of church and the world she had created within it. Her husband, a believer, prayed for her every night and supported her decision to leave her position as pastor. She's still struggling to find a new space she can call her own.

For many atheists these kinds of stories would merely confirm their belief that religion is filled with intolerant souls who refuse to accept difference. Adherence to doctrine and unquestioning love of God is apparently required for obedient church duty. Hope can certainly be destroyed when compassion and understanding are absent, but I believe we must resist making sweeping generalisations about religion because of the bigotry of the few. Atheists are hardly immune from similar outbursts of hatred.

Hope and resistance can be fuelled in the most difficult of circumstances. Gay Australians of Middle Eastern descent can face beatings from family and friends. Psychologist Sekneh Beckett told *Good Weekend* magazine in April 2012, 'Most of the young people I meet are presenting from extreme violence experienced at the hands of their families in response to knowing their sexuality.'[82] She explained the family's response: 'They believe they are trying to save their child from the wrath of hell. But they create hell for their child.'

However, despite the best efforts of reactionaries to suppress homosexual expression in the Arab world, change through hope has occurred in the last decades. Lebanon and Turkey are showing signs of a gay spring. Club Arak, a dance party in Sydney for 'a bunch of lesbians and gay guys', opened in 2002 and continues to this day.

Alyena Mohummadally is a Pakistani lawyer in Melbourne who in 2004 started an online forum for queer Muslims in Australia. She told *Good Weekend* she was determined to use new technology to show she could be out and proud:

> That's important for people in the Muslim community but it is also important for people in the non-Muslim community not to make the assumption that you live in that religion with crazy Taliban people going around chopping each other's heads off. People ask, 'Why would you want to identify as a Muslim?' I say I don't identify with their version of Islam and most people I know don't. I identify as Muslim, but I am very much queer as well. They are two halves to the whole.

Hope lives.

None of this is to excuse or ignore the blatant crimes committed against gays or minorities in the name of religion. It shames both the faith itself and those who remain silent about it. But what inspires me, especially when so few fellow Jews publicly challenge what's being done in their name in Israel and Palestine, are people who aren't paralysed by communal pressure when human rights abuses are committed by 'our' side. It's far easier to retreat into a tribal bubble and simply repeat platitudes we hear from a friend, synagogue or newspaper.

Jewish, atheist hope comes for me in the form of a random selection of beliefs that include a moral framework I was taught as a child by my liberal, Jewish (and still believing, if less so) parents. I dismissed the less tolerant parts of this upbringing and became compelled to challenge what I felt was unthinking bigotry. I didn't possess huge amounts of knowledge but I couldn't sit silently while my cousins spouted racism.

My difficult relationship with my father during my teens forced me to find companionship and hope on my own as an only child. Judaism was never part of this belonging. If anything, I felt estranged from Jewish friends who loved Israel despite most of them never having been there. Hope came in the form of understanding grandparents and a school-friend who lived down the road. In the days before the internet and mobile phones, isolation was far easier to hide.

The secular Western world can imagine a world without religiously inspired hope. The 2011 Australian census found that increasing numbers of citizens are turning away from faith. Close to 4.8 million people said they had no religious affiliation.[83] Islam, Hinduism and Buddhism were the only religions that experienced a boost in numbers. These figures probably reflect a welcome assertiveness of multicultural Australians in admitting their religion. For example, there were 40 per cent more Muslims in this census since the last one and this almost certainly was because Muslims were reluctant to state their religion in the years after September 11, 2001. There are now 476,291 Muslims in Australia, 2.2 per cent of the population.

How do these numbers affect hope in a nominally secular nation? They certainly show a divide between believers and the rest. But hope is a personal mission, a desire to attain peace in a complex world. Whether that strength is gained through prayer and belief or the mere words of an inspiring friend or relation, what matters is the final outcome. Hope is like a field that constantly needs tending. It's never fully satisfied, rarely ever complete. Hope can come crashing down in an instant or it may take a lifetime to develop.

I fear a day where I no longer feel hopeful. If that time ever comes I'll likely not refer to my atheist or Jewish beliefs but instead turn to friends or family, something more tangible yet potentially fleeting. I almost envy believers in a higher being for allowing themselves to outsource hope to an entity over which they have no control. They can imagine what they want God to be saying or believing or telling them to do. That doesn't preclude independent thought but it also doesn't allow complete intel-lectual freedom. In such an environment, can God disappoint and not provide hope and the answers? Surely, yes.

Hope, as Karl Marx said of religion, may be an opiate for the masses. It's never content, always demanding more and inevitably destined to disappoint. 'I'm hoping for the best' is a statement we utter on a regular basis, but implicit in such a belief is faith. I like to believe that hope can be a wholly secular outlook, utterly separate from relying on religious doctrine to be satisfied. It ebbs and flows and relies on inner power to thrive.

I'm acutely aware, having spent time in war zones across the world, that the definition of hope differs between the comfortable, indulged West and everywhere else. A poor man in Afghanistan, who has only ever known conflict in his life, will hope for some stability and peace. A teenager who lives in a decent suburb in inner Melbourne may hope for an iPad for Christmas. The former will probably use his Muslim faith to pray for change while the latter is more likely to pray to the secular God of commercialism.

Hope is never entirely absent but neither is it ever entirely present. We delude ourselves by thinking hope is anything but a transient state that requires regular care.

Simon Smart

ABC TV's *Four Corners* recently ran a program on growing up poor in Australia, one of the wealthiest countries in the world. A suburb that began three decades ago as a social experiment in public housing was profiled, revealing the dreadful cost for children of generational unemployment, alcohol abuse, domestic violence and social dislocation.

Twelve-year-old Jessica, already getting into trouble at school, articulated a bleak view of her imagined future. She could still dream of a decent job and a happy family, where she could be a good mum and be married to someone who wasn't violent, but she held no illusions as to how likely those things were. 'That would never happen,' she said. This was a picture of hopelessness if ever I saw one.

But it's not only disadvantaged twelve-year-olds who express a lack of hope these days. I once interviewed Professor Louise Antony, a leading philosopher from the United States who also happens to be an atheist. At the end of a wide-ranging, fascinating discussion, I asked her if there was a longing of the human heart not available to her because of her non-belief. After pondering this for a few moments, she suggested that *hope* is the thing that is missing for her.

'I think it's a struggle for people that don't have this belief that something is ordering the universe,' she said. 'It's a real struggle to keep going in the face of the probability that things are going to get worse.' Louise Antony had opted for the brave life in the face of harsh reality.

Where has hope gone? It would be wrong to imply that everyone in the West feels profound hopelessness, but I sense there is a huge lack of the sort of hope that I want to talk about here.

We see this deficit of hope in modern music, literature and film – and very often in the best quality examples of those artforms – where world-weary cynicism and bleak storylines dominate. Narratives of global Armageddon – either ecological or economic – are reflective of such a spirit. Cormack McCarthy's devastating novel *The Road,* for instance, depicts a ravaged, hope-less world that cannot be put right again.

How did we get here? Theologian Miroslav Volf from Yale University believes that with significant shifts in Western thinking has come a diminution of hope. In the fifth century, philosopher and theologian St Augustine, who was enormously influential on the West, wrote about God being the source of all that is good, true and beautiful. According to him, people live lives of deep and lasting satisfaction when they seek things that fit with the character and will of God, who is in essence love. The supreme good that makes people fulfilled is to love God and love other people.[84]

In the eighteenth century a distinct shift away from a transcendent God and towards a focus on human affairs without reference to a higher power ushered in a period of a new humanism and its corresponding understanding of the good life. Solidarity and goodness towards others were the ideals of this period, along with an assumption that there was no need for a God to reference what this might look like.

A further shift in the late twentieth century saw the notion of human flourishing increasingly defined as experiential satisfaction where the experiences themselves came to be the measure of a good life. Moving from an understanding of the vast expanse of an infinite God, the West's sense of human life was reduced to the more limited human community and then even more substantially contracted to the confined and paltry self, says Volf.[85] In this movement there has been a parallel diminishment of human hope. Hope has been reduced to 'the scale of self-pampering'.[86]

Is it this rejection of an ultimate story to which we belong that makes hope so hard to come by? Many believe so and it afflicts a wide variety of people. The philosopher Alasdair MacIntyre says: 'I can only answer the question "What am I to do?" if I can answer the prior question, "Of what story or stories do I find myself a part?".'[87]

Without an overarching account of reality we have been cast adrift on an ocean of individual interest and self-reflection. The problem is most of us feel the need for something more substantial. In his book *The Longing for Home*, Frederick Buechner writes, 'No matter how much the world shatters us to pieces, we carry inside us a vision of wholeness that we sense is our true home and that beckons to us.'[88] It's that vision that produces in us that sense of longing that we all know, for things to be different and better than they currently are. We long for peace, for community, for lasting and healthy relationships. We desire forgiveness, fresh starts and acceptance. We long for rest from constant striving and relief from anxiety. We long to be known and to be part of something larger than ourselves.

Whatever you make of the story of Adam and Eve and their expulsion from the garden, the story acts as an archetype of the distance all humans feel from the harmony we wish for. Jesus's parable of the prodigal son from Luke's Gospel is surely one of the richest and most dramatic expressions of a homecoming. The son staggers back to the family farm after years away ruining his life and wasting his inheritance on profligate living, only to be showered with love and kindness. It's a powerful expression of redemption, total acceptance and the love of a parent: the love of God. It's full of hope.

When I talk about the hope my Christian faith gives me, I mean something more than the everyday expectation that good things can come as a matter of course, and I also mean something far greater than optimism. Optimism is to do with good things unfolding into the future, but they are things that are already there. Optimism involves a consideration of the past and the present and, as we make a judgement about what's likely in the future, if it looks good we're optimistic.[89]

Hope, on the other hand, in the Christian sense, is to do with good things (and, importantly, new things) that come to us from outside – as a gift from God. This hope is dependent on the promises of God and his faithfulness, related to his redemptive purposes for the world and his commitment not to give up on us. What seems impossible becomes real, giving birth to hope.[90] A baby born in the most obscure and inglorious circumstances turns out to be God in the flesh, coming to be among us. A brutal and humiliating crucifixion that apparently brings to a swift end the brief career of a little-known Jewish rabbi, is actually the path to salvation and the key to human life.

When the Bible talks about a 'hope that doesn't disappoint' it relates a profound and abiding sense that an assured future has invaded the present such that we need never give way to despair. This is a relational hope, which at its heart is about the 'flourishing of individuals, communities, and our whole world'.[91] It's all about the restoration of broken things – of fractures between us and God, each other and the world itself.

Such an idea has obvious connections with Antony's belief in hope being located in relationship, and the love of friends and family. That's certainly part of it, but it just doesn't seem enough to me. It's one part of the puzzle, but lacks the central and defining element of God's place in our lives, on which everything else rests. Where Antony believes that hope can be found wholly separate from a belief in God, I believe what he talks about is not truly hope, but merely a pale and unsatisfying reflection of it. And the idea that hope relies on an inner power to survive appears self-defeating to me. If I have to rely on my internal resources to give me hope I'm not confident I could muster a whole lot. If there really is a personal creator of the universe in whom true hope resides, then my own efforts to conjure something meaningful have to look paltry by comparison.

All of this might sound overly theoretical but I know I've been sustained by the hope my faith has offered me. This hope is not based on some idea that God will give me or my family an easy life. I'm old enough to have sat with plenty of friends and members of my family as they've had to go through almost unendurable circumstances. Many of them with faith in God would testify that their faith doesn't offer them a way to sweep their misery under the carpet, but hope within their pain. It's the sense that while heartbreak and hardship – even death – are all too real, those things will not have the final word.

I once heard a summary of Christian joy as a 'defiant nevertheless', and this rings true for me. It's the feeling that even when things get really tough, as they inevitably do, promises are made – reliable promises, made by God himself – that mean a future reality can and does shed a light on the present. Having experienced that perspective as very real it's impossible for me to ignore it.

The grand story of Christianity is one of redemption and restoration of what has been lost. You can think of that equally in terms of the universe and our individual lives – all the things that are not as we would wish them to be. And this is a vision of a world that will be put right.

The source of hope I believe in and write about here must look like make-believe to some (Antony included). I don't agree. But there is one aspect of the Christian story that shares something with the fairy tale genre: the denial, not of sorrow and failure, but of universal, final defeat. It's what J. R. R. Tolkien described as 'a fleeting glimpse of Joy, Joy beyond the walls of the world, poignant as grief'.[92]

These days those who are not completely turned off Christianity will sometimes say that the story of Jesus is a good one to hang on to – for the kids. But it's worth noting that adults read and remember kids' stories with a childlike longing that they be real. The wish for happy endings, miraculous escapes, punishment of wickedness and saving of the innocent, of places where evil is conquered and justice restored, where twelve-year-old girls are not trapped in a cycle of poverty and violence, where order emerges from chaos, where death is not the end and where hope triumphs – these are things that never quite leave us.

I'm left wondering whether those who dismiss outright the Gospel accounts of Jesus's life, who of course have their own desires and hopes and fears, ever consider this 'story for the kids' and wonder whether it might also be true, whether it has anything more than sentimentality to offer us as we navigate life's big questions and struggles.

Jane Caro

The American wit Dorothy Parker once said, 'Hell is other people.' On some occasions I've found myself wholeheartedly agreeing with her, but far more often I find that hope is other people. All through my life, just when things have felt hopeless, someone has said something, done something or made me laugh at something that has kept hope alive.

One of the things I care passionately about is public education. Simon is also an enthusiastic supporter and often takes the time and trouble to send me a short email responding encouragingly to something I've written or said on the topic in the media. His responses, and those of others like him, not only give me hope, they also help me carry on with what can feel like a losing battle. Encouragement from others – literally the passing on of courage – is one of the most reliable sources of hope.

When I began speaking out about the plight of Australia's public schools – and I don't intend to get into the rights and wrongs of the issue here – I often felt like a lone voice. When I decided to back up my beliefs in the importance and high standards of our public school system by sending my daughters to a co-ed, comprehensive public high school, I was hit with a barrage of criticism and disapproval. The most common criticism was that I was 'sacrificing' my children for my principles. I have since learnt that many other parents, particularly those with the means to do otherwise, who have sent their children to ordinary old public schools – particularly when their kids reach high-school age – receive similar criticism and feel obliged to defend their decision. I'm quite aware that many of my friends, neighbours and colleagues thought me (probably still think me) a bore on the subject. But I continued to state my case. Not because I'm noble or brave or anything, but because when I feel strongly about something I'm almost constitutionally incapable of keeping my mouth shut about it. I've also absorbed the idea – from my parents, no doubt – that if you don't speak up for your beliefs, particularly when you hold an unpopular or controversial point of view, then there's really no point having them.

As with all tough fights, in the fifteen years or so that I have been advocating for Australia's public schools, things have not got much better. When I first started writing about the issue and began my steep learning curve about the facts, I naively thought that all I had to do was tell people all about them and they'd immediately slap themselves on the forehead, realise the error of their ways and fix it. I've learnt – the hard way – a great deal. Despite all my very best efforts and arguments, including co-authoring two books on the subject, public schools remain underfunded and – almost worse, as I discovered when I sent my own kids to them – sneered at by many. Canberra, for example, is now the first place in Australia where more high-school-aged children attend private schools than public ones, although – as I remind myself when I get too gloomy – there are opposite trends as well. All the public schools, both primary and secondary, on Sydney's wealthy North Shore, for example, are now so full that the Education Department is considering hiring empty office space to house excess students.

In general, however, fighting for public education – as it is for all sorts of other unpopular causes – has been at best a bumpy ride. Recently, even battle-scarred old warriors like me allowed ourselves to get our hopes up a little when the Gillard federal government promised to pass the very sensible Gonski reforms, which would fund students according to real need and so – given that public schools educate the overwhelming number of disadvantaged, non-English-speaking background, Indigenous and disabled kids – it looked like our public schools would finally be getting some much-needed support. No sooner had we allowed ourselves to hope a little, however, than our hopes were dashed when the New South Wales, Queensland and Victorian state governments immediately announced cuts to school spending, the bulk of them in public schools, that would pretty well cancel out any anticipated largesse from Gonski. Public funding for private schools, of course, thanks to their powerful and sophisticated lobby groups – often, sadly, church-based – will remain more or less untouched.

I still haven't given up hope, however, and that's because of the responses from other people – people I know, like Simon and some of my fellow agitators, but also people I don't know and will probably never meet again, whose casual generosity of spirit I come across constantly. People send me letters, emails, Facebook posts and tweets urging me to continue, offering ideas and telling me stories. And people often pass me in the street or at a shopping centre and make an encouraging remark: 'Keep up the good fight' or 'Thanks for all you're doing for public schools' or 'Love your work'. They say these lovely things as they walk by, without breaking their stride, wanting and expecting nothing in return. They just want to pass on hope and courage – and they do.

Rachel Woodlock

One of the things that differentiates human beings from the rest of the animal kingdom is our ability to conceive the far-off future and imagine outcomes, both good and bad. It's this that gives us the ability to hope. From an Islamic perspective, hope is ultimately about attaining divine felicity. This is because, for all the wonderful things that might happen to a person, nothing beats God's good pleasure. It's more fabulous than getting a promotion or winning the lottery. Shaykh Ebrahim explains that, like Adam, we have complete and immediate unconditional access to God's forgiveness, mercy and loving kindness. It's not about keeping score, it's about changing our actual character and thus our deeds. How is it possible not to be hopeful with such a glass-half-full theology?

Hope is tempered, however, by what the Qur'an calls *taqwa*. Sometimes translated as 'the fear of God', it means to protect yourself from the harmful effects of your wrongdoing. It's the awareness that life brings consequences for what we do. For example, like most teenagers I thought I was pretty invincible; it never occurred to me that I could get hurt or die any time soon. I was staying in Innisfail in Far North Queensland, and some friends took me for a splash in a gorgeous rain-forest swimming hole. I gave not a moment's thought to my safety as I scrambled up some wet rocks to dive into the water. Halfway up, my bare feet slipped slightly and, as I wobbled and adjusted, I was struck by the sudden realisation that this was bloody dangerous. I could slip on the rocks, fall, crack my head open and drown. Before I had followed my similarly foolish friends up the rock face, I had lacked *taqwa*.

It's the same with the spiritual effect of the things we do. The correct Islamic attitude is to have *taqwa* – by attempting to live a balanced and integrated life – and hope in the mercy, forgiveness and loving kindness of God. 'Given a merciful and just God, and the solidarity of character called *taqwā*, human well-being is provided for' explains the great modernist scholar Fazlur Rahman (d.1988).[93]

I want to digress for a moment, to mention the hope that keeps me going in the face of almost constant negativity about Islam and Muslims on the part of so many politicians, shock-jocks and bloggers. In 2007,

I observed the Australia Deliberates: Muslims and Non-Muslims in Australia conference, in which a representative sample of 329 Australians met to discuss issues about Muslim settlement and integration in Australia. They had been polled prior to the conference and then asked the same questions afterwards, the results of which showed that interaction between Muslims and non-Muslims, and the opportunity to have open and frank discussions, led to a decrease in numbers of people wanting to reduce Muslim immigration, an increase in those willing to welcome and respect people from culturally diverse communities, and a decrease in people thinking that Muslims negatively impact Australian society.[94] This means that when ordinary Australians whose only exposure to Islam comes from the likes of Alan Jones, Andrew Bolt, Pauline Hanson or Cory Bernardi get a chance to actually interact with their fellow Muslim citizens, they are generally willing to change their minds. The 'Green Menace' meme collapses when people meet actual flesh-and-blood Muslims.

But Muslims make up only 2.2 per cent of the Australian population,[95] which is why it is important that we get out and about in the community, being of service to others. And there are some fabulous examples of Muslims doing exactly that. The Al-Ghazzali Centre runs the Mizaan project in which young Muslims spend the first Saturday of each month helping to clean up and regenerate the Cooks River environs. The Jewish Christian Muslim Association of Australia, whose current president is Shaykh Riad Galil OAM, is an interfaith group that runs conferences, meetings and other events promoting positive relations between followers of the three main Abrahamic faiths. Benevolence Australia organises a variety of volunteering activities including helping out at soup kitchens, with newly settling refugees, and providing activities for youth. So, although I sometimes despair at the way Muslims are vilified and stereotyped in the national discourse, I cling onto the hope that Muslims can effect real change by a jihad for goodness in everyday life.

DOESN'T RELIGION CAUSE MOST OF THE CONFLICT IN THE WORLD?

Rachel Woodlock

'Well, duh!' is my first response to the question 'Doesn't religion cause most of the conflict in the world?' Religion is powerfully motivating, and humans, belligerent by nature, fight over it. Heck, religion has caused conflict even in my diverse and tolerant family.

Taking our daughter overseas to visit her Irish-Catholic relatives for the first time, I impressed upon my husband that he should warn his mother not to give any pork to her grandchild for religious reasons. Like Jews, Muslims steer clear of bacon, pork chops, trotters and anything else with an oink. In Ireland, however, even desserts come with a side of ham. My gentle, peaceable mate, wanting to avoid one of those conversations, instead said: 'Mam, Yazzy doesn't like pork so don't give her any.' A few days later, my beaming mother-in-law, who had been on babysitting duty, proudly announced: 'She does like pork. I gave her some sausages and she ate them right up!' I can tell you it took a few days for my blood pressure to return to normal.

Then again, humans also fight over small bits of compressed carbon, tracts of dirt, addictive mind-altering substances and soccer matches. Greek mythology tells of the Trojan War, started because of the beautiful Helen's abduction. The Yellow Turban Rebellion in second-century China was due to unscrupulous landowners oppressing starving peasants. England's Wars of the Roses were fought between noble houses over royal succession. The American Civil War was fought over slavery and states' right to secede. The First World War, between European imperial powers, was sparked by the assassination of Archduke Franz Ferdinand of Austria. The Vietnam War was inflicted on South-East Asia to halt communism. Racism fuelled the Hutu genocide of Tutsis in Rwanda. State-imposed atheism was a defining feature of brutal twentieth-century regimes led by Stalin, Tito, Mao Zedong, Pol Pot, Kim Il-sung and Kim Jong-il, all of which resulted in the suffering and murder of millions. To give one example, tens of thousands of Russian Christians were executed for their religious beliefs by atheists intent on purging religious belief from the Soviet Union.[96] So maybe we should pause before simplistically attributing 'most' conflicts to religion.

Yet religion has been a major feature in some historical conflicts and the most recent wave of modern terrorism. Religion has taken on extra significance today because globalisation is challenging and changing everything. Religious identity not only survives but can take on heightened significance when national and political alliances break apart, as happened in the former Yugoslavia in the early 1990s, when Serbs, Croats and Bosnians were divided along Orthodox, Catholic and Muslim fault lines. Ethno-religious violence has occurred between Hindus and Muslims in Kashmir; Jews, Christians and Muslims in Israel and Palestine; Christians and Muslims in Nigeria; Sunni and Shi'i Muslims in Iraq; and Catholic and Protestant Christians in Northern Ireland. Not even warm and fuzzy Buddhists are exempt, as can be seen from the violence between Buddhists and Muslims in Thailand and Myanmar, and Buddhists and Hindus in Sri Lanka.

The Qur'an recognises this propensity for religious conflict when it says: 'Were it not that God repels some people by means of others, monasteries, churches, synagogues and mosques – wherein God's name is oft-mentioned – surely would have been demolished' (Q22:40). In the earliest period of Prophet Muhammad's mission, the Muslims suffered years of hardship, indignity, persecution and martyrdom at the hands of the Quraysh in Mecca. The Quraysh hosted the pagan pilgrimages to the Ka'ba and benefited economically from their status. As elites they were largely indifferent to the suffering of those on the margins – slaves, widows, orphans, travellers – and became alarmed at the ramifications of Prophet Muhammad preaching monotheism and social justice (Q107:1–7, Q90:12–18).

When the persecution became intolerable, some of the Muslims sought refuge in Abyssinia, which was ruled by a sympathetic Christian king. Later, the Prophet and his followers were invited to move to Yathrib (now Medina), making a pact of mutual protection with local tribes: 'Permission [to fight] is given to those being fought, because they were wronged,' the Qur'an informed the émigrés (Q22:39). Although Medina was not a state in the modern sense of the word, the Prophet and his followers were no longer individuals suffering religious persecution, but were collectively responsible for assisting their hosts in protecting

Medina and her inhabitants. Thus began a period of war between the Quraysh and the Muslims and their respective allies that eventually resulted in Muslim success and the Prophet's triumphant return to Mecca.

The Qur'anic justification for military jihad after all efforts to negotiate peace have failed is that religious freedom should be protected, because 'oppression is worse than killing' (Q2:191). From this, Muslim scholars developed a just-war theory that included protection of non-combatants and the environs of war, although admittedly in the ensuing centuries jihad was also used to further the territorial ambitions of ruthless leaders, just as today it is twisted and distorted to justify terrorist bombings. Like law and politics, religion can be used to defend the oppressed *and* to oppress the defenceless.

Unfortunately, despite the Qur'anic commitment to religious freedom and diversity, we Muslims over the years have done our fair share of denying freedom to others. Muslims believe the Qur'an, following hot on the tails of Jesus' message, was the blockbuster conclusion to God's heavenly series. But in the nineteenth century two Persians claimed to be bearers of new divine revelations. God had spoke again, they claimed. Apocalyptic fervour ran riot in Persia, lots of people converted to the new movement – Babism, which evolved into what is now known as the Baha'i Faith – and this really annoyed the Muslims, especially when some prominent religious figures converted. For 170 years, the Baha'i Faith has been a thorn in the side of the Islamic world.

As a child, I was not fully aware that people belonged to different religions. I just assumed everyone was Baha'i, like my family. That was until the 1979 Iranian revolution happened, and Baha'is began fleeing systematic state persecution. Almost overnight, the small and ethnically diverse Australian Baha'i community found its ranks swelled by Iranian refugees bearing horrific tales of midnight raids, holy places razed, businesses looted while authorities looked the other way, schoolkids harassed by their teachers and fellow students, prison torture and even executions.

Nine-year-old Taraneh,[97] who would become my best friend, spoke of how her well-off family had to abandon their home suddenly and flee.

The authorities were looking to arrest her father, a known Baha'i who was in hiding, and her mother had been tipped off they were coming to raid the house that night. In her new, sparsely furnished, tiny bedroom in suburban Melbourne she told me 'We couldn't take anything', but she was grateful to be alive. I imagined becoming a refugee, leaving the warmth and comfort of my home, abandoning my favourite dolls and pet goldfish to save my life. It was beyond my childish comprehension.

Another family friend, Mr Ahmadi, was a small, portly man with a warm smile and thinning hair. In all the years I knew him, I don't think I ever saw him out of a neatly pressed business suit, and it was hard to visualise him escaping on the back of a camel in the dead of night, cold and shivering, wondering whether he'd make it out of Iran alive or be mugged and murdered on the way.

Then there was Mona's story, which every Baha'i knows by heart.[98] She and ten other Baha'i women were martyred, executed by Iranian authorities for their religious beliefs. In 1982, Mona was an intelligent, gentle, quiet sixteen-year-old who would not have harmed a fly. She was also very religious, the Baha'i Faith her animating passion. She was arrested with her father because the revolutionary guards raiding the family home found religious material in her bedroom. After being imprisoned, prevented from praying, interrogated and tortured, she was given a mock trial and executed with the other women. The so-called Islamic Republic of Iran had become modern-day Quraysh.

Muslims persecuting Baha'is is an example of what Charles Kimball calls 'corrupted religion'. Because all the great traditions teach love of the transcendent and compassion towards others,[99] where there is violence, barbarity, prejudice and hatred, it is a sign the tradition has been corrupted. In *When Religion Becomes Evil: Five Warning Signs*, he outlines five markers of religion gone wrong:

- Absolute truth claims: when zealots elevate their doctrines, or more precisely their particular interpretations of the faith's doctrines, to the level of absolute truth.
- Blind obedience: when believers abdicate intellectual and moral responsibility to manipulative charismatic leaders.

- Establishing 'ideal' time: when ordinary political events are viewed as portents of an approaching apocalyptic period.
- The end justifies any means: when affirming religious values are cast aside to protect sacred space, reinforce group identity against threatening outsiders or perceived dissidents, or protect the image of religious institutions at all costs.
- Declaring holy war: when war itself is cast as holy, an end in itself, or to justify grubby political ambitions. [100]

Kimball also argues that wholesale rejection of *all* religion is a type of fundamentalist absolutism,[101] because religious traditions are understood and practised differently by different people in different contexts. It's more informative to compare differences in interpretation and orientation towards peace or violence, than to simply castigate religion as conflict-prone. There's a world of difference between Nobel Peace Prize winner and human rights lawyer Shirin Ebadi, and terrorist Osama bin Laden, just as there is between Christian cultist Jim Jones and civil rights leader Martin Luther King Jr.

The problem of corrupt religion has attracted the criticism of many prophets and saints. In a passage reminiscent of condemnations by biblical figures such as Ezekiel and Jesus, the Qur'an censures religious hypocrites:

Among the people there is he whose discourse on the life of the world pleases you, and he calls on God as witness to what is in his heart, yet he is an unyielding and antagonistic adversary. When he turns and leaves, he walks about corrupting the earth, destroying crops and livestock – God loves not corruption. When it is said to him, 'be conscious of God' his pride drives him to sin. Therefore, hell suffices for him, such a vile resting place (Q2:204–206).

According to the exegetes, this verse was revealed to be about al-Akhnas ibn Shariq, who waxed eloquent about his religious faith, but then set fire to some Muslim-owned crops and cruelly hamstrung the cattle. The verse could well apply to Saddam Hussein, who made a show of praying on television, but gassed and bombed Kurds and was a tyrannical dictator. Religion, unfortunately, provides a useful cover and powerful motivator for the evil-hearted. That religion can be so markedly different in the hands of the power-hungry and corrupt, as opposed to the altruistic and virtuous, really says more about human psychology than it does about religion. That's why so many human conflicts unfortunately involve religion.[102]

Antony Loewenstein

Alain de Botton, philosopher and author of *Religion for Atheists*, is worried about fundamentalism. 'To say something along the lines of "I'm an atheist: I think religions are not all bad" has become a dramatically peculiar thing to say,' he told British journalist Bryan Appleyard in 2012. 'If you do say it on the internet you will get savage messages calling you a fascist, an idiot or a fool. This is a very odd moment in our culture. Why has this happened?'[103]

Neo-atheism, the belief that science is the only path to truth and all religions are equally deluded and destructive, has taken hold in much of the debate over atheism. The movement, whose keys figures include Richard Dawkins, the late Christopher Hitchens, Sam Harris and Daniel Dennett, is an ideology that arrogantly celebrates an understanding of everything through supposed reason and proof. It allows little doubt or questioning about the unknown. It also happens that some of these key figures, including Ayaan Hirsi Ali, who appeared at Melbourne's Atheist Convention in 2012, are backers of state violence against Muslim countries since September 11, 2001.

I find myself partially agreeing with Sayeeda Warsi, chair of Britain's Conservative Party, who wrote in London's *Daily Telegraph* in February 2012:

> one of the most worrying aspects about this militant secularisation is that at its core and in its instincts it is deeply intolerant. It demonstrates similar traits to totalitarian regimes – denying people the right to a religious identity because they were frightened of the concept of multiple identities.[104]

It's clearly an exaggeration to suggest atheists are rampaging through the streets demanding the end of religious belief – a pipedream that goes against the numbers in vast swathes of the world where faith is only growing – but the last decade has seen an ever-increasing number of atheists feeling the need to ridicule or damn people who do believe in a god. I'm not one of them but it's undignified, intolerant and ignorant to suggest because a man or woman believes in a higher being they're somehow a lesser human being in need of help or pity. Such arguments will do little to convince others to join the atheist cause. Instead, the reason religion is dramatically falling in popularity in the West is the rapidly decentralised nature of power in our societies, multiculturalism, countless church scandals and better education. Ideological rigidity can occur in any of us and should be rejected.

Richard Dawkins, at a dinner with de Botton and others in London in early 2012, recounted a conversation he'd had with Christopher Hitchens. 'Do you ever worry,' Dawkins asked, 'that if we win and, so to speak, destroy Christianity, that vacuum would be filled with Islam?'[105] It's a curious question that reflects both the vicious hatred of Muslims by many so-called new atheists but also a creepy utopian nightmare that is apparently idealised by them.

Destroy Christianity? Because the Catholic Church has committed innumerable crimes, opposes abortion and birth control, refuses to accept female priests and hides sex offenders in its midst? To be sure, the institution is dysfunctional, but wishing for its disintegration reflects a savagery that will only inflame, not reduce tensions. Besides, even the Catholic Church isn't solely defined by incendiary decisions made in the Vatican.

None of this is to excuse the undeniable barbarity unleashed by religionists over the centuries. The misogyny, beheadings, terrorism, killings, beatings and cruelty are real. They continue. Today we see a growing battle in the Middle East between Shi'ite and Sunni; a Jewish state unleashing militancy against Christian and Muslim Palestinians; a church in many Western nations that refuses to take responsibility for hiding and defending paedophiles; and an anti-gay crusade led by some Jewish, Christian and Muslim leaders that threatens the sanctity of life itself.

That there is corruption within religion, as defined by Rachel, is true. Countless theologians have acknowledged the problems inherent in trying too neatly to define faith or human nature solely by what is dictated in a holy book. Values change. For example, the desire for many gay Catholics to remain inside the church is a painful journey, one filled with official condemnation but occasional local support and understanding.

I've been guilty of claiming religion is the source of the world's evils, but it's a careless comment. It's far too easy to blame the Muslim faith for honour killings. It's lazy to believe that because the Pope opposes gay sex the solution is to abolish the Catholic Church. I'm under no illusion about the fact that religion is routinely used to justify the more heinous crimes, such as murder, torture or war. But the twentieth century is filled with examples, namely Stalin's Soviet Union and Mao's China, that didn't need God as an excuse to commit genocide against a state's own people.

A close confidant of former British prime minister Tony Blair alleged that Blair's Christian faith was a driving force behind his desire that 'good should triumph over evil'. It allowed Blair, according to John Burton, Blair's political agent in his Sedgefield constituency for twenty-four years, to support and defend the 2003 invasion of Iraq, the war in Afghanistan, the Israeli wars against Lebanon and Gaza and a possible military strike against Iran. Burton argued:

> I truly believe that [Blair's] Christianity affected his policy-making on just about everything from aid to Africa, education, poverty, world debt and intervening in other countries when he thought it was right to do it. The fervour was part of him and it comes back to it being Christian fervour that spurred him into action for better or worse.[106]

But none of this means that Christianity is itself inherently violent or colonialist and demands its followers to pursue ideas that lead to the death or subjugation of fellow human beings.

I surprise myself with this defence of religion. I believe that demo-cratic states and their policies should not be dictated by faith-based people. I vehemently oppose the idea that because some of religious faith believe a woman shouldn't have the right to an abortion we should accept this rationale and outlaw the procedure. The opposite is neces-sary: an even stronger understanding that secular values are vital in a modern world but religious ideas must be part of the conversation. Not just tolerance but active encouragement. To dismiss those with religious faith, of any kind, means that a state and community will only be hearing perspectives that may conform to their own beliefs.

In our hypersensitive age, we're told that conflict is always bad. It's not. Violence against civilians is wrong but robust discussion is essential to better understand issues. Conflict can bring clarity and purpose and assist our own ways of deciding what's right and wrong. To imagine a world without it sounds as appealing as an atheist utopia.

Jane Caro

On 11 October 2012, the day before I began writing this, my 21-year-old uni student daughter returned from her part-time job upset. It wasn't about anything that happened at her work, it was about a news story she had heard on the radio.

Fourteen-year-old Malala Yousafzai is an outspoken advocate for the education of girls in her area, the strife-ridden Swat Valley region of Pakistan. Such activism in that part of the world takes a degree of courage and determination beyond anything ever required of any of us – of any age – in our comfortable secular world, as was dramatically demonstrated. As Malala sat on a bus in the grounds of her school, a Taliban gunman boarded the bus and shot her in the head. After proudly claiming responsibility, Taliban spokesman Ehsanullah Ehsan told the world's news media that the teenager's work represented 'a new chapter of obscenity, and we have to finish this chapter'. Two other teenage schoolgirls were also wounded in the attack. And what was the 'obscenity' that had to be 'finished'? It was the education of girls.

In the modern secular world, anyone shooting a fourteen-year-old girl in the head would know that what they were doing was unjustifiable on any level, unless they were either certifiable, a fanatic, or, sadly, importing a tradition from theocratic societies (like Pakistan) – the so-called honour killing. To their credit, the government and population of Pakistan have been as outraged by the crime as the rest of the world, and the authorities have declared that they will not rest until they find and punish her attackers.

But that doesn't change the fact that the Taliban and their spokesmen feel absolutely no shame. They know that what they have done is right and just, because their god tells them so. Religion, throughout the millennia, has been used to justify almost any cruelty that human minds can imagine, from burning heretics at the stake and stoning adulterers to crucifying Jesus himself.

Recently, also in Pakistan, an intellectually disabled eleven-year-old from a Christian family was set upon by a Muslim mob because she was accused of having desecrated the Qur'an. The scenes of this bewildered child having to be rescued and protected from adults baying for her blood were deeply distressing. She was held in a maximum-security prison for two weeks for her own protection under threat of a charge of blasphemy, which carries a possible death sentence in the Islamic Republic of Pakistan. It was later revealed that the burnt pages of the Qur'an had been planted in the child's bag by a Muslim Imam, Khalid Chishti, who allegedly told a witness that this was 'a way of getting rid of Christians'.

On the other side of the world, Anders Behring Breivik slaughtered seventy-seven mostly teenage Norwegians as a (hideous) protest against the 'weakening' of Europe due to multiculturalism. Although he killed mostly non-Muslims, Breivik seems to have seen his murderous spree as a way of getting rid of Muslims. He was called a Christian fundamentalist at first, but his 1500-page manifesto revealed, at best, a weak attachment to religious belief – although it's safe to say he expected that if any god existed it would be a Christian god. To Breivik, Christianity seems important mainly because he sees it as white. Breivik has been declared sane by the Norwegian courts, and, like the devoutly religious Taliban, he also appears to feel no shame for his horrific crimes.

The men who flew passenger planes into buildings on 9/11, the tribal Pakistanis controlled by more sophisticated terrorists on mobile phones who went on a murderous rampage in Mumbai (a witness said they appeared not to know how to turn on a tap), and the Bali bombers, all killed as many people as they could in the name of their religion. Breivik did it in the name of his race. Timothy McVeigh, who killed 168 people and wounded 800 others, hated the government. All saw their mass murder as a political act of protest and all felt justified.

Conflict is caused by an irreconcilable clash of world views, and people with all sorts of beliefs have committed evil acts. Atheists like Mao Zedong, Stalin and Pol Pot have starved, tortured and murdered millions in the name of political totalitarianism. Hitler, raised a Catholic, used a quasi-mystical racist philosophy to justify his exploitation of the ancient hatred of the Jews by Christians. Modern technology allowed these men to conduct murder on a massive scale. I heard somewhere (and I've never been able to discover where) that terrorism occurs when you combine a sense of military and economic inferiority with a sense of moral superiority, an explanation that made a lot of sense to me. Religion is very good at conferring a sense of moral superiority on its followers.

Indeed, while the religious have murdered throughout history in the name of their god, I've been unable to find any evidence at all of atheists (or anyone else) killing anyone in the name of atheism. Atheists are no more nor less capable of evil than anyone else, but it seems that murder, particularly mass murder, including war, is a sin of commission rather than omission. In other words, human beings are generally only prepared to fight and kill in the name of something. It can be a god, but it can also be a political philosophy – centralised, totalitarian philosophies like Nazism or Communism, or their opposite, fear of centralised government like that motivating McVeigh or the Unabomber. It can be in the name of patriotism: many fight wars for their country or for their tribe – Tutsis versus Hutus in Rwanda – or race, as Breivik has demonstrated. Some kill because they're psychologically disturbed, like Martin Bryant or the various school shooters who seem to have infected the United States, but none – so far – in the name of atheism.

So, while I don't agree that only religion causes conflict or even the worst conflicts, I would argue that all mass murder and war are fought in the name of some kind of bigger-than-self philosophy or idea. Atheism, which is simply a lack of belief in a supernatural god, has not yet proved compelling enough on its own to motivate anyone to murder, and that's entirely to its credit.

So far no one has gone into a crowded public space with a backpack full of explosives and detonated them while shouting, 'No god is great!'

Simon Smart

In his book *God Is Not Great*: *How Religion Poisons Everything*, Christopher Hitchens doesn't waste time making his position clear:

> We believe with certainty that an ethical life can be lived without religion. And we know for a fact that the corollary holds true – that religion has caused innumerable people not just to conduct themselves no better than others, but to award themselves permission to behave in ways that would make a brothel-keeper or an ethnic cleanser raise an eyebrow.[107]

When Christopher Hitchens says religion poisons everything, he means everything! Later in the book he tells us that all religion is 'Violent, irrational, intolerant, allied to racism and tribalism and bigotry, invested in ignorance and hostile to free inquiry' and 'ought to have a great deal on its conscience'.[108] Many of the believers among us wince as we read these words, not only because of the flamboyant, lively writing, but because we suspect they are partly true. We fear that, despite our deeply held beliefs, Hitchens is not totally wrong.

But we also want to keep the conversation going. There's much more to be said about this topic to give us a full and accurate picture. Antony talks about the new atheism, of which Hitchens is a good example – it might be entertaining, but it's ultimately intolerant and comes to partially resemble the monster it sees itself as trying to destroy.

Hitchens and the new atheists are not alone in their assessment of religion as an essentially violent force. Anthropologist Maurice Bloch, in his book *Prey into the Hunter*, argues that the 'irreducible core of the ritual process' involves 'a marked element of violence or . . . [a] conquest . . . of the here and now by the transcendental'.[109] Religions, therefore, are by their very nature violent.

Is this true? Like Rachel, I have to concede that religion has been implicated in all sorts of conflict and violence throughout human history. There's blood on the hands of those claiming faith, and no avoiding the fact that in the service of the wrong people, religion can be a means of enhancing the violent attempts of the strong, deluded or wicked to impose their will on others.

And as far as Christianity goes we can read stories, pretty much from the time of Constantine's conversion in the fourth century, of supposed followers of the crucified Christ perpetrating gruesome acts of violence under the sign of the cross.

When power shifted away from the pagans and to the Christians in the time of Emperor Theodosius I (AD347–95), the pendulum swung fairly abruptly from persecution of Christians to the pagans copping it. We can tell stories of monks plundering pagan sites and raiding peasant villages.[110] Having said that, the conversion of the Roman Empire from pagan to Christian actually happened without much violence at all. The Christians of early centuries were best known for peacefulness, generosity, and care for the poor and sick.[111]

There have been times over the centuries, though, when the seasons of Lent and Holy Week have been for the Jews a time of fear as Christians perpetrated terrible crimes against them. Muslims might also associate the cross with violence, recalling the rampages of the Crusaders pouring across Europe and into the Middle East with Christian banners out in front of their infamous pilgrimages.

There's plenty of material at the disposal of those who wish to call into question the integrity of the whole Christian faith due to the violence of its history. It seems a bit of a sport these days to highlight the sins of the Christian past – witch hunts, the Inquisition, the Crusades, Christian support of slavery, and the oppression and mistreatment of women (see 'Doesn't religion oppress women?').

But as Rachel has so clearly explained, the picture is much more complex than is often implied. If we look at the history carefully, it's really not as straightforward as the relentless religious violence and barbarism that is so frequently served up by those most eager to bring religion down.

An example of this would be the Inquisition, rightly remembered as a terrible episode in Christian history. Dinner party guests are likely to nod in agreement when someone mentions the 'millions killed' at the hands of the church, but the latest figures from historians suggest around 5000–6000 over a 350-year period. That's less than eighteen a year. One a year is terrible, but the reality appears a long way from what we often hear.

Similarly it's extraordinary how many times I hear it said out loud that 'most of the wars of history have been caused by religion'. This is demonstrably false. The vast majority of wars have been conducted in the pursuit of profits or conquest or power or territory, even though it's clear that religion has frequently been caught up in those pursuits. The secular nation-state, especially in the twentieth century, has been responsible for violence of all kinds and on a scale that dwarfs past conflicts.

Asked by the BBC to conduct a 'war audit' to see how many wars had been caused by religion, Greg Austin, Todd Kranock and Thom Oommen concluded that there have been few genuinely religious wars in the last hundred years. Further, they found that you have to go back to the Islamic expansion beginning in the sixth century, the Crusades beginning in the eleventh century and the Reformation beginning in the sixteenth century to find wars that could reasonably be labelled 'religious' rather than be linked to other political causes.[112]

We have to ask ourselves about the underlying causes of conflict. Very often any evil committed by a religious person becomes an argument against the entire tradition itself. If we accept that humans are, broadly speaking, driven by violence, greed, hatred and the desire for power, we won't be surprised that if those things get into religion, the practice of the faith will be corrupted. But there's a very real sense in which religion can moderate those forces. On this subject David Hart writes:

> Does religious conviction provide a powerful reason for killing? Undeniably it often does. It also often provides the sole compelling reason for refusing to kill, or for being merciful, or for seeking peace; only the profoundest ignorance of history could prevent one from recognising this. For the truth is that religion and irreligion are cultural variables, but killing is a human constant.[113]

I can't let Jane get away with the claim that no one has killed in the name of atheism. Presumably this stems from her idea that atheism is merely a lack of belief with no positive entailments. The millions killed at the hands of the twentieth century's worst dictators might beg to differ. To say that Mao, Stalin and Pol Pot's murderous totalitarianism had nothing to do with their atheism is to completely misunderstand them and the ideologies on which their actions rested.

But on the question of religion and violence – and especially Christian history and violence – I think Yale theologian Miroslav Volf is especially helpful, with his idea of 'thin' and 'thick' religion. Have Christians been guilty of terrible violence over the centuries? Indeed they have. But it is abundantly clear that the story of Jesus gives absolutely no warrant for this violence. Anyone behaving that way is disobeying the one they claim to be following.

The Apostle Paul wrote that people who follow Jesus are to imitate his life in the here and now. As Christ died in self-giving love for the godless, Paul urges Christians towards non-violent engagement with the world. According to this teaching, to seek to conquer evil with evil is to be conquered by evil; evil can only be overcome with good.[114]

Christianity will only be violent, says Volf, if it is stripped of its content – *thinned out* – and infused with a different set of values. This is often what happens when Christianity is employed to legitimise violence. God is declared to be 'on our side' and people see themselves as soldiers of God. Faith is commandeered for ambitions and conquests that are extraneous to the faith, and it's a lethal combination. Volf writes:

> The more we reduce Christian faith to vague religiosity which serves primarily to energise, heal and give meaning to the business of life whose content is shaped by factors other than faith (such as national or economic interests), the worse off we'll be.[115]

The answer, he argues, to violence perpetrated in the name of the cross, is not less Christianity but more – that is, Christianity not depleted of its meaning but full of its original moral content, which is at its heart non-violent and a force for good.

Finally, some have objected to the key part of the Christian story – the crucifixion – as violence carried out on an innocent which inspires violence elsewhere. But Christianity doesn't glorify violence, it just understands that violence is part of our world and that Jesus was not spared it.[116]

Christian belief holds that the cross was not a *demonstration* of violence but a message about a love stronger than death. Crucially, the crucifixion of Jesus also says that violence will not have the last word.[117]

New York pastor Timothy Keller reminds us that when Martin Luther King Jr confronted racism in the white church in the South – and he found plenty there – he called on those churches not to become more secular, but more Christian. He called on white Christians to be *truer* to their own beliefs and to hear what the Bible teaches. King knew that the answer to racism and violence was not less Christianity but a deeper and truer Christianity.

I have come to understand this episode in world history as emblematic of Christianity at its best. Despite Christopher Hitchens' ludicrous claim that Reverend Martin Luther King was only nominally Christian, it's clear that MLK gained his inspiration and motivation from the one who said that those who follow him must turn the other cheek, love their enemies and pray for those who persecuted them. It's why King could inspire thousands of others to refuse to bow to ignorance and hatred, but equally be determined to resist with non-violent self-sacrifice. Only in such a way could the believers among them obey the one they claimed was their ultimate leader. It remains a fine example of love triumphing over hate, of costly and courageous resistance against evil and of religiously inspired social action that made the kind of difference everyone can appreciate.

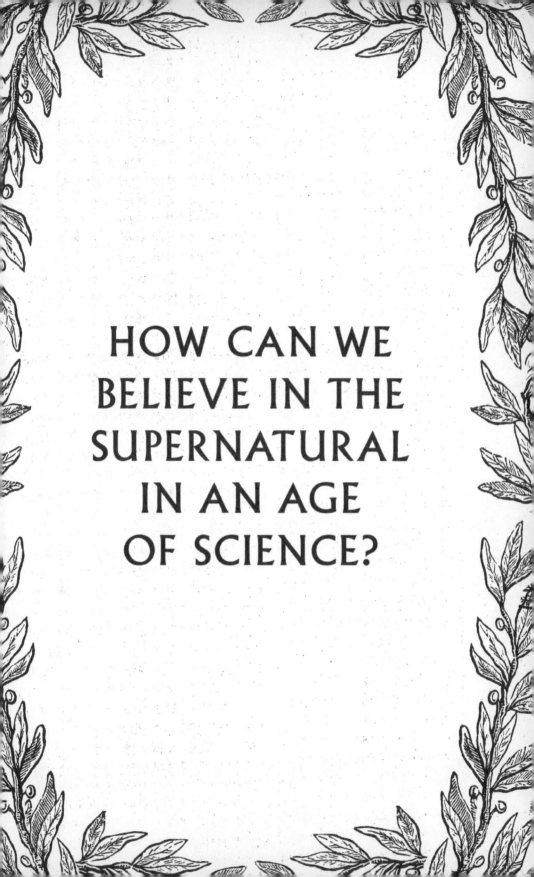

HOW CAN WE BELIEVE IN THE SUPERNATURAL IN AN AGE OF SCIENCE?

Jane Caro

We all create narratives around our own lives. We tell ourselves stories about the world and our place in it from the earliest age. As a small child, so my mother tells me, I had both an imaginary friend who lived in the light (I think her name was Brigid) and – much more irritatingly – an imaginary electric train set my poor mother was constantly inadvertently stepping on. (What a little fascist I must have been!)

My youngest daughter, when aged about two, had her own imaginary friend called Mrs Fireworks, who had a very loud voice and a beautiful garden full of colourful flowers. Charlotte had an intense fear of fireworks and her green-fingered friend helped her manage that fear. Perhaps I was afraid of the dark and that's why I created Brigid. What fear I was trying to assuage with the imaginary train set, I cannot imagine.

It's completely understandable to me that human beings living in a world they couldn't explain or understand would have coped psychologically by creating stories that made the world explicable and so helped manage their fears. Indeed, all cultures have done precisely that, and the stories they created are rich and beautiful. From those stories, I believe, have grown all the world's great religions and all of human culture, from the Dreaming of the Indigenous Australians to the transubstantiation of the Catholic mass. The nature of these stories is that they are so deeply trusted and believed, so helpful to the psychological health of their followers, that they're considered sacred. Indeed, even a sceptical old atheist like me has the greatest possible respect for the ingenuity and creativity of my own species and our ability to manage the world regardless of how much we actually know about it. No doubt the many religious and sacred stories that human beings have told themselves throughout time have been integral to our survival. Other animals are lucky. They're ignorant of death and of their own individuality. We're not. That's our genius and, of course, our curse.

But as our ever-curious species has explored the world, the universe and our place in it, we've developed both technology and knowledge. Where once there was mystery, and so the need for an explanatory story, now there's knowledge and the need for the story has retreated.

Although many argue that science and religion are not in opposition to one another and many of the religious have been entirely prepared to accept scientific explanations like the theory of evolution, for example, and live quite comfortably with both their religious belief and scientific understanding, I think it's arguably true that scientific understanding has adversely impacted on religious belief and influence.

Perhaps a reaction to the perceived threat of science is why the fundamentalist tendency in some religions is experiencing a resurgence; after all, as a very famous scientific thinker once proved, for every action there's an equal and opposite reaction.

Non-belief is growing exponentially. In Australia, according to the 2011 census, the number of people who declared they had no religion rose by 29 per cent to 22.3 per cent of the population. This may be partly because it's now much more respectable to admit to having no religious belief, and even to bluntly declare yourself an atheist, than once it was. Indeed, there have probably always been secret non-believers in every religious community. According to the *Sydney Morning Herald*, a recent survey conducted by the Australian National University suggests that:

> ... this could describe a quarter of people attending church monthly or more. The 2009 poll found 13 per cent believed in a personal god but had their doubts, while 6 per cent subscribed to a 'higher power' instead. A further 1 per cent said it was impossible to know if there was a god, 3 per cent sometimes believed and 2 per cent didn't at all.[118]

And that's just among the few believers who actually regularly attend church. Damon Young had further bad news for religion:

> According to the National Church Life Survey (NCLS), approximately one in five Australians go to church once a month ... And in only five years, from 1996 to 2001, the NCLS reports that church attendance dropped 7 per cent.[119]

There's no doubt that, at least in the developed world, religious belief is on the decline and has been for a very long time. I suspect this is not because science has directly targeted religion or belief in the supernatural per se, but simply that, as knowledge has given us the real stories about how the world works, how we work and how the universe works, we have less need to create supernatural narratives to protect us against the nothingness. Human beings cannot bear a vacuum. In place of no story or information we'll create one. We have less need to do so now because we understand so much more.

The response of some religious groups to this decline in the power of all religious stories in the face not just of scientific knowledge but also the unbelievable technology it has given us, has been to pull the blinkers ever more firmly over their eyes.

Lifelong Republican Mike Lofgren, in his book *The Party Is Over: How the Republicans Went Crazy, Democrats Became Useless, and the Middle Class Got Shafted*, blames the rise of the religious right in America for the fact that Americans are closer to Iranians and Nigerians in terms of their beliefs about such things as creationism; the literal meaning of scripture; and angels and demons, than they are to Canadians or Europeans (or, indeed, Australians). He argues that the involvement of the religious right in the Republican Party has normalised what used to be extreme religious beliefs. Worse, he argues, that as a result many in the United States are now suspicious of science, academic research and evidence.[120]

It seems it's not just possible for many people to believe in the supernatural in the age of science; it has become such a psychological imperative they've closed their eyes to anything else.

The consequences of this 'hostility to science' in the age of climate change could be devastating.

Rachel Woodlock

I'm rather glad false prophets aren't burnt at the stake any more! They've been predicting the imminent demise of religion since the early eighteenth century, and it hasn't happened yet. In fact, the secularisation thesis is 'one of the great predictive failures in the history of the social science'.[121] The American sociologist of religion Rodney Stark cites Thomas Woolston in around 1710 as the first to predict the death of Christianity, then later Voltaire, Auguste Comte, Friedrich Engels, A. E. Crawley, Max Weber, Sigmund Freud and a number of twentieth-century prophets all confidently asserted religious belief was just about to disappear.[122] You wouldn't want any of them to pick your lotto numbers.

Stark reckons there never was a hyper-pious past now in decline due to education and science. Jane is probably correct when she says the non-religious are simply more comfortable admitting it these days. I'm delighted to say this is because of a shift in the coercive power of religious organisations. As Australian sociologist of religion Gary Bouma writes:

> In secular societies religion and spirituality have seeped out of the monopolistic control of formal organisations like churches. This has resulted in vastly increased diversity of both organised religion and private spiritualities.[123]

Jane writes that non-belief is growing at an exponential rate. However, fewer bums on pews is not the same as the death of belief in the supernatural. My husband, for example, ticked 'no religion' on the latest Australian census in 2011. He has always held intensely private spiritual beliefs and doesn't feel the need to declare them on a census form – even if there was an appropriate space to describe them. The 'nones' may not belong to particular religious traditions, but as the American researcher Robert Putnam pointed out when he was in Australia in 2012:

> Most of them are not atheists, these are not people who've been convinced by the new atheism, so-called, of Dawkins and others.

Most of them say they believe in God, most of them were raised in religious homes, many of them still pray, some of them say that religion is an important part of their lives, but they are very alienated from organised religion, that's the crucial thing.[124]

Rather than dying, religion is evolving.[125] It has always been variegated, constantly and slowly changing as societies shift. Today, the modern world is becoming increasingly individualised, a process that certainly challenges traditional religious authority structures. Belief in the supernatural, however, has been an integral part of human experience since the dawn of time, and I suggest will ever continue to be so.

★

Another unsupported idea of the secularisation thesis is that religion is for primitive tribes, the uneducated, brainwashed cultists or irrational Liberal Party voters. Although modern anthropology was forced to recant the 'religion is for primitive minds' claim once real fieldwork was undertaken, the vestige of religion as anti-science lives on.[126]

Interestingly, despite the popular perception that science and education destroys belief in God or the supernatural, Rodney Stark, Laurence Iannaccone and Roger Finke report that, at least in the United States, the slightly lower levels of religiosity among the university-educated precedes scientific training, and that university staff and students in the 'hard' sciences tend to be *more* religious than those in the 'soft' sciences.[127]

But the notion that science conflicts with religion was never as big a problem for Muslims as it was for European Christians. There was no 'great divorce' between faith and science; indeed, the West owes a debt of gratitude to the Islamic world. As a young student I remember my music theory professor standing at a lectern, peering over his glasses, and telling us we have Muslims to thank for preserving and developing the ancient Greek musical scale system, which the Catholic Church had banned.

But the substantial contribution of Muslim scientists, mathematicians, philosophers, engineers, doctors, musicians, and so on – many of them religious scholars as well – remained unacknowledged in the

West until very recently. They were inspired by popular sayings attributed to the Prophet Muhammad such as 'seek knowledge even unto China', 'knowledge is the stray camel of the believer, take it wherever you find it', 'the ink of the scholar is holier than the blood of the martyr', and 'seeking knowledge is a duty for every Muslim male and female'.

The 'science in the Qur'an' genre of literature is exceedingly popular with Muslim proselytisers, but I've always thought it twee when Muslims try to prove the Qur'an's divine origin by pointing to verses containing scientific 'facts' unknown to seventh-century Arabs. It's an inherently dangerous activity, given that scientific theories are subject to constant revision. It also risks turning Qur'anic cosmology into a superficial hodge-podge of pseudoscience, when its real purpose is to draw us closer to God.

Ignoring scientific facts about the physical universe and asserting literal creation accounts has made some religious folk a laughing stock. Christian creationism has been picked up and regurgitated by a Turkish author who writes under the pseudonym Harun Yahya, and I cringe whenever I see his glossy pamphlets being handed out. Yet long before Darwin, Muslim scientists like Nasir al-Din al-Tusi (d. 1274) espoused evolution theories.[128] Our earliest ancestor who was fully human both physically *and* spiritually emerged at a specific point in the much longer story of primate evolution. Given that according to some Islamic traditions, it took forty thousand years for the creation of Adam, this pivotal moment in evolutionary history is, theologically speaking, God breathing the spirit into our already animated clay. Put simply, evolution is the tool by which God unfolds creation.

When we speak of the universe in the scientific sense, we mean the observable, material universe. This realm, as Jane is correct in pointing out, is subject to critical examination of propositions that must live up to tests of evidence and reason. But as Simon I'm sure would agree, theists argue there are worlds existing beyond the material universe, and these are not under the remit of science. No microscope, telescope or spectrohelioscope (say *that* one three times quickly) will reveal God to us.

Huston Smith argues, in *Why Religion Matters*, this is because we can only scientifically observe that which is intellectually inferior to us. The 'hard' sciences of geology, biology, chemistry and so on can tell us a great deal about rocks, plants and lab rats, but the 'soft' social sciences and humanities are much fuzzier. We already find it difficult to design repeatable experiments that precisely measure data about human behaviour. When it comes to observing beings superior to us, we wouldn't have a hope. Smith says science cannot 'bring them to view for the sufficient reason that if they exist, it is they who dance circles around us, not we them. Knowing more than we do, they will walk into our experiments if they choose to; otherwise not.'[129]

As important as rationality is, human beings possess other faculties for figuring out what to believe or discount. Al-Ghazali discussed the problem with presuming that reasoning is the sole or best determiner of what's true. In his autobiographical work *Deliverance from Error*, he first points out that we think our senses — sight, hearing, touch, taste and smell — provide us with accurate information about reality, yet reason shows us our senses can be tricked into believing something that isn't true. If intellect can falsify our sensory perception, who's to say there's not a super-intellect that can falsify our intellect?

Even fake religious experiences can be artificially manufactured, as atheist Derren Brown demonstrated in his television special *Fear and Faith*.[130] He used a combination of psychological and neurolinguistic programming tricks to artificially create a religious conversion experience in Natalie, a scientist and atheist. Sitting with her in a church, chatting, Brown prompted Natalie to recall feelings of love and awe. He associated these with an embracing, idealised father figure who might have a plan for her life, and affirmed faith as a positive thing. Then Brown triggered what Natalie reported as an overwhelming experience of love. Later she recalled it was as if: 'all the love in the world had been thrown at me . . . as though that love had always been available to me, but I'd kind of pushed it away, or mistreated it somehow by not letting it into my life. It's as if my spectrum has just been broadened.' She initially attributed it to a supernatural source, which puzzled her as an atheist.

When Brown revealed his manipulation to Natalie, she looked disappointed and perhaps a little embarrassed. But she needn't have felt upset. Brown didn't disprove God in the riveting hour-long program. I suggest he was acting like a neurosurgeon who can stimulate someone's brain to artificially perceive smells, music or memories, by poking a probe into various parts during a craniotomy. That a person can hear Beethoven when a neuron is zapped doesn't disprove the symphony orchestra performing at the city concert hall.

So, the senses can be fooled and the intellect can be fooled. But we can become aware of the effects of the supernatural realm on this universe, not only through emotional experiences, but also through cultivation of intellectual and spiritual virtues. I'm not saying that atheists are not virtuous. At the risk of using that well-worn phrase of the narrow-minded, some of my best friends are atheists, and they're lovely, principled people. But insofar as anyone practises humility, curiosity, honesty, detachment, patience and wisdom, to list a few requisite attributes, they're fostering a special facet of human awareness. It is, as Simon discusses below, the heart's ability to discern truth and become cognisant of the divine realm.[131]

Simon Smart

There are plenty of people today who will say that the modern world's progress in science and technology has made the supernatural claims of the Bible redundant. According to this way of thinking, if you've grown up in the world of jet aeroplanes, the internet, open heart surgery and satellite navigation, you're not going to be impressed with reports of the parting of the Red Sea, Jesus turning water into wine, the blind being made to see and the lame being able to walk. If you're a true child of modernity you'll certainly struggle to accept anything like an actual resurrection from the dead.

But is this true? Is it the case that you have to either believe in the supposed hard facts of modern science *or* be open to the possibilities of the supernatural? The whole question boils down to a fairly simple but profound clash of world views. If you're open to the idea of the universe being the deliberate work of a personal God who created all things out of nothing, who preserves and governs the universe, then it won't be much of a stretch to think that sometimes he might choose to intervene by producing amazing works of power that are 'signposts' to him. But if you're not open to the possibility of that kind of being, then you'll have a hard time accepting miracles and a spiritual dimension to life.

For this discussion Jane has gone for the idea that religion is essentially humanity's creation of myths and narratives to assuage and manage our fears in the face of a complex and daunting world, and the frightening prospect of our own death. In doing so she's joining some formidable opponents of religion who regard it as a human construction emanating from our deepest fears, hopes and dreams. There have been various permutations of this idea from the nineteenth century onwards when Ludwig Feuerbach posited that God was the product of human wishes.

Others ran with this, producing their own slant on the idea. For Karl Marx religion was a substitute for living a life of drudgery in a factory while others got rich. Sigmund Freud told us faith was a projection of repressed desires and disappointment with our dads, while Erich Fromm felt it was a symbol of human potential. Like Jane, these writers saw belief in God as an immature fantasy out of which humanity is slowly emerging.

This whole 'religion as a human construction' idea sounds potentially devastating for believers until you realise something can be both a human projection *and* a reflection of reality at the same time. Australian author Robert Banks, in his book *And Man Created God: Is God a Human Invention?*, argues that the general wishes of humans, such as an infant wanting food, a lover wanting sex, a person longing for knowledge (or for the Sydney Swans to win the premiership), all have counterparts in the real world.[132] The projection of the belief or the wish is reflected in reality. This is highly suggestive. Might not this also apply to the human hope in a transcendent presence giving meaning to our lives?

Jane would get support for her theory from some strands of the scientific study of religion, such as evolutionary psychology and cognitive science. But as philosopher Alvin Plantinga argues, many of the claims of these disciplines when it comes to religion are highly problematic.[133] Even if we were to come up with a convincing 'natural' origin for religion, that in no way discredits it. Merely describing where religious belief comes from and the cognitive methods involved does nothing to count against the truth of the belief.

Christians (or theists generally) believe that God created us all in such a way that we can know him and have a relationship with him. He could have done this in any number of ways, and presumably could have organised things so that 'our cognitive faculties evolved by natural selection ... in such a way that it is natural for us to form beliefs about the supernatural ... and God'.[134] That is surely possible.

Thinking about Freud, it's even feasible that God makes us aware of his presence by way of a mechanism like wish fulfilment. We so want to be in God's presence and feel his love that we come to believe this is possible.[135] That's feasible too. The point is, to identify (as much as that has been done successfully) a natural or physical source of religious inclination is not in itself a defeater of religious belief.

And it cuts both ways. Disbelief in God could just as easily represent a form of wish fulfilment as belief. After all, religious commitment has the inconvenient habit of challenging desires, demanding sometimes-costly personal change and urging us to put the needs of others ahead of our own. It requires commitment to a community made up of all sorts of people, some of whom you might otherwise choose to avoid. It's not unreasonable to think that some self-interest could play a part in a decision to consign the divine to the status of imaginary friend.

A person who places their faith in the Christian story does so out of a conviction not that they have merely employed their capacity for reason to answer existential puzzles (as important as that is), but also that in some measure God has revealed himself to humanity in a way that we can respond to him. It's about an event in time and space, a record of a life that represents a moment of communication between God and people.

Jane acknowledges that for many people of faith there is no conflict between their beliefs and the work and progress of scientific discovery, and I'm glad she does. But she also implies that the trajectory we're on in the modern world is one of religious belief diminishing at the hands of ever-growing scientific knowledge about how things work, suggesting a kind of inherent clash between the two realms – the scientific and the religious. But is this so?

Oxford University professor of mathematics John Lennox is obviously no enemy of science, but he's clear about its place and its limits. In an interview at the Centre for Public Christianity, Lennox explained that science is great at the 'why' questions of function, but doesn't really deal with the question of intention or purpose. Lennox says you can see the limits of science very easily in that it cannot address the simple questions of a child – Where does life come from? What am I here for? What's the meaning of my life?

I share Jane's concern about the rise of fundamentalism of all kinds, and she's right that when some people feel their world view is under threat they bunker down in an unreflective extremism that is ultimately dangerous to civil society. We see this from religious people for sure and, as Jane mentions, in the disastrous way religion has become intertwined with right-wing politics in the United States. Jane neglected to mention Islamic extremism, which appears to be growing and presumably is of concern to her as well.

But fundamentalism is not the exclusive domain of religious fanatics, and I have my own worries about the posture of some of the most fanatical atheists towards people of faith, and what appears to be a positively evangelical trust in science as the answer to all of humanity's woes. We all live by one story or another, and some choose the narrative of humanity-on-an-ever-upward-trajectory, and place their trust in scientists to aid us on that path. But this can begin to look like its own desperate form of faith.

Jane is far from alone in being among those who believe that religious faith is essentially the result of us not understanding things about the world. As knowledge increases, so she tells us, the need for the explanatory power of a mythical story recedes into the background as clearer thinking prevails. Well, that might explain away an ancient story of how thunder and lightning are the result of a cosmic battle between angry deities, but it hardly accounts for the complexity and intellectual richness of the world's religions today. It can't be a simple case of becoming more sophisticated. Too many of the greatest minds across the centuries and still today have also been devoted believers for that argument to hold water.

It's true that in the West the church has been in decline for many years and large numbers of people have abandoned the institution and perhaps the belief (although that part is not as clear). Is that because we know more about the world and the universe and have gained clarity about what's real and true and good? Or is it because we have bought into a different myth, one that's superficially attractive and certainly less demanding – the myth of the self-determining individual in command of his or her destiny and the author of his or her life?

I happen to be very glad to live in an era of air travel, iPods, cars that don't break down and pain-free dentistry! But I can't bring myself to put all my eggs in the scientific basket. There's a lot science can give us to make life better, but it can't deliver what all of us need – meaning, a purpose and a coherent understanding of our lives.

And this belief that progress and human values are inherently part of humanity's increased knowledge just doesn't cut it. As British philosopher John Gray explains, the twentieth century reveals the opposite.

Human beings will use the power of scientific knowledge to support the goals and values they already have. That might involve relieving suffering and overcoming obstacles to human flourishing, or it might just as easily mean building death camps, more destructive bombs or economic practices that enslave. 'Science made possible the technologies that powered the industrial revolution,' writes Gray. [136] 'In the twentieth century, these technologies were used to implement state terror and genocide on an unprecedented scale. Ethics and politics do not advance in line with the growth of knowledge – not even in the long run.'

Jane believes that life holds less mystery these days and consequently we are in less need of an explanatory story, but I would argue the opposite. Life remains mysterious in all the areas that really matter, and, as has always been the case, we humans need the power of story to provide us with grounding, purpose, perspective and hope. Such a story needs to include the spiritual dimension to life because we're more than physical beings.

Albert Einstein called Blaise Pascal, the sixteenth-century mathematician, inventor and philosopher, the smartest man to have lived in Europe in the last thousand years. Among other things he invented the calculating machine, the barometer, the hydraulic press and the syringe. He also wrote a defence of Christian faith titled *Pensées* (*Thoughts*). In this work, Pascal argued that while reason is important in coming to a point of faith in God, reason alone is not enough: 'The heart has its reasons of which reason knows nothing: we know this in countless ways. We know the truth not only through our reason but also through our heart.'[137]

Pascal believed it was principally through the heart that we perceive God. Reflecting on this and the way the longings of the human heart point us to God, Dr Brian Rosner writes:

The human heart seeks transcendence, is impressed by antiquity, searches for wisdom, yearns for justice, needs hope, loves beauty, senses its own darkness, is appalled by evil, repulsed by death and aches for the reassurance of a satisfying story to make sense of our existence.[138]

This unchanging human longing and my own satisfaction in the Christian story to meet those desires make me think that, in an age of fast-paced technology and scientific endeavour, it's not only possible, but essential, to believe in and to know of life beyond the purely material realities of everyday existence. Of course, I believe that to be not some vague spirituality but a person who is also God, the source of all life, all meaning and all hope.

Antony Loewenstein

God is personal. Intolerance breeds hate.

These seemingly uncontroversial statements have taken on a different significance since the terror attacks on New York and Washington on September 11, 2001. Militant Islam has caused a fundamental shift in secular assertiveness. Many Westerners feel under attack, rightly or wrongly, from individuals who hold strong beliefs acutely at odds with their own. The desire to stress the 'rational' and 'sensible' has led to an uncomfortable and unnecessary push to rival Islamists' rhetoric.

British journalist Peter Popham, writing in *The Independent* in 2012, argued that the debate over identity had become inflamed by the very individuals who've learnt little from twentieth-century utopian nightmares:

> The fanaticism of the Islamists has provoked an equally intolerant and intemperate reaction from secular and other quarters, with the ban on headscarves in France and on mosque-building in Switzerland and the rabid anti-Islam rhetoric in the Netherlands; while in Britain it has produced a sudden lurch of opinion among our noisiest public intellectuals against any and all religion. All religions are wrong, goes the argument, everyone knows they are wrong, and their time has expired. As [Richard] Dawkins put it at the Jaipur Literature Festival last month, faith is 'a virus'; he looked forward, he said, to the 'complete death of organised religion' in his lifetime.[139]

Although we live in an age of remarkable scientific breakthroughs, satellite technology and globalisation, the material world may not be enough to satiate the human mind and soul. The above comment by Dawkins is so spectacularly ignorant, arrogant and militant I hope the audience in India, a nation of comparatively few secularists, laughed in his face. The issue isn't one of believers versus non-believers – that dichotomy is too simplistic when it comes to religious belief – but one of assuming there's far more we don't understand than we grasp. If this is the supernatural, then count me in as a believer.

I write this as someone who takes no solace in an afterlife or deities I can neither see nor feel, but I can't so easily dismiss individuals who don't accept that the world is only literal. Spirituality can be separated from religion and assume a position of comfort within a secular framework. Take meditation and yoga, actions with some religious pedigree but today fully accepted by many Westerners as a way to unwind and find nourishment.

In his essay, Simon argues for a life that goes beyond the obvious, the explicable and the scientific. It's hard to disagree with him when he calls for a more rounded understanding of the human condition. Simon needs something more than what he can see or even understand. I share this need, though I don't turn to religion, Christianity or God for the answers. Besides, there are countless ways for religion to survive without the often-suffocating embrace of an established church, mosque or synagogue. Religion of the mind is a perfectly reasonable pursuit.

I was struck by an article in the *New Yorker* in November 2012 about the American celebrity pastor Rob Bell. His journey towards a better understanding of the world around him, as a smart, engaged and sometimes extreme man in the United States, is a moving example of how increased intelligence need not play a part in eschewing God. Bell struggles with understanding the significance of hell. In his bestselling book *Love Wins*, according to the magazine:

> he was dreaming of a world without Hell, but he was also dreaming of a world without arguments – as if the right book, written the right way, would persuade Christians to stop firing Bible verses at each other and start working to build Heaven on earth.[140]

It failed, of course, but it was inspired by debates that seem strange to me and utterly removed from my daily life. This doesn't mean that I don't in many ways find these conversations intriguing.

Bell, who has led a number of Christian communities across America, told one congregation, 'You're either headed to Heaven or you're headed to Hell. It's just that simple.' But he soon started to doubt the certainty of the Bible and question the literal translations of passages. He claimed to

have seen hard evidence of the Bible helping young couples and struggling drug addicts, and this convinced him there was an ability to heal
human beings with messages that weren't delivered by doctors. Like a
version of the bestselling book series *Chicken Soup for the Soul*, Bell could
never accept that God would be merciful until we're dead and then not
let the next conversation begin until the afterlife.

I've wondered why I find Bell's story so compelling. I can't relate to
his life or his message. I find his moralising patronising. And yet when
his spiritual path is revealed and I can feel the angst he feels when old
certainties are lost or challenged, I believe this goes to the heart of why
a supernatural existence, however it's defined, is much more satisfying
than simply believing what's in front of us. For billions of humans on
the planet, increasingly non-Western and a world away from the lives
of Richard Dawkins or Christopher Hitchens, the ability to understand
pain, suffering and joy without a higher being or power is limited if not
non-existent.

The age of science is upon us and irreversible. For this we should
be thankful. But the atheists among us should also acknowledge that
striving to understand the chaos in the world and beyond isn't necessarily a sign of irrationality or madness but merely the human spirit and
mind at work. I agree with British philosopher Julian Baggani, who
champions secular values in government and the law but resists attempts
to completely obliterate religious symbols or traditions. 'If secularism has
come to be seen as the enemy of the religious when it should be its best
friend,' he wrote in *The Guardian* in February 2012, 'then we secularists
must share at least some of the blame.'[141]

Baggani's key point, and one often forgotten by militant atheists who
believe religion poisons everything, is that a society that dismisses or
ignores anything other than the visible or scientific will be a very dull
society indeed. 'The central mistake is simply to lose sight of the fact
that secularism is really a very specific principle about the workings
of public and political institutions,' he argued. 'As long as they operate
without granting privilege to any particularly comprehensive worldview, secularism has nothing to say about how religious the rest of
society and public discourse should be.'[142]

If that means a friend takes comfort from a mystical passage in the Qur'an after the death of a parent, then so be it. The fundamental error that must be avoided by those of us who preach a secular tolerance is not to allow others to believe in the fantastical or even absurd.

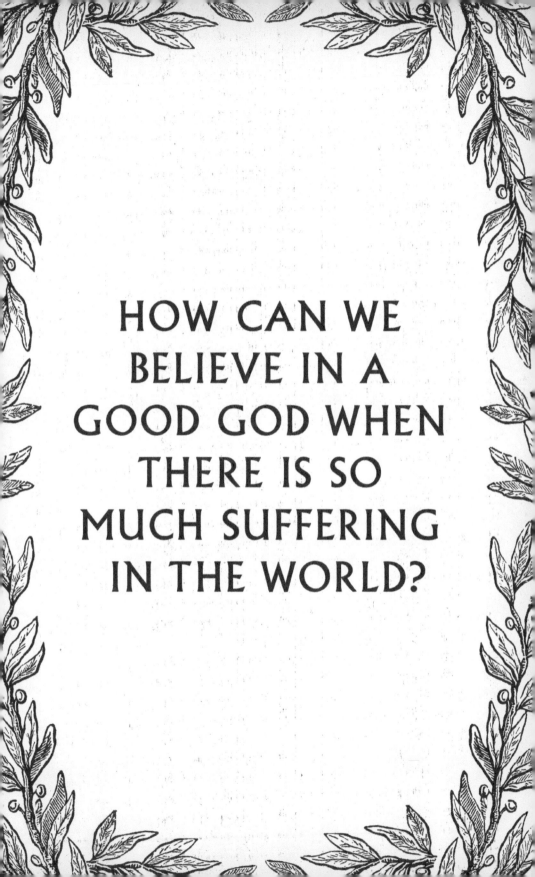

HOW CAN WE
BELIEVE IN A
GOOD GOD WHEN
THERE IS SO
MUCH SUFFERING
IN THE WORLD?

Simon Smart

On Boxing Day morning in 2004, while Australians nursed Christmas hangovers in the cooling waters of preferred holiday destinations, a massive undersea earthquake off the coast of northern Sumatra violently and abruptly lifted the ocean floor several metres. This triggered devastating tsunami waves that surged across the Indian Ocean, striking land with merciless speed and force, killing more than 230,000 people in fourteen countries.

A few years after this event I interviewed the CEO of World Vision Australia, Tim Costello, about his experiences of being on the ground in Sri Lanka forty hours after the wave tore through the countryside, destroying everything in its path. 'There were apocalyptic scenes with bodies everywhere, particularly kids,' he said. 'There were people standing there staring out to sea hoping against hope that someone was coming – being washed back alive.' Costello, a deeply committed Christian, admitted that he was pushed to the very limits of his faith. 'At that point you say to yourself, "Where is God?" That's the question you ask, "Where is God?"'[143]

You could justly ask the same question of any number of human catastrophes, great and small. Whether it is conspicuous catastrophic suffering of the kind described here, or something less than that, we all know that even a good life is eventually littered with sorrow, disappointment, strained relationships and heartbreak of one sort or another.

As the title of this chapter suggests, the 'problem of evil and suffering' is indeed a problem for those who believe in an all-powerful, good God. It's the most problematic thing for me as a believer and, more than anything else, gives me reason to doubt at times. Importantly, it doesn't seem to say anything about God's existence, though – if God exists he could simply be uninterested or perhaps remarkably cruel. But pain and suffering do go straight to the heart of God's character and whether he is in fact good.

If you have a faith, there's an intellectual problem with the possibility of God being good and all-powerful and yet somehow still allowing suffering to continue. Philosophers have wrestled with this question for centuries. The horror of the extravagant evil and misery that we all know is a daily part of the human experience frequently leads to a desire for justice and a longing that things be made right.

But just because we can't see or imagine a good reason why God might allow something to happen doesn't mean there can't be one. Furthermore, unless we have some sort of divine, eternal perspective upon all of time, it's clear that, on this issue, we can't draw conclusions that could 'disprove' God's existence from our own finite experience and knowledge. Nevertheless, I'm conscious that when it comes to real, personal suffering, those sorts of arguments don't help much. If you lose someone very close to you, if you suffer an enormous loss of some kind, there's a personal element that isn't touched by intellectual debates.

So what are we to make of the reality of suffering and pain?

Buddhism, an increasingly popular philosophy in the West, developed directly in response to the question of suffering. The answer in the Buddhist framework is that attachment to things and people – which are actually an illusion – is where the problem lies and hence the solution. Suffering is part of the grand illusion of existence, therefore Buddhism proposes a *disengagement*: a recognition that ultimately our lives are a chain of cause and effect. There is no real 'you'. Remove the self, or just recognise that there never was such a thing, and suffering will disappear.[144] This, according to the Buddha, is how we deal with the pain of life.

What about for Islam? I'm sure Rachel will want to say something about this but, putting it crudely yet I hope accurately, for the Muslim ('one who submits' to God), all events in history are absolutely determined and controlled by the will of Allah. Events that cause suffering, therefore, such as disease, wars, a car crash and so on, are the direct result of the specific finger of Allah. Suffering thus becomes an opportunity for the faithful to 'submit' to Allah's indisputable will, and to reaffirm the central creed that Allah is the 'Cause of all causes'.

For those who self-consciously identify as atheist, the reality is that suffering is just part of life, and there can be no real objection to it. According to this view, what's wrong is that we live in a world subject to chance and uncontrolled processes, which is why Richard Dawkins concludes that what we have is exactly what you'd expect if there were no God. When Christopher Hitchens started to write about the illness that eventually claimed his life, he wrote, ruefully, 'In whatever kind of "race" life may be, I have very abruptly become a finalist . . . To the dumb question "Why me?" the cosmos barely bothers to return the reply: "Why not?".'[145] As Hitchens recognised, to complain about suffering is nonsensical when there is no one to complain to. And nor can there be any hope in the face of either the pain of life or the jolting finality of death.

So what about my faith? First, it's particularly striking to note that there's enormous space within the Christian framework for 'lament' – a passionate expression of grief or sorrow and also protest – in response to suffering. The Bible is full of people – some of them the most faithful of God's followers – who come to him with lament, baffled questions and objections. Lament is not only allowed but is modelled all over the place.

All of this should tell us something of the Christian response to suffering. It's hard-edged. It sees suffering as an aberration – something to rail against. It takes into account the reality of people's lives and yet it offers hope. The laments of the Bible are offered by those who believe they know God, which is precisely why they protest – because of the jarring contrast between what they know of God and what they see around them. This, after all, is the God who, we are told, 'has compassion on all he has made' (Psalms 145:9). It's appropriate to ask, then, 'How can he *not intervene* when hundreds of thousands of people are killed in an earthquake?'.

Secondly, the story of Christianity contains within it an ancient (and admittedly mysterious) account of a profound alienation from God that has wounded creation to its uttermost depths and reduced all things to a pale glimmer of the world God truly intends. This is a world enslaved to spiritual and worldly powers hostile to God.[146] While Christian believers debate over the exact nature of the early chapters of Genesis and how they should be read, they all agree that the story of the fall of humanity refers to an immense fracture in the relationship between humans and God, between humans and each other, and even between humans and the world itself.

This certainly matches my own experience. The evil and brokenness of the world distorts and infects good things and frequently renders them ugly, oppressive and life-sapping.

This account of reality includes each and every one of us as part of the problem – we are all bound up in a fallen existence, and we also contribute to this brokenness. Our own suffering might never make the evening news, or even Twitter, but we all know and sometimes contribute to the damage brought on by pride, resentment, bullying, selfishness and petty jealousies. Only the most wilfully blind optimism can deny that we live in a world of not only earthquakes, tsunamis, droughts and disease, but also human-induced injustice, cruelty, violence and hatred. In the West, while we gorge ourselves and throw food away, somewhere else on the globe, every five seconds, a child dies of hunger. 'We know that the whole creation has been groaning as in the pains of childbirth right up to the present time,' writes the Apostle Paul,[147] and if we are alive to the truth of the human experience we can all say Amen to that!

When a Christian stops to consider the struggle of human existence they will want to point to the story of the death and resurrection of Jesus as the centre of a very long story of how God launches a rescue plan to save the world from its misery.

There were lots of crucifixions around the time of Jesus; there'd be nothing remarkable in this famous one except for the nature of the person on the cross. The claim is that Jesus is God incarnate, or God in human form. If that's true, we might not have many answers to suffering in any exhaustive sense, but we do know this – God has not remained aloof from the suffering but has become part of it.[148] We're talking about an engaged God.

The crucifixion, therefore, is not an explanation of evil and suffering, but the account of the event where God deals with it – Jesus taking on the darkness and, in an ultimate sense, defeating it. The resurrection of Jesus tells a compelling story of God condemning all the things that have destroyed life, and promising a day when the weight of history and all the centuries of human cruelty, sadness and loss will be overcome.

The biblical picture promises a new beginning, when murdered children will be raised up and restored, and families torn apart by violence will find peace and harmony again. It presents a vision of a time where crushing loneliness will be a thing of the past, where bodies broken and ravaged by disease or old age will be restored to strength and vitality, where people who have experienced grinding poverty will find abundance, where children ripped from their mother's arms in a tsunami will be ushered into new life. Every aspect of this vision is predicated on Jesus rising from death. If that didn't happen, then it's right and proper to throw the whole thing out the window.

As a Christian, I have plenty of unanswered questions to do with suffering. But the biblical picture is big on the present reality of the God who suffers and that God being with you in your struggles. I and many others can testify to that. And it's also big on a future hope.

But there's an important point to add to this picture of future hope, and that is the belief that the 'age to come', or the future age, overlaps with the present. That's why those who follow Jesus see themselves as taking part in God's redemptive action in the world and are motivated to play a part in relieving suffering now. I don't mean to suggest that all Christians are good at this, or that they're the only ones doing this sort of work, but such action is part of a long tradition begun by the church in the first century – known as it was for radical service to those in need, bringing healing and protection to the most vulnerable people.

This brings to mind my friends, Allan and Sheena Gaston who, at middle age, left a comfortable existence in Northern Ireland to work with children in South African public hospitals. Almost all of these children have only one parent, or in many cases none, and they are all extremely poor. Some are dying of AIDS. Many are suffering terrible burns and some are victims of rape.

Allan and Sheena run an organisation called Zanini Bantwana (Zulu for 'Come Children') – a team of people dedicated to show love and care for these desperately poor, sick and lonely kids. The team sit with the children, play with them, read to them and keep them company. They provide a basic education.

Their motivation? They believe that God is love, and that they want to be part of his redemptive work, bringing healing and grace to their small corner of the world.

In the end Christianity is a story of the denial of the powers of darkness and violence and cruelty and hatred and heartbreak – and in their place the victory of goodness and mercy, kindness and love. Sometimes we might think of this as a flickering light in the darkness, but it is a light, one that promises to burst into a glorious blaze. That's a vision I'm hanging on to.

Jane Caro

As someone who – as Simon rather oddly puts it – 'self-consciously identifies as atheist' (why is it self-conscious for me but not for a Christian, Muslim or Jew?), I have no problem with the question that forms the basis for this chapter. I don't believe in a god, good, bad or indifferent.

This means my expectations are at best realistic and, if happiness is all about managing expectations, it certainly seems to be working. I'm fully aware that disaster could strike at any second and I don't worry about it. If and when it strikes, I'll deal with it as best I can. But when it does, I won't torture myself further by worrying that the misery visited upon me or those I love is some kind of malevolent punishment. Nor, if great good fortune comes my way, will I regard it as some kind of reward. For me, it's just the way life is. I pays me money and I takes me chances.

Recently, my husband and I, who now both have the privilege of working for ourselves, managed to sneak a couple of days midweek at our country property. One beautiful spring morning we heard a knock at the front door. This was extremely unusual, because no one ever comes to the front door. If a neighbour visits they always come round the back. Indeed, it had been so long, we had great difficulty forcing the old hinges open. Once we managed it, there, on the doorstep, looking somewhat hot and bothered and very much out of their natural habitat, were a couple of young Americans in white-collared shirts and black ties. Yes, a couple of those poor, misguided Mormons who get shipped around the world to proselytise to the uninterested had washed up on our front doorstep, at the end of 11 kilometres of dirt road, four causeways and a 55-minute drive from the nearest shop.

If there is a god, and he is the Mormon's god, surely he would not be so cruel as to – out of all the gin joints in all the world – make the two of them take such a long trip only to end up facing me? Even I was forced to feel a little sorry for them.

They started with their spiel and my husband – who'd diplomatically elbowed me out of the way – informed them we were atheists and they'd wasted their journey. The Mormons were not about to give up so easily. First, they tried the 'Look at your beautiful surroundings, isn't that enough evidence of God's existence for you' argument and were met with short shrift. Then they rapidly switched from carrot ('Praise God for all this beauty') to stick – 'You'll burn in hell for all eternity if you don't believe as we believe'. That particular line of persuasion goes down especially badly with me, so I'm afraid I yelled at them over my husband's shoulder.

'You mean that no matter how exemplary a life I may lead, if I don't believe in your god he's going to consign me to the flames?'

They nodded, solemnly.

'What a nasty, vain, judgemental, narcissistic, infantile [there may have been more] small-minded god you worship.'

They beat a hasty retreat.

Forget about gods permitting suffering. The bigger problem believers have is that god doesn't simply permit indifferent nature and flawed humanity to cause us misery. He threatens to inflict it upon us after our deaths, personally. Gods use suffering as a selling tool.

Rachel Woodlock

The Qur'an gives us an account of Moses and his mysterious spiritual guide known to Islamic tradition as al-Khidr, 'the green one'. Don't look for an equivalent tale in your Bible, folks, you won't find it. The text doesn't tell us whether the enigmatic immortal is a prophet, an angel or even, as Muhammad Iqbal suggested, symbolic of Moses' self.

Anyway, as the story goes, Moses is guided to meet al-Khidr, who possesses esoteric knowledge given to him directly by God. Moses asks to accompany the wanderer to learn from him, but al-Khidr warns that his prospective pupil would not be patient enough, not being in possession of all the facts. Nevertheless, al-Khidr agrees as long as Moses promises not to ask questions until his guide is ready to explain. Al-Khidr then does three things that confound Moses, who, unable to contain himself, objects each time.

First, al-Khidr scuppers a boat the pair had boarded; next al-Khidr kills a young man they meet; and lastly al-Khidr rebuilds a collapsing wall gratis for some inhospitable townsfolk. At each stage, Moses objects to the seeming injustice of al-Khidr's actions: the boat's owners may drown on the scuppered boat; the lad is innocent of any wrongdoing towards al-Khidr; and the townspeople who'd refused them food should have at least paid for al-Khidr's work.

Because Moses has failed to keep silent they part ways, but not before al-Khidr explains to Moses the meaning of each event:

As for the boat, it belonged to some poor mariners and I wanted to damage it because there was a king after them seizing every boat by force. As for the young man, his parents were faithful believers and we had reason to fear he would overburden them with his rebellious transgressions and ingratitude. So we intended that their Lord would instead give them a better son, purer and nearer in affection. As for the wall, it was for two young orphan boys in the town, underneath which was a treasure intended for them. Their father was a righteous man and so your Lord intended that they reach their maturity and then unearth their treasure, as a mercy from your Lord. I did not act of my own accord. That is the explanation of what you were unable to bear patiently (Q18:79–82).

This allegorical tale emphasises how we have limited knowledge about the injustices and tragedies that occur in our lives, but that if we possessed God's full knowledge and wisdom, we would understand that everything happens for a good reason. There's meaning and ultimate justice that encompasses all reality, beyond even space-time, but, as Simon says, we just don't have God's divine, eternal perspective.

What I find difficult with Christianity's position is the claim that Jesus' death on the cross is a victory, that it's God's way of dealing with suffering and defeating it. But I am not sure exactly *how* that occurs? I can't understand how God dying on the cross means death is defeated.

From an Islamic perspective, the reason suffering and death isn't seen as a failure on God's part is that Islam's theology attributes a variety of characteristics to him that are all in balance. He has names of beauty as well as names of majesty, and Islamic theology abhors one side being emphasised at the expense of the other. Not only is God *al-naf'i* 'the source of good', *al-wadud* 'the loving', *al-muhyi* 'the life-giver' and *al-muqit* 'the nourisher', he is also *al-darr* 'the afflicter', *al-mudhill*, 'the humiliator', *al-mumit* 'the life-taker' and *al-muntaqim* 'the avenger'.

From an Islamic perspective, everything we experience, the good and the bad, has its reason. Life is like a big school, with tests and trials as lessons for us to learn and exams for us to pass. 'We divided them into communities on the earth, some of them are righteous, and some of them fall short. We tested them with good and bad that they might return (Q17:168).' Simon is correct in his succinct paraphrase of how Muslims understand suffering. We each need patience to withstand our own difficulties, learning to be grateful to God even when it seems everything is going wrong, because each breath is a gift from the universe.

I know there's nothing worse than a do-gooder who tells you 'It's all for the best' or 'This is just God's will' when you're suffering almost unbearable distress. People who utter pithy aphorisms just want to alleviate the discomfort *they* feel, facing a soggy, crumpled mess of snot, tears, rage, pain, frustration, bleakness and despair. Maybe it's not possible to make meaning out of the suffering another person experiences, only your own. Instead, our response to other people's suffering must be to do everything in our power to help, while remembering that everything that happens to us is according to God's will.[149]

Antony Loewenstein

It takes a certain kind of Jew to write the following:

> Yes, all criticism of Israel is anti-Semitic. Yes, it is so because of specific historical circumstances. Yes, it is inescapable. Yes, it holds true however well-intentioned such criticism may be. Yes, it holds as true for Jewish as for non-Jewish critics of Israel.[150]

Tel-Aviv based writer and author Benjamin Kerstein wrote this in the *Jerusalem Post* in May 2012. His ability to frame any and all Israeli actions as defensible and inherently good, and therefore beyond criticism, proves to me that a kind Zionist God is a contradiction in terms. We're all suffering because of this Jewish constipation.

I use this example slightly in jest. Kerstein certainly argued this point but we can hardly damn all Jews because of the actions of one, or indeed many, who share his politics.

We react to suffering when it's close to or caused by us. Distant pain – how many Westerners know or care that millions of Congolese have been murdered in the last twenty years? – affects us in a way that's far easier to ignore. As an atheist, I don't view a deity as a barometer of what's good or destructive in the world. I have my own values that allow me to do that.

I agree with Jane that 'Gods use suffering as a selling tool'. Far too many religions hold over believers the threat of punishment for supposed misdeeds. That's not a community, it's blackmail. We're not born with sin; we emerge into the world as a clean slate. For me it's not about finding the right god or a good god, or even a god. It's not hoping and praying that an unknowable figure can understand what I'm experiencing. What humans see and feel is far more personal than appropriating a god that millions of others also use for their own purposes.

There are times when I know believing in God could be easier. It may give me comfort. It may help when I visit Afghanistan and see men high on opium looking at me with a vacant stare. It could assist my anger when I witness the destruction wrought on Palestinians by my supposed Jewish brothers and sisters in the occupied territories. I've too often heard the invocation of God and Jewish suffering when listening to explanations of why Israel must brutalise Arabs. We don't want to, I hear, but we have no choice. They make us do it to them.

If I imagine a good God, my mind is filled with a benevolent being who doesn't judge. But that's a fantasy no religion accepts. Instead, I refuse to entertain the idea of suffering being caused by a god, or of a god being capable of stopping it. Suffering occurs because people inflict it for a million reasons. God may be given the blame but that doesn't mean it's rational or fair to the faceless creature who lives in the hearts and minds of billions globally.

The desire for gods to be imagined dangerous, edgy, hot, toxic, brutal or tolerant is a creation of a human mind, not religion itself. Communities have the possibility of change. It's surely a sign of progress that growing numbers of North American Jewish organisations embrace lesbian, gay, bisexual and transgender (LGBT) people, whereas until recently such individuals would have been told there was no room for them. The Jewish Organization Equality Index found in 2012 that 50 per cent of non-profit Jewish groups received the highest score for 'inclusion' and were taking steps to welcome LGBT men and women.

Although I'm not in that world, and I can't imagine the pain of being gay and excluded from a synagogue I so desperately wanted to be a part of, I welcome the growing awareness among traditionally conservative and God-believing Jews to alleviate suffering.

If I ever see signs that a god – good, bad, indifferent, clean-shaven or bearded and pretty or slim – has entered the world and knows how to reduce or even eradicate suffering, I may become an instant convert.

HOW DO WE ACCOUNT FOR EVIL?

Jane Caro

I don't believe in evil. I absolutely accept that there are evil acts and evil consequences, but I don't believe in the concept of a devil or in evil as a kind of entity in itself. I don't even believe there are evil people. In fact, I completely agree with the Christian concept that while we can hate the sin we should never hate the sinner.

I'll never forget the ghastly sight of people who no doubt regarded themselves as 'good' baying for blood as a police van supposed to be carrying the then ten-year-old killers of Jamie Bulger passed them on its way to court. These adults literally howled abuse at the boys they thought were inside and some lunged ferociously at the vehicle, hammering on the sides. Whatever the two boys had done, and their crime was heinous indeed, they remained human and children themselves. It seems evil acts often beget evil behaviour.

The intense desire of many to punish those children – often cloaked in self-righteousness – I found bewildering, even in its less ferocious incarnations. A woman I worked with took it upon herself to start a petition to have the two ten-year-olds tried as adults. For the life of me, I couldn't see why. The crime had happened on the other side of the world, she didn't know anyone involved, and we knew nothing about it except what was in the papers. Why was she so full of hate and the desire for revenge? Needless to say, I refused to sign. Such was the intensity of passion their behaviour aroused in the community, however, that, once they had been tried and convicted, both boys had their names changed when they entered the juvenile detention system.

Self-righteousness frightens me. I wouldn't call it evil, exactly, but it often leads to evil acts. No doubt the religious zealots who throw stones at some poor woman accused of adultery are fuelled by a sense of their own rectitude.

Such are the complexities of human psychology, however, that I often can't help wondering if punitive self-righteousness isn't actually a cover for unacceptable impulses and desires inside ourselves. In the ad business we're trained to 'follow the benefit', an accepted concept in other branches of human psychology. And it has struck me occasionally that the self-righteous desire to punish others for horrible crimes (or even just sexual behaviour that's deemed taboo) is so energising because it presents the perfect opportunity to externalise the hidden parts of ourselves we find shameful, while still allowing us to claim the high moral ground. The benefit of self-righteousness, then, is in our ability to separate our own sins from ourselves by punishing them in others. Just for a moment, perhaps, we feel cleansed. None of this is conscious, by the way, and that's precisely why it's so dangerous.

Socrates said 'The unexamined life isn't worth living', but I think it may be worse than that. I think that evil behaviour and the great harm it causes often come from the parts of us that have remained unexamined, the parts we've buried because we believe they're unacceptable or shameful. Originally, particularly if damage or trauma has occurred in our childhood, we may have repressed the overwhelming emotions that accompany such suffering simply to survive.

Alice Miller, a controversial German psychiatrist, believes that it's precisely this 'splitting off' of childhood trauma that can give rise to evil. She relates the fact that Hitler once told his secretary he experienced exactly this kind of dissociation. He said that during one of his regular beatings from his father he was able to stop crying, feel nothing and count all thirty-two (thirty-two!) of the blows. In the same article she explains how this response to childhood abuse manifests in adulthood:

> In order not to die, all mistreated children must totally repress the mistreatment, deprivation, and bewilderment they have undergone because otherwise the child's organism wouldn't be able to cope with the magnitude of the pain suffered. Only as adults do they have other possibilities for dealing with their feelings. If they don't make use of these possibilities, then what was once the life-saving function of repression can be transformed into a dangerous destructive, and self-destructive force. In the careers of despots such as Hitler and Stalin, their suppressed fantasies of revenge can lead to indescribable atrocities.[151]

Maybe evil actions are simply the unexpressed, unacknowledged agony of a damaged and abused child wreaking havoc where they can once they have more power as a disturbed adult. When I worked as a volunteer telephone counsellor we heard a lecture by a psychologist who specialised in sexual deviancy. He explained that as the strongest motivation in men is the sexual drive, damage and abuse in boys often expresses itself through sexual deviancy when they grow up. The paedophile, he explained, is usually fixated on children of a particular age – almost always the age at which the paedophile himself was first abused. Chillingly, he also explained that the most serious and violent sex offenders had often been traumatised when they were preverbal, and that was why the consequences were so profound and so impossible to treat, because they could not be expressed. Is evil, therefore, just the result of the unheard cries of abused children echoing down through the generations and the centuries? When adults abuse a child the way they were themselves abused, is that how we perpetuate evil? Instead of condemning, if we want to stop evil, should we instead start listening to children and damaged adults so we can begin to understand?

I think compassion is the opposite of self-righteousness. When we're in the grip of self-righteousness, we feel superior to the object of our condemnation. Indeed, if I'm right that self-righteousness is a way to disown our personal sins and humiliations through punishing them in others, then that sense of superiority is precisely the point. Compassion, on the other hand, is defined by its humility. When we feel compassion we recognise our shared humanity and accept our common weakness and vulnerability. Far from seeking to punish the sinner and distance ourselves from them via our loud (sometimes to the point of shrieking) condemnation of their actions, we see the tragedy of the situation and feel the pity and the terror of both the wrongdoer and the wronged. We identify with the sinner, in fact. We don't dismiss them as evil monsters but recognise them for what they are: flawed and damaged human beings.

Perhaps compassion is the only real antidote to evil we have. After all, if the devil really did exist, what a tragic and pitiful figure he would be.

This doesn't mean that I believe we should simply shrug our shoulders in the face of evil acts. In fact, I believe the precise opposite.

I believe that through compassion, through understanding that nobody – however horrific their behaviour – is wholly and irredeemably evil, we give ourselves some chance of reducing evil in the world while remaining civilised ourselves. If we fall into the same trap as the evildoer – by dehumanising or demonising the perpetrator – it becomes easier to do evil ourselves. We run the risk of believing that if we simply eradicate the person we see as wholly evil, we have eradicated evil itself. Actually, when we do that, what we really do is perpetuate evil in the name of defeating it. As Gandhi said, an eye for an eye makes the whole world blind.

I don't think I'm naive, optimistic or wilfully ignoring the problem of evil by approaching it compassionately. Indeed, I'd argue that I'm staring it unflinchingly in the face by acknowledging it as part of my responsibility, as someone who tries to be a decent human being, to recognise that all humanity is capable of evil, including me.

Simon Smart

On 16 March 1968, 120 American infantrymen from 'Charlie Company' attacked the Vietnamese village of My Lai. Most people know of the story.

When Charlie Company arrived in their helicopters, the Vietcong battalion they planned to attack was not in the village. Despite the fact that they were not shot at once in the whole day, Charlie Company went on a rampage of killing and destruction. Every house was burnt down. Women and young girls were raped and then shot. Dozens of people at a time, including old men, women and small children, were machine-gunned into a ditch. In four hours, nearly 500 villagers were killed. Some had their scalps cut off, others their hands and feet and tongues. Pregnant women had their stomachs slashed open and were left to die.

The men who committed these acts were normal young American men. They were brought up in average American homes. Fred Widmar, who killed two small children, says of his involvement:

> Why? Why did I do that? That's not me. Something happened to me. You reach a point where you snap . . . Somebody flicks a switch and you are a completely different person. There is a culture of violence, of brutality, with people all around you doing the same thing.[152]

There are too many of these sorts of stories: the massacre of over 200 people in the Guatemalan village of Dos Erres in 1982, the slaughter of more than 8000 Bosnian Muslims in Srebenica in Bosnia Herzegovina in 1995. What's perhaps most disturbing about them is that they're not drawn from some ancient barbaric past but recent memory, and were carried out by people who mostly lived unremarkable, regular lives. They're a reminder that, given the right circumstances, all kinds of people are capable of all kinds of evil, cruelty and darkness.

Every language has a word for evil, but when we use the word what do we mean? Most people think of evil as something that occurs but *ought not to* and is unexpected. Evil is *disorder.* It oppresses and is oppressive. It's the sense that the world is *not the way it's supposed to be* and hence we react to evil with indignation, protest and disgust.[153] What's interesting to me is that any discussion of evil presupposes a standard against which we can measure acts as closer to good or evil. It's worth asking where we think this standard comes from, and on what basis we make our judgements.

I take Jane's point that evil acts beget evil behaviour, and she's no doubt right when she says that many evil actions are the agony of an abused childhood finding expression in adulthood. But I don't think this is an adequate account of the scope of evil we're discussing here. The 'unheard cries of abused children echoing down through the generations and centuries', as Jane describes it, certainly explains much of the misery of the world, but this description takes us nowhere in understanding the source of evil, nor its nature. I just can't agree with those who wish to excuse or explain away the worst excesses of cruelty and monstrous brutality by attributing them to a terrible upbringing or limited opportunities. Is that what was going on at Srebrenica? This seems like avalanche-dodging to me. Ethicist Margaret Somerville says we have to face 'the fact of evil' and not try to make it disappear by redefining it as sickness.[154]

I understand Jane's concern about ugly self-righteousness, and in this she'd find an ally in Jesus, who rejected all forms of sanctimonious behaviour, especially by those who are religious. He warned against worrying about the speck in someone else's eye without paying attention to the plank in your own. Jane mentions religious zealots who throw stones at women accused of adultery, which of course brings to mind exactly the situation Jesus defused by imploring anyone 'who is without sin' to throw the first stone. At the same time Jesus expected people to make assessments of right and wrong and in that sense to make judgements. The key for him was any judgement of another must be motivated by love and not derision or condemnation.

Evil might appear too dated a concept and have too much of a ring of absolute judgement and simpleminded certainty for some, but it's revealing that many of our greatest artists and writers have found it necessary to plumb the depths of this topic. It appears to them to be such an unavoidable question and an area of deep human complexity that it demands attention. Most have recognised evil not only to be a reality but also, at least to some extent, to reside within each of us.

Reflecting on his experiences in a Russian gulag, dissident writer Alexander Solzhenitsyn said life would be much simpler if there were easily identifiable evil people we could separate from the rest of us. But it was clear to him that:

> the line dividing good and evil cuts through the heart of every human being[155] ... Even within hearts overwhelmed by evil, one small bridgehead of good is retained; and even in the best of all hearts, there remains a small corner of evil.[156]

Jane's take on evil I find simply inadequate. It shares some characteristics with what philosophically could loosely be called *optimism*. It involves a kind of rational reflection and acceptance of evil acts in such a way as to place humans within a totality that cannot be other than it is. This has the effect of, as Etienne Borne writes, 'removing the evil from evil, *i.e.* of excising what appeared to be unjustifiable about it,' or to strip evil of its character.[157] For the one who is able to see sufficiently broadly and far, evil doesn't actually exist. You get this sort of thinking in the Vedas or even in Christian Science. The difference between good and evil is abolished, as we are all identical to the absolute. There have been lots of (sometimes modified) versions of this way of thinking over the centuries. At the time the New Testament was written the Stoics were highly influential in the Graeco-Roman world and represented a kind of optimism labouring under strain – unable to overlook evil but determined to do so.[158] The parallels with Jane's assessment of this question are obvious and I can't help feeling she lays herself open to the charge of wishful thinking by evading what she cannot accept.

The desire to confront evil and see something done about it forms the shape of so many of the stories we tell ourselves in literature and film. But, as theologian Tom Wright points out, we know that in real life innocent people get convicted and guilty people are let off. Companies destroy people's lives and walk away scot-free. Sometimes people spend the rest of their lives coping with the hurt and bitterness caused by the cruelty or carelessness of another. Millions of people are murdered or starved to death in the labour camps of despots and never get to see those responsible brought to trial. Our hopes to achieve justice are only ever partial, and often fail completely.[159]

The biblical story takes evil very seriously. It is unrelenting in denouncing the reality and danger of evil,[160] and yes, it does attribute evil to the evil one, the adversary, the prince of darkness. According to this picture, evil is something contrary to the will of God, but is, for a time, permitted by him. It's not part of how God originally intended things, and it's neither really 'something' nor really 'nothing'. It's opposed to all the good things of life God created and is therefore, by nature, destructive.

Jane says that if the Devil did exist he would be a tragic and pitiful figure, and indeed that's the picture the Bible ultimately gives us. As Sebastian Barry writes, the devil's own tragedy is that he is the author of nothing and the architect of empty spaces.

Evil is divided within itself; it's disorder and a functional perversion. It's parasitic in that it lives by means of good things. Evil takes a positive thing – human sexuality, for instance – and turns it into something ugly and oppressive, like the sex slavery of poverty-stricken teenage girls. The wonders of human ingenuity and technical brilliance can be used to create the A380 airliner or a life-support machine, but can also be commandeered in the production of chemical weapons and cluster bombs.

The Bible won't allow us to reduce evil to single acts that are wrong, but rather tells us that evil has a momentum whereby the whole becomes much greater than the sum of its parts. Evil can be institutional and systemic. For example, we live in a world where in 2011, 6.9 million children died before reaching their fifth birthday. Almost two-thirds of them – 4.4 million – died of infectious diseases, nearly all of which were preventable.[161] All of this goes on while in the West we continue to die from overconsumption and drown in excess. The sum total of individuals living like this produces results that we know to be evil.

Frederick Buechner says that when the Bible turns its light on us the Christian story is bad news before it is good news: 'It is the news that man is a sinner, to use the old word, that he is evil in the imagination of his heart, that when he looks in the mirror all in a lather what he sees is at least eight parts chicken, phoney, slob.' But while Christianity depicts evil as a serious problem it also offers hope. Buechner adds that the Gospel is also the news that us 'slobs and phoneys' are 'loved anyway, cherished, forgiven, bleeding to be sure, but also bled for'.

It is in the cross that hope lies, not just for us as individuals but also for our world. 'The impenetrable mystery of evil meets the paradoxical mystery of the cross,' is how French theologian Henri Blocher puts it.[162] Jesus's crucifixion and resurrection tell us of God's mastery over evil and his plan to ultimately defeat it once and for all. At the cross God's Kingdom comes about not by weaponry or power but by a spirit of sacrifice, not by subjugating people into slavery but by the service of God himself.[163] Blocher says that, ironically, it is in what looks like the ultimate defeat, the cross, that evil is crushed, turned back on itself; conquered in the end by love and the fulfilment of justice.

While evil is all too real, both around us, and to some extent within us, there exists in the Christ story a defiant hope and a promise of ultimate justice, restoration and the renewal of all things. It's a vision that has inspired and encouraged countless millions in the centuries since.

Antony Loewenstein

My family never saw it coming. When Adolf Hitler came to power in Germany in 1933, most Jews thought it was a passing fad, an extreme reaction to economic troubles. My father's parents were living in Dresden at the time and my grandfather used to tell me that initial concern at the rise of the Nazis was muted by the belief that Jews had been an integral part of German society for so long; one cousin even fought on Germany's side during the First World War.

In the stunning book by Erik Larson, *In the Garden of Beasts*, about America's first ambassador to Hitler's Germany, William E. Dodd, the writer explains that there existed in 1933 a perception that the Nazi government would not endure.[164] Hitler himself wasn't seen internationally as a menace ('a temperate actor') and US President Franklin D. Roosevelt was scared of speaking too strongly about the 'Jewish problem', fearing a mass influx of Jewish refugees from Germany at a time when America was recovering from the Depression. There was a thought across America at the time, writes Larson, 'that such reports [of Hitler ordering brutality against Jews, Communist and other opponents] must be exaggerated' though the State Department's reports were graphic in their detail.[165]

The darkness soon descended in Germany – Jewish businesses were boycotted, including my great-grandfather's hat shop in Dresden, eventually forced into bankruptcy – and my uncle in Toronto, Herbert Lowe, writes that by 1936 my family realised they 'must start planning on moving to another country'. In November 1938 many males in my family were picked up by the Nazis, thrown into jail and put in trucks. 'We found out later that we were very lucky,' he explains. 'The jail was used as a holding area until more people could be shipped to concentration camps.' Luckily, they were all released after a number of months behind bars, and some obtained visas, to Australia and Canada, but the vast bulk were not so lucky and were murdered.

History is full of strange, unexpected quirks. Herbert, whom I recently saw in Toronto and is now ninety-two, says that the day before the war was declared in 1939 he received in the post a visa for England. 'By noon

I took the last direct train to Holland. I said goodbye to my parents –
never to see them again.'

What happened next is unarguably the most documented genocide
in history. It brought suffering and cruelty on an unimaginable scale,
alongside resistance and bravery, and a decimated Europe that emerged
in 1945 to rebuild, slowly but surely.

Fast-forward to 2011 and one glorious, bittersweet moment
completed a paradoxical trajectory from 1945 to the twenty-first
century. I was in the German consulate in Sydney, receiving my German
passport, just one way a chastised German government has attempted
to repair the damage it caused in the 1930s and 1940s. Jews were made
stateless on departure and my grandparents arrived in Australia in 1939;
because I was able to prove this, the authorities in Berlin were keen to
offer me citizenship (my father, after rejecting it for many years, initiated
the process a few years earlier).

I had tears in my eyes when presented with my passport. The official
representative asked how I felt. I responded, or likely mumbled, that it
was a surreal feeling to be a German citizen only a short time after the
country wanted nothing to do with Jews or my family. But it felt like
a victory of sorts, a just outcome, the best kind of revenge for what
the Nazis had tried and failed to do.

The extermination of millions, Jews, gypsies, gays, blacks and countless others, is routinely cited as the epitome of evil, the pinnacle of
horrors in the modern age. The mechanised form of death remains
unparalleled in history.

But calling it evil is a mistake, too simplistic. There were acts of
extreme violence and industrialised killing, but the word 'evil' merely
conjures up blackness, an incomprehensible reality no one can explain.
And perhaps that's the point: not every German was complicit but too
few spoke out in opposition. If it's not evil, what should it be called?
I can't think of another clear word to describe the horrors that occurred,
and yet it seems inadequate, too neat.

Evil can be so broadly defined – surely the Holocaust was one of
the worst cases of genocide in history, but it wasn't the only one, and
other horrific events on a much smaller scale, like Catholic priests

having sex with minors, are also repugnant – that trying to impose a religious framework to its magnitude is perhaps a natural reaction. But it still doesn't offer anything close to clarity and seems only to muddy a principled emotional and psychological response.

My story is both unique and common. Millions of Jews have similar tales of pain and redemption. They tried to kill us. We survived and thrived. The question is what lessons are learnt from the trauma. For many, it's to blindly support a Jewish state that oppresses Palestinians in the name of security. For others, it's to act when minorities are oppressed in the name of a fundamentalist ideology.

Many Jews during the Holocaust renounced their belief in God, claiming that no deity could stand by and watch while an entire people were slaughtered. Some strengthened their love of a higher power because they survived Auschwitz or one of the other death camps.

In his essay, Simon talks about the lessons of Jesus in understanding the reasons behind evil. He makes some compelling points, not least when he argues that too many in the West live overly comfortable lives and remain oblivious to the suffering of millions around the world, but I wonder if his adherence to what appears in the Bible is simply the latest form of postmodernism gone wrong. It's a very progressive reading, and I share his views in some ways, but surely Simon ignores that the definitions of evil have changed greatly over the centuries.

Take the issue of abortion. It's a relatively common procedure in many countries, despite still having a certain social stigma in some circles because elements of the Christian church and Muslim faith want it to. For them it's about maintaining control over a woman's body, not allowing her complete freedom over what she does to her womb after sex. Relying on the Bible to find a moral code about this or other modern procedures seems odd considering the fact that women's rights in that text are secondary to men's.

I accept that the Bible can be viewed as a transformative and non-literal text, but using it to justify present-day acts feels like an intellectual stretch. The reason many in the West are turning away from organised religion is the constant inability of faith representatives to appear relevant to people's lives. The Bible can't explain everything. The Bible was written by men, and one of the vast differences in today's world is the fulfilment of Enlightenment values and a rejection of black-and-white morality. Amen to that. When it comes to female rights and reproduction, the Bible should be the last book consulted.

'It is in the cross that hope lies, not just for us as individuals but also for our world,' Simon argues. But Jesus on the cross was designed as a redemptive gesture, meant to bring atonement and salvation. When evil occurs, in Cambodia, Rwanda, the Democratic Republic of Congo or Pakistan, the offered justification should be viewed through the prism of history, personal responsibility, society, peer groups, the economy and nationalism. Applying biblical values, as opposed to humanist ones, should be resisted as creeping morality: a judgemental attitude is inevitably involved.

Absolving ourselves of sin is a key tenet of Christianity, as if the mere act of daily living and breathing inevitably brings a stain to be washed away. Jews don't have this belief but Yom Kippur is the annual Day of Atonement. It can be useful to reflect on the year that's past and try to improve in the coming period, but a framework for moral and healthy living is far more important than an overly convenient stop in a busy schedule to feel better about ourselves, like takeaway food after a long day at the office.

An interesting study published in 2005 by the Kripke Centre found that the 'more secular, pro-evolution democracies [Japan, France and Scandinavia] have, for the first time in history, come closest to achieving practical "cultures of life" that feature low rates of lethal crime, juvenile-adult mortality, sex-related dysfunction, and even abortion'.[166] The results aren't conclusive, but they do indicate that societies with more evolved and less religion-based morality are achieving better results for their citizens. Can secular people do terrible things? Of course, for a range of reasons, but the evidence would indicate that repressed social and political environments become more likely places for dysfunction.

I've never thought the worst crimes in history were carried out by religious beings. China under Mao, the Soviet Union under Stalin and Cambodia under Pol Pot confirm this fact. There's nothing inherently wrong with using religion as a way to cope with grief, evil or hurt – whatever gets people through the day and night – but we should be very careful using a deity as an explanatory tool.

I acknowledge that if I personally suffered through a horrific incident I don't know what I would use to manage the pain. It could well be a form of liberal Judaism. My atheism has a flexibility I'm willing to admit.

Rachel Woodlock

I didn't grow up believing in Satan, and I venture to say that, like Jane and Antony, many people in the modern world don't believe such a character literally exists, even if some do believe in God. Pretty much everyone who believes in some sort of an afterlife thinks they're going to heaven; very few people are honest enough to admit they could be destined for the *other* place. Believing in the reality of a diabolical figure implies hell as a concrete possibility. Who wants to run that risk? Even the word 'evil', as Antony mused, seems to have lost most of its punch. It's easy to name Pol Pot and Saddam Hussein as evil, but thankfully most of us are shielded from such devastating malevolence. They seem like rarities who belong in a horror-movie script, although reading about Antony's family killed in Nazi Germany makes the damnable real.

It was only after I read a number of M. Scott Peck's books that I began to take the possibility of Satan seriously. He defines evil as that which seeks to kill love and life. It is, Peck argues, the principle that sacrifices others in service to its narcissism. His book *People of the Lie: The Hope for Healing Human Evil* is specifically devoted to the subject. He presents cases drawn from his work as a psychotherapist – not ordinary cases of mental illness or even of mundane sinners who might have done something terrible, but cases involving people who had crossed some invisible line into consistent evil. People like the parents of 'Bobby', who gave him for Christmas the very rifle his own brother had used to commit suicide. Peck persuasively argues that evil is not locked up in jails, it walks among us.

Because evil cannot bear to admit its own wickedness, it has to deny and hide its abuse. Evil people are 'utterly dedicated to preserving their self-image of perfection, they are unceasingly engaged in the effort to maintain the appearance of moral purity'.[167] What better place to hide, then, than in religion?

When a powerful church is more interested in preserving its image and finances than truthfully admitting its institutional sins and helping victims who suffered abuse at the hands of its representatives, that's evil. When a religious institution circumvents its own consultative processes to dis-enrol members it perceives as challenging its dictatorial control of believers, that's evil. My life experience has taught me the truth of Peck's claim: God does not work through organisations, he works through people. Satan, on the other hand, has a grand old time with religious bureaucracies, if you ask me.

★

I've sensed tangible evil and it made me want to flee. Many years ago, I was elected on to a committee for an Islamic group. An outgoing member had booked premises for an event under the committee's name, which a concerned friend told us about. 'You should probably look into this,' she said, 'they're pretty hard core.' The event was due to happen the next night, giving the committee little time to meet and decide what to do, so a couple of us attended to keep an eye on things.

Men with harsh faces milled about the entrance, and I could see they had segregated the doors, which was not particularly unusual for Islamic events. Nevertheless, this time I decided to accompany my husband through the men's entrance. I was getting a weird vibe and I didn't fancy being separated from him. When one fellow started to challenge me, I asserted, 'That's okay, I'm coming in this side with my husband.' He looked a little confused as I kept walking, but didn't try to stop me.

We took seats and waited as the hall filled up with more harsh-faced men, women, and a few children here and there. The lights were dimmed and speakers introduced. I felt a growing sense of unease as each one spoke, their words including the truly bizarre claim that Australia's lack of rain was proof of being cursed by God. Given that Saudi Arabia, where the twin holy cities Mecca and Medina are located, gets less rain than Australia, I found the speaker's logic difficult to follow. Trepidation, confusion and distaste grew into alarm when they dimmed the lights and played a graphic movie of real-life violence: soldiers beating a man nearly to death. I could not believe they were showing it to us, let alone in the presence of children. And why didn't the parents quickly get up and leave?

There were angry shouts from the audience cursing the soldiers, and when the lights were raised a speaker began to shout into a microphone while deputies moved around the audience with buckets collecting money. People threw in notes and coins to the speaker's pricelist of bullets and guns. The evil was palpable, devils whispering gleefully into the ears of everyone present, all supposedly in the name of God. Horrified, I quickly left and rang another of the committee members to inform him. I was in no position to stop the gathering, but we had to do something.

In an emergency meeting with representatives of the organisation that held the event, a smooth-voiced man informed us that we were mistaken. 'The brother is just passionate; we were raising money for our group, not for jihad,' he said with an oily ease. Either this man was lying to us at that moment, or the speaker had been lying to the collected audience. I was gobsmacked that people claiming to be Muslim, claiming to do God's work, were unruffled by the easily produced falsehoods. But then, the modus operandi of evil is to sacrifice ethics at the altar of ends-justify-means.

★

In the Qur'an, evil is personified as Iblis, who appears in the creation myth disobeying God by refusing to bow before Adam. Iblis haughtily protests, saying, 'I am better than him. You created me from fire while you created him from clay' (Q7:12). God condemns Iblis for his pride, and expels him from his presence. Iblis falls into hopeless despair and asks God for permission to oppose human beings, by making sin and evil appear attractive to the weak-in-faith. This is granted him, and as Satan he becomes man's inveterate enemy until the day of judgement. On that future day he will disclaim any power, saying, 'I had no authority over you except that I called to you and you responded to me. So do not blame me, but blame yourselves' (Q14:22). In Islamic doctrine, Satan is not the opposite of God, but of human beings.

It reminds me of Jim Henson's movie *Labyrinth*, the tale of a young girl emerging into adulthood. Sarah lost something precious – her brother, stolen by Jareth, the Goblin King – and in order to win him back she must successfully navigate the labyrinth before thirteen o'clock. Jareth throws obstacles in her path, and it seems the challenge is terribly unfair, but with the guiding help of friends she meets along the way, she comes to realise the truth of a half-remembered poem: 'You have no power over me!' I loved that movie when I was young, and frankly, I think the only reason it got bad reviews is that the critics were cranky old men who could never understand what it is to be a teenage girl!

The movie is a parable for all of us trying to win the precious prize of reunion with God. We, too, must navigate the twists and turns of life, which can seem labyrinthine and unfair. We're given only a short span of time, an eye-blink really, before the angel of death comes for us. Satan throws down obstacles to distract us from the right path, but we have guidance in the form of the friends of God – prophets, saints and right-eous companions. Ultimately, we'll discover that Satan has no real power over us other than what we give him. If we can remember God, Satan's ability to distract us evaporates.

Satan, then, is the means by which we can learn to choose good from evil, because the one contrasts to the other; he is necessary, even though God does not approve of him.

The traditionalist philosopher Frithjof Schuon (d.1998) wrote that our response to evil has seven elements:

- Don't allow evil to disturb our relationship with God, because this is what evil does – tempts us away into entropy.
- Understand the metaphysical necessity of evil, that without it we would never delight in the good.
- Remember the relativity and limits of evil, as it is God who has the last word.
- Be stoic about what we encounter as destiny; it couldn't have been any other way. In other words, there's no point stressing over what you cannot control.
- Realise that life isn't about having it easy. God uses trials to prove us. Our 'muscles' of virtue will not become strong if we don't exercise them against resistance.
- We're only accountable for what we have control over, what we do. God won't hold us accountable for anything else.

- Pure happiness and unimpeded bliss are not for this world, they're for the next.[168]

That's not to say that we do nothing in the face of evil, dismissing it as the will of God – quite the opposite. In a creedal passage, the Qur'an defines virtue as a mixture of faith, action and patience with the divine will. We must have certitude in God as well as in that future day when he'll answer all the whys that plague us in this life, and we must know that this physical world isn't the limit of reality, that there's an unseen angelic realm. God's guidance, which helps us distinguish good from evil, is given to us via scripture, borne by prophets. The passage then shifts to the practical expression of that belief in defining virtue as giving generously to family, orphans, the needy, travellers, those who ask and to free the slaves. The virtuous pray, give in charity, fulfil their promises and are patient when the going gets tough (Q2:177).

DOESN'T RELIGION OPPRESS WOMEN?

Antony Loewenstein

The New York City area has around 250,000 ultra-Orthodox Jews, the largest such community away from Israel. 'They are more afraid of the outside world than the deviants within their own community,' said Samuel Heilman, a professor of Jewish studies at Queens College, in the *New York Times* in May 2012.[169] 'The deviants [such as child abusers] threaten individuals here or there, but the outside world threatens everyone and the entire structure of their world.'

This fear of modern society was revealed very publicly when more than 40,000 Orthodox Jewish men filled Citi Field stadium in New York in May 2012 to fret over the allegedly negative aspects of the internet. 'The siren song of the Internet entices us,' spokesman Eytan Kobre announced. 'It brings out the worst of us.'[170] Women weren't invited to the major event but parties in Orthodox neighbourhoods in Brooklyn and New Jersey allowed them to view proceedings.

At the same time, serious allegations emerged that community rabbis and a Brooklyn district attorney were refusing to report accurately the depth of child abuse and sexual assault against women because tradition dictated the problems be solved internally. The reputation of the community was more important than justice for the victims.

Allegations against some ultra-Orthodox defendants included groping women on public transport and the placing of a penis on a woman's shoulder. Young girls and boys were molested over many years, and countless abusers escaped justice.

This is clearly a case of religious zealotry and official collusion gone mad. A powerful segment of the Jewish community claims the right to maintain ancient traditions and ignore the values of the contemporary world when it comes to the rights of children and women.

We've had similar outrages within the Catholic Church, Islam, Scientology and a range of mainstream and cultish fads. Sadly, it's neither unique nor new. It's unsurprising when patriarchal traditions trump common sense, decency and gender equality.

But none of this means religion inherently oppresses women though so many religious men and women do so. People with religious beliefs routinely discriminate against others, but so do individuals with no spirituality or faith. Some priests, rabbis and mullahs preach on a daily basis an ideology of hate, intolerance and misogyny. The ancient texts of all major religions contain passages of horrific sexism, racism and violence. It's impossible to read the Christian Bible, for example, and not be deeply offended by the incessant homophobia. Death is seen as too good for gay people. Any person in the twenty-first century who isn't infected with the fundamentalist gene won't tolerate these attitudes, and that's why there's a healthy and growing gay movement inside the various denominations of Christianity to bring acceptance and change.

It would have been unimaginable even a few years ago for a conservative British prime minister such as David Cameron to tell a reception for the lesbian, gay, bisexual and transsexual community in 10 Downing Street in July 2012 that legalised gay marriage is inevitable. More importantly, he said that the church should not 'be locking out people who are gay, or are bisexual or are transgender from being full members of that Church, because many people with deeply held Christian views are also gay'.[171]

It should be uncontroversial to say that the Catholic Church hierarchy is misogynist. It must be necessary to challenge the inherently sexist preaching of the Pope and his refusal to accept the ordination of women. It's essential to condemn the vile misogyny of Saudi clerics who insist women have no right to drive or work, or be heard or seen.

It's equally important to oppose West Bank rabbis who refuse to allow women to participate in local elections because, according to Rabbi Elyakim Levanon of the Elon Moreh colony in May 2010, they should only be heard through their husbands. I feel shame as a Jew when I read that fundamentalist Jewish leaders in occupied, Palestinian territory insist that male Israel Defence Force soldiers be allowed to boycott events where women are singing. This isn't Judaism, it's the Taliban.

I've spent the last few years travelling the world and witnessing the reality of life under religious dictatorships. Women in Gaza, Iran, Saudi Arabia, Pakistan, Afghanistan and Palestine all suffer in various ways in a system that is legitimised and defended as devout and supported by the word of God. Because in all these nations Islam is reinterpreted by various leaders, bodies and governments, this proves that a religion isn't set and is open to interpretation. Only a blind person would ignore the glaring inequalities between the sexes across much of the Muslim world.

My hesitation in arguing that religion itself is the sole problem here is that I believe it's far too simple an explanation. Christopher Hitchens, in his much-discussed book *God Is Not Great*, argues the religious are inherently irrational because 'believers claim not just to know, but to know everything. Not just to know that God exists and that he created and supervised the whole enterprise, but also to know what "he" demands of us – from our diet to our observances to our sexual morality.'[172]

It is arguably only on the last point that Hitchens is correct. For a man who enjoyed, in his last decade before death, saluting and celebrating the worst excesses of American empire and the bombing of countless Muslim nations by his friends in the Bush administration, his secular certainties took him to the ugliest of places in the name of 'reason' and 'humanity'.

Soon after September 11, 2001, Hitchens expressed 'exhilaration' and excitement about a 'battle' 'until the last day of my life' against 'theocratic barbarism'.[173] The slaughter of countless Muslim women in this noble fight didn't concern him in the slightest. Near the end of his life, Hitchens called without hesitation for the bombing of Iran.

That this man was held up as a leader of a new atheist movement says more about the movement than it does about atheism itself. Hitchens wasn't demanding the bombing of the Vatican or other Christian nations, places where repression against minorities and women are facts of life. No, his venom was reserved for Islamic states that often oppressed women – and yet invasion, attack and occupation have only made those realities worse.

But Hitchens' point about religions dictating the rights and wrongs of sexual behaviour is undeniably true. All major religions refuse to accept or promote sexual freedom out of wedlock. Promiscuity is opposed. Finding a perfect mate and bearing children is the ultimate goal. Guilt over feelings of sexual desire is encouraged. Besides, it's impossible to ignore the incessant naming and shaming in our society over legal sex acts, which derives from a time when religion had far more power than today in the West and adulterous behaviour was severely punished. All too often there are public stonings in Muslim nations of women who've supposedly sinned and brought shame to their community. The decision to exercise this ultimate punishment always comes from men.

These pressures and limitations restrict a natural human urge to flirt and play with men or women for the simple reason that we can. I've lost count of the number of people I've met in my overseas travels, particularly Muslims, who can't understand that I've had a number of girlfriends over the years and remain happily unmarried. I can have sex without guilt. I don't have to worry about an oppressive Jewish morality guiding my personal life and restricting my choices. If sexual acts are consensual and inflict neither physical nor mental harm, a truly progressive religion should encourage them, as part of the pursuit of pleasure, which should be a key human goal.

But they don't. There remains an inability and unwillingness, both wilful and deluded, to surrender control over human bodies and what we do with them in our own private lives. Historically, religious leaders knew that a majority of people who attended a service would take their advice on family matters. But today, in the second decade of the twenty-first century, the Catholic Church hierarchy can't even officially support the use of birth control in countries where HIV/AIDS runs rampant. The Pope claims it's about saving the sanctity of life but in reality it's motivated by a fear that women, that group of people who can never reach the upper echelons of the institution, will have ultimate control over life itself.

Religious oppression of women is undeniable, but billions of believers will interpret doctrine in their own way. To argue, as the new atheists do, that religion poisons everything and a secular world is inevitable, takes a Western-centric world of history and the present and ignores political shifts. Take the ramifications of the Arab Spring as an example. Islamists are gaining power and strength in a range of countries, such as Egypt, Libya, Tunisia and Syria. Secular forces exist in these nations but they're small and politically weak.

Consider Israel, a state established through ethnic cleansing in 1948, now proudly eschewing a secular future and embracing a Jewish, militaristic and racist outlook that will inevitably drive out non-religious forces and those demanding gender equality.

But these cases don't prove that religion is inherently bigoted. Many adherents may be, and I write this as a proud secularist who wants no overt religious influence in the running of my country, but the challenge surely lies in reforming traditions that still bring comfort to billions of global citizens.

Jane Caro

The prima facie evidence that all religions are man-made is their treatment of women.

The idea that women are fully human is something man-made religions seem to struggle with. I love the paradise offered to Islamic *jihad* warriors. Apparently, as martyrs for Allah they'll receive their reward in heaven by disporting themselves with innumerable virgins. As one wit put it, imagine all those obedient, god-fearing Muslim women who keep themselves pure behind all-encompassing clothing out of their devout worship of their God, only to find that, when they die, their reward for all that virginal vigilance is to end up as a whore for terrorists. My own response when I heard about this extraordinarily male-centric view of the eternal reward was to wonder what appalling sin those poor virgins must have committed to require such punishment. In other words, the terrorists' heaven was clearly the virgins' hell.

Perhaps Rachel will argue that this is a false interpretation of Islam – I certainly hope she will – but, to be honest, I don't think that kind of argument ever quite works. Religion seems to be quite regularly misinterpreted by its followers – indeed, they seem to spend more time arguing with one another about the 'correct' way of following their gods than they do arguing with atheists like me. Maybe religions are like Marxism – they sound lovely in theory but once they interact with real flesh-and-blood human beings they mostly create oppression and misery.

The Islamic *jihad* fantasy of heaven, by the way, illustrates religions' use of a classic advertising trick: they create fear of damnation in the powerless – women, slaves and the poor – then offer them hope of salvation, but only after they're dead. Religion has been used this way to keep all sorts of people in their place, but it has made its greatest contribution in increasing human misery among women. Why? Because women, unlike slaves, the poor or – as Antony points out – homosexuals, are not a minority group. They're more than half the human population. Keep them down, limit their life options, make them ashamed of their very existence and you make the majority of human beings less happy than they might otherwise be. Women, after all, also make up many of those (if not the majority) who are slaves, living in poverty and homosexual. Indeed, it's arguably the characteristic fear and hatred of the feminine among man-made religions that leads them to be so prejudiced against homosexuality. The oppression of more than half the population of the world cannot be dismissed as a minor issue or glossed over. It's the most important problem in the world today.

We know, for example, that if you educate a girl it has a huge positive effect not just on her own life and opportunities, and on those of her own family, but also on those of her entire community. Many religious believers are wholly on board with the international antipoverty movement that has been dubbed 'The Girl Effect', but it's nevertheless entirely valid to ask who has been holding girls down until now and so counterproductively restricting their access to education and economic independence. And the answer to that question takes us directly and unequivocally into the still enormously controversial area of reproductive rights.

For women and girls to control their lives they must be given control of their fertility and the ability to choose how many children they'll bear. This is not an opinion, it's a fact. Wherever the standard of living is high, the birthrate is low. Yet female reproductive rights remain controversial. Why? There really is only one honest answer to that question, and it is man-made religion. Let's be absolutely clear: reproductive rights mean easy access to effective contraception and safe, legal abortion. And it's spurious to argue that because presumably half the foetuses that are terminated are female, this represents a persecution of women. Feminists, unlike many of the religious, do not value one gender's life more than the other. And the fact that some cultures (almost always religiously based) value male children over female ones so much that they use technology to identify female foetuses so they can be aborted, while horrific, seems to me yet another argument that proves religions – all of them – are often deeply and intractably misogynistic. Indeed, what would life be like for those girls if we compelled their parents to bear them? Indeed, what has life been like for girls throughout history who were born into cultures – often theocracies – that so deeply despised and undervalued the feminine?

Unloved, unwanted and treated as possessions ('Do not covet thy neighbour's wife' is a commandment that reveals a world view where only men exist as sentient beings and women are mere possessions, owned as surely as livestock). For many of the world's women there's no doubt that there are much worse fates than never having been born. And we can thank religion for that.

It's easy for men to argue that women should put their own deeply held ambitions, delights and dreams aside if they become pregnant. It's not a sacrifice they'll ever be asked to make. I'd ask them to remember that to force a woman to carry, gestate and then bear a child she doesn't want for nine months is an outrageous interference in her fundamental liberty. To do so is to literally colonise another human being's body. That's why the secular believe that where there's a conflict of rights, the rights of the sentient being must take precedence over the rights of the potential being.

Almost every religious tradition has or does oppose both contraception and abortion, and by doing so they can do nothing else but oppress women – because they restrict her liberty. Those who fight for women's rights around the world know that their opponent is almost always a god.

Religions have also made women responsible for male sexual responses to them, hence the almost universal religious concern about the way women 'flaunt' their apparently uniquely dangerous and explosive bodies. In extreme cases, women are forced by male-centric religions to carry their own prisons around with them in the form of niqabs and burqas. The lack of logic in blaming women for male sexual behaviour is easily revealed if we simply ask whether any religious tradition holds rich men responsible for being robbed by poorer men because they've tempted them by 'flaunting' their greater wealth. Of course the answer to that is an unequivocal no. In making excuses for the bad behaviour of men, religions have made women over-responsible and men under-responsible, and neatly prevented all of us from properly growing up. Secular common sense puts the responsibility back where it belongs; if the mere sight of a woman gives a man an erection that's entirely his problem, not hers.

Conveniently for the blokes who invented them, gods of all kinds are entirely happy to see one half of humanity held in subjection to the other half. According to many of their earthly messengers, they have approved of and even commanded that women be beaten, raped – at least in marriage – and sold as property, either to husbands or masters. Gods have stated that a woman's testimony and word are worth less than a man's, that she is not to be permitted to speak in public, take part in public life, take 'headship' over a man, preach religion or, in extreme cases, even appear in public. It was religious belief that drove what may be the longest pogrom in recorded human history: the persecution and execution of (in the vast majority of cases) vulnerable women accused of witchcraft across Europe between the fourteenth and seventeenth centuries.

The mere fact that most of the world's religions reserve their various priesthoods and holy men roles for, well, um, men, is another indication that they simply assume male superiority. If there are any female ayatollahs, imams or muftis in Islam currently, I'm yet to hear of them. The Catholic Church has its female saints but resolutely rejects the idea of female priests. The only good women are dead women, perhaps? Some of the Protestant denominations have grudgingly accepted female ministers, deacons and bishops but, because not all of them have, we won't see a female Archbishop of Canterbury any time soon.

My assumption that the opportunity to climb your chosen religion's priestly hierarchy is one way of judging its attitudes to women can be dismissed as Western, white colonialism. But if there was a religion that said people of colour, for example, were all very well in their way – you know, equal but different (the very phrase that was used to justify apartheid in South Africa) – but that they should never take leadership over white people, what kind of judgement would we or should we make about the attitudes of that religion to people with darker skins? Why, then, the double standard for women? Call me a colonialist all you like, but if you wouldn't accept such limitations for your sons, why on earth is it fair to do so for your daughters?

In some parts of the world, in theocracies, we still watch gods deny women and girls the right to work, travel, drive, get access to health care or even walk the streets unaccompanied. In 2002, fourteen school-girls died in a fire in Mecca after being forced back into a burning building by religious police because they were not properly covered. In November 2012, Savita Halappanavar died in agony of septicaemia in Ireland because doctors at the hospital she went to in distress refused to give her the abortion that would have saved her life, even though they knew and admitted that her slowly miscarrying foetus could not survive. Chillingly, as she and her husband begged for the lifesaving abortion, a doctor refused them by saying Ireland was a 'Catholic country'.

Women's lives only began to improve in most of the West when feminism emerged thanks to the secular Enlightenment. Mary Woll-stonecraft, author of *A Vindication of the Rights of Women*, could not provide a greater contrast to that first Mary, the so-called mother of God. No virgin, she was a vulnerable and suffering human being. Blessed (if you will excuse the term) with a shining intellect and the clear-eyed courage it took to see through millennia of male hypocrisy, she was despised and vilified in her own time – most often by the religious.

But her words took hold, and in the 300 years since she first put pen to paper, the lives of women and girls, at least in the developed world, have changed unarguably for the better. By almost any objective measure, women in the secular West are better off than they have ever been before. In terms of longevity, mental, physical, reproductive and emotional health, economic independence and human rights, today's woman leaves her female ancestors for dead. Unfortunately, however, at almost every step, representatives of gods have resisted women's progress. While this may be dismissed as Western feminist colonialism by some, the hard statistics about income, educational achievement, earnings, political representation and longevity are hard to brush aside with just an insult.

The religious have variously opposed higher education for women; higher status employment for women; their right to vote; their right to enter parliament; their right to their own earnings, income and property; their right to their own children after divorce or separation; their right to resist domestic violence; their right to learn about their own bodies; their right to refuse sexual intercourse in marriage or agree to it outside marriage; and their right to contraception, abortion and sexual information. Less than a century or so ago, if a woman was so badly damaged by successive child-bearing that doctors advised against further pregnancy, churches resisted her right to use (or even know about) contraception and she had to rely on the goodwill and restraint of her husband to avoid further catastrophic damage or even death. Only last year a nun was excommunicated for allowing the US hospital she ran to give an abortion to a woman who would have died without it. Presumably, therefore, the good Catholics who condemned Savita Halappanavar to death by refusing the same request in Ireland will be lauded by their church for protecting the so-called sanctity of life.

When chloroform was first used as an anaesthetic in the nineteenth century, doctors immediately heralded it as a boon for birthing women. Church leaders condemned it because they believed women's suffering in labour was ordained by god as punishment for Eve's original sin. Fortunately for labouring women, the then head of the Church of England was herself a birthing mother. Queen Victoria ignored her spiritual advisers as she gave birth to her eighth and ninth children, and grabbed chloroform with both hands, immediately making pain relief in childbirth acceptable.

To be fair, as women have made gains in the secular and developed world, many religious believers and leaders have changed their opinions and been persuaded of the universal benefit of female equality and opportunity. Many religious feminists, and Rachel is certainly one of them, argue passionately that there's nothing necessarily godly about the oppression of women, but – if as the Bible says, 'by their fruits shall ye judge them' – even today they're on shaky ground.

It's no coincidence that societies where women enjoy high levels of personal freedom are the richest and most stable in the world. As I pointed out earlier, we now know that when you educate women and girls the benefits accrue to the entire family and society, rather than simply the individual. There's even research to indicate that in societies with more women in positions of power and influence, men have longer life expectancy. Can it also be a coincidence that these societies are among the most secular and, apart from the United States, are often cited as those where belief in a god is dying most rapidly? Looked at from that perspective, it's almost as if gods and women's rights are diametrically opposed to one another. As one rises, the other falls. Women who are unfortunate enough to live in theocracies universally have their human rights curtailed, limited and denied. The fact that gods and women appear to be so firmly in opposite corners is yet another indication to me that gods are all about men.

It's impossible to do justice in a couple of thousand words to the fearful price women have paid as a result of man-made religion. I don't have time to mention the decimation of women by HIV in Africa, helped along by wicked and paranoid misinformation promoted by the Catholic Church about the permeability of condoms. Suffice to say, four out of ten girls in Kenya are now HIV positive – many of them god-fearing virgins infected on their wedding night. For me, however, it's not just the gross history of religion's treatment of women that informs my atheism. It's simply the one-eyed nature of all the world's religions that finally convinces me all gods are man-made. Yes, even Buddhism, that last refuge of the fashionable Western mystic. After all, why hasn't the Dalai Lama ever been reincarnated as a girl?

Rachel Woodlock

You know when a creationist says something like 'If we're descended from apes, how come there are still monkeys and baboons, hah!' and scientists give a collective sigh of exasperation, wondering how it's possible our modern education system can produce graduates so completely ignorant about the basics of evolution? That's how it feels when Islam is reduced to: women have to imprison themselves because men are too horny and suicide bombers get seventy-two virgins in paradise. To use a Twitterism: facepalm!

If you want to find awful interpretations of Islam, then sadly they exist. But Antony is correct when he says religion isn't inherently oppressive. It's like saying politics oppresses women. If a bunch of misogynists are in government then you get laws that are bad for women. If a bunch of misogynists claim to speak for God, you get religious justification for oppressing women. But, when women are in the game – politics, religion or anything else – things look very different. The real question for believing women isn't whether religion oppresses women but how can we reclaim the right to speak for ourselves?

I've lost count of the number of astonished looks I receive when I say I'm a Muslim feminist, as if Islam and feminism are mutually exclusive. When one of my relatives discovered I was researching the experiences of Muslim women, she touched my arm and with a voice full of compassion, said, 'Oh, I'm so glad you'll be able to help them.' Forced veiling, genital cutting, honour killings – why would any woman in her right mind choose to be a Muslim?

Islam, perhaps more than any other religion, is viewed as quintessentially anti-women because it has long served as the inverse mirror of Western self-imagery. Western women have dynamically won their freedom; Muslim women are perpetually enslaved victims. It's so frustrating for non-Western feminists when white secular feminists assume their own particular experiences and aspirations are universal and they need to rescue the poor, brown, Third-World woman. They flatten the wide diversity of other women's experiences over time, culture, class, geography and so on in a way they never do for their own.

Over the last few decades, Lila Abu-Lughod, Leila Ahmed, miriam cooke, Yvonne Haddad, Mohja Kahf, Saba Mahmood, Chandra Mohanty and Gayatri Spivak, among others, have developed a devastating critique of this patronising 'colonial feminism' that has serviced Western imperialism, like when former first lady Laura Bush justified the US invasion of Afghanistan by saying, 'The fight against terrorism is also a fight for the rights and dignity of women.'[174] I wonder what the thousands of Afghan women killed, maimed or displaced as a result of Operation Enduring Freedom think about that.

Once upon a time it was enough for missionaries to write disparaging accounts of life under Islamic oppression to accompany and justify European colonialism. For example, in this 1907 book charmingly titled *Our Moslem Sisters: A Cry of Need from Lands of Darkness Interpreted by Those Who Heard It* we read: 'the condition of women under Islam is everywhere the same – and . . . there is no hope . . . except to take them the message of the Saviour'.[175] These days we have native informers – Ayaan Hirsi Ali being the current darling – who present their wretched life stories as evidence of the terrible oppression of all Muslim women everywhere, claiming redemption can only come through abandoning Islam/their culture and embracing whatever Western political goals are currently in vogue. As Abu-Lughod notes, 'One can hear the uncanny echoes of their virtuous goals today, even though the language is secular, the appeals not to Jesus but to human rights or the liberal West.'[176] Actually, Hirsi Ali is on record as suggesting Muslims should convert to Christianity, even though she herself is an atheist.

What's so damn frustrating is that the paternalistic approach of colonial feminism disempowers real Muslim women and men working to challenge specific local instances of oppression that are the result of a complex web of interacting sociopolitical forces, at times justified in the name of religious interpretations. Christina Ho makes this point in her discussion of the Australian experience: 'When the defence of women's rights is bound so closely with anti-Muslim racism in public discourse, Muslim women's own concerns with patriarchal practices risk fuelling further racism.'[177]

Colonial feminism also ignores indigenous feminist movements that arose in parallel to Western ones, in which women have often drawn on their religious beliefs for inspiration. For example, Nana Asma'u (d. 1864) led a massive women's education movement in Nigeria's Sokoto Caliphate, based on the Islamic emphasis on acquiring knowledge. 'The potency and power of the *'yan-taru* movement has been borne out by its continued existence to the present day.'[178]

Asma'u drew on Islamic teachings to promote women's education, which was dear to the heart of Prophet Muhammad, not that you'd know it by the way the Taliban act. He was reported as observing, 'How praiseworthy are the Ansari women: their modesty does not prevent them from attempts at learning and the acquisition of knowledge' (Sahih Muslim). Indeed, the University of Qarawiyyin – the world's oldest university – was founded by a Muslim woman, Fatima al-Fihri (d. 880).

Asma'u's younger contemporary was the Persian heroine Fatimih Baraghani (d. 1852) known by her titles Qurrat al-'Ayn (consolation of the eyes) and Tahirih (pure). When I was younger, I desperately wished my parents had named me after her, she seemed so exotic, powerful, intelligent and delightfully rebellious. Tahirih was a leading figure in the Babi movement, which preceded the emergence of the Baha'i Faith. As Negar Mottehedeh writes:

In contemporary historiography, the Bábí movement is, however, chiefly renowned for its egalitarianism and particularly for its impact on the status of women in Iran. This is perhaps because of the public visibility of one of the Bábí movement's female leaders, the poetess Qurrat al-'Ayn Táhirih.[179]

Today, the United Arab Emirates is training female muftis, there are female imams who base their legitimacy on the Prophet's deputising Umm Waraqa in the role, and a variety of women had been elected to lead modern Muslim nation-states long before Australia had its first female prime minister.

What Muslim feminists like me argue is that all religion is mediated through a wide variety of cultural expressions, many of them

patriarchal: that's just the reality of human history. The Qur'an prag-
matically acknowledges this, and provides context-limited legislation for
those environments in which women are dependent on men. However,
importantly, it does not *prescribe* patriarchy, rather it promotes an ethic of
equality to which we should aspire:

> The believing men and believing women are protecting friends of
> one another. They enjoin what is right and forbid what is wrong,
> they observe the prayers and pay alms, and they obey God and his
> apostle. Those upon whom God will bestow mercy, verily God is the
> mighty, the wise (Q9:71).

Because of this, Muslim feminists reclaim powerful feminine role
models who challenge stereotypical views of women. The plethora of
examples includes:

- scriptural and legendary archetypes such as Hagar, who initiated
  rituals still followed by Muslims today; the Queen of Sheba, who
  acted as a consultative ruler; and Mary, the mother of Jesus, who had
  access to the holiest place in the temple
- the Prophet's wives and female followers, such as Khadija, a
  businesswoman who employed the Prophet and proposed marriage
  to him; 'A'isha, a central Islamic figure who interpreted religious law
  and taught men and women; the daughter of the Prophet, Fatima,
  who plays an especially important role in Shi'i veneration; Umm
  'Umara who fought on the battlefield and was injured shielding
  the Prophet; Umm Waraqa, a Qur'an expert whom the Prophet
  deputised to act as imam and lead her clan in prayer; and teacher
  Shifa' bint 'Abd Allah, who was appointed market inspector by the
  second caliph 'Umar
- women who lived in the succeeding generations, such as seventh-
  century Ghazala al-Haruriyya, a battle commander who led her
  troops in prayer; Rabi'a of Basra (d. 801), one of earliest and most
  influential Sufis; Sayyida Nafisa (d. 824), a scholar of the Qur'an,
  hadith and jurisprudence; Fatima of Nishapur (d. 849), whom the

Sufi master Dhu al-Nun ranked as the most excellent person he knew; Wallada bint al-Mustakfi (d. 1091), a somewhat controversial Spanish poet; Queen Arwa of Yemen (d. 1138), much beloved for her philanthropy and benevolent rule; Shahdah the Writer (d. 1178), a calligrapher and hadith authority; Rabi'a bint Abi Bakr (d. 1216) whose husband founded the Rifa'i order and who was a *shaykha* (master) in her own right; Ibn 'Arabi's twelfth-century teachers and peers, including Nizam bint Makin al-Din, Fatima bint al-Muthanna, Yasmina Shams Umm al-Fuqara, Zaynab al-Qal'iyya, and a slave girl of Qasim al-Dawla; Sultana Roxelana (d. 1558), who wielded political clout and was a noted philanthropist; Chand Bibi (d. 1599) known as the invincible lady of Ahmadnagar; Nur Jahan (d. 1645), a Mughal empress and benefactor; Raju Hijau (d. 1616), Queen of the Patani sultanate and her sister successors; Indonesian freedom-fighter and later Qur'an scholar Tjut Njak Dien (d. 1908); Kurdish leader and patron Adela Khanum (d. 1924); Gulrukh Hazrat Babajan (d. 1931), who was a teacher and healer; and Fatima Jinnah (d. 1967), known as the mother of the nation for her important role in the founding of Pakistan

- contemporary role models, such as Munira Qubeysi, who founded the largest women-only religious education movement in contemporary times; Meihua Jin, imam of one of China's women-only mosques; Ingrid Mattson, first female president of the Islamic Society of North America; Amra Bone, who sits on the Sharia Council at Birmingham Central Mosque; Salma Yaqoob, former leader of Britain's Respect Party; Tayyibah Taylor, who founded the well-known *Azizah* magazine for Muslim women; Aisha Rafea, an Egyptian writer, researcher and teacher of Islamic spirituality; Shirin Ebadi, human rights activist and winner of the Nobel Peace Prize; Australian educator and activist Silma Ihram; Aheda Zanetti, a pioneering designer of sports clothing for Muslim women, including the 'burkini'; academic and television personality Susan Carland; and Islamic studies experts such as Leila Ahmed, Fatima Mernissi, Amina Wadud, Dalia Mogahed, Azizah al-Hibri, Asma Barlas, Ziba Mir-Hosseini, Asma Afsaruddin, Zainah Anwar and Katherine Bullock, among many others.

The reason why secular feminism has not had much traction in the Muslim-majority world, except perhaps among the elites who have benefited by throwing in their lot with Western kingmakers, is that religion remains important in the lives of ordinary people. Abdicating religion only leaves it in the hands of the most strident. The history of colonisation in Muslim-majority nations has seen Muslims rejecting the expectation they should abandon their beliefs and cultures to adopt Westernisation instead. Exit the Taliban, Afghan women did not throw off their burqas en masse. Why? Because it was a cultural mode of Pashtun dress predating that fundamentalist phenomenon.

In Muslim cultures that practise segregation (which varies from culture to culture), veiling is a form of portable privacy providing women with agency to move in the public space.[180] Furthermore, Islamic law has traditionally had much more to say about men's appropriate modest clothing, and it was the Muslim man's turban that was seen as the 'divider between unbelief and belief'.[181] But it's true that female dress has become a cause célèbre for both anti-Islam activists and fundamentalists who have politicised veiling as an anti-Western statement. Interestingly, research recently published in the *European Journal of Social Psychology* found that our brains are wired to view sexualised male and female bodies differently,[182] which supports the Muslim feminist argument of veiling as a rejection of the panopticon of the public gaze, something to consider given the hypersexual expectations placed on Western women, as evidenced by the multibillion-dollar beauty, fashion and porn industries.

Islamic teachings de-emphasise sexuality in public but celebrate it in private, which shocked the proverbial out of medieval Europeans, leading them to accuse the Muslims of being lascivious. I have collected a wealth of interesting factoids I like to bring out at boring parties to spice up the conversation a little. For example, some scholars ruled husbands may not practise contraception (in those days, coitus interruptus) without permission from their wives, on the basis that women have a right to sexual enjoyment and children. Or, if a pre-modern Muslim woman needed an early term abortion, she could take certain abortifacient medicines on the basis that, theologically speaking, ensoulment doesn't happen until quite some time after conception. And did you know that Arabic has a word for a woman who isn't satisfied merely with penetrative sex in her quest for multiple orgasms. I particularly like the tradition where the Prophet informed the Muslims that God rewards sex with one's spouse.

To answer Jane's question about false assurances to would-be martyrs, murderers who blow up innocent people do not get rewarded – no virgins, no silk robes, no one-way ticket to Paradise. As professor of law and contemporary Islamic scholar Khaled Abou El Fadl has written, as classical law developed:

> Muslim jurists considered terrorist attacks against unsuspecting and defenceless victims as heinous and immoral crimes, and treated the perpetrators as the worst type of criminals . . . Most important, Muslim jurists held that the penalties are the same whether the perpetrator or victim is Muslim or non-Muslim.[183]

Speaking of consequence-parity, God rewards both men *and* women who successfully manage to navigate life while avoiding becoming terrorists:

> Verily, the Muslim men and the Muslim women, the faithful men and the faithful women, the obedient men and the obedient women, the truthful men and the truthful women, the patient men and the patient women, the humble men and the humble women, the charity-giving men and the charity-giving women, the men who fast and the women who fast, the modest men and the modest women, the men who remember God much and the women who remember God much – God has prepared for them forgiveness and great reward (Q33:35).

The Qur'an promises them delights couched in metaphor: heavenly companions, golden bracelets, rivers of milk, wine and honey (Q47:15, 3:15). It's through allegory that we understand paradisal companionship with mysterious heavenly creatures called the *huri* (who are not recycled human virgins, by the way) and ageless male youths (Q56:17–38). The Qur'an says of itself: 'in it are verses absolutely clear, they are the foundation of the book, and others are allegorical' (Q3:7). God uses symbolic language because we simply have no ability to comprehend the supernatural realm when we are on this side of the grave, as a famous tradition explains: 'I have prepared for my righteous servants that which no eye has seen, nor ear has heard, nor that which has occurred to the mortal human heart.' I mean, what would you *do* with a literal river of honey?

The Qur'an uses sexual metaphors to describe the afterlife because, as the great mystic and philosopher Ibn 'Arabi explains, the closest intimation we have to the felicity of the soul's reunion with God is the orgasmic delight of lovemaking. In sex as an archetype, the male annihilates himself in the female and she brings forth new life. 'The witnessing of the Real[184] in women is the greatest and most consummate witnessing. Marriage is the greatest union.'[185] In other words, although from one perspective God is utterly transcendent and unlike anything in creation, from another perspective, in which all his attributes are reflected in the cosmos, fantastic sex teaches us about God. Karma Sutra, eat your heart out![186]

Simon Smart

There's something fabulous about a young woman free to be who she is, unselfconscious, and unencumbered by prejudice and restriction.

But many people, Antony and Jane being good examples, would say that the female cause has prospered despite religion and not because of it – that religion has suppressed the talents and abilities of women and prevented them from flourishing as full human beings. The reality is that these days religion is associated with the subjugation of women. At various times and places, for my own faith and for others, that reputation has been deserved.

I must admit I'm pretty depressed reading Antony's and Jane's essays on this topic, partly because I agree with quite a lot of what they write. Religion has and does oppress women. That's obvious, though Rachel makes the good point that the forces that oppress women tend to do remarkably well without the aid of religion. Even today, some parts of the church are completely male-dominated – and blithely unaware of male privilege. Where expressions of faith have made women feel less than fully equal to men, it's simply unjust, and I feel that injustice keenly – though clearly not as much, it has to be said, as the women around me.

But my despondency also comes from my belief that the overall picture Antony and Jane paint is misled and misleading. If my own faith tradition fits into the picture of religion they paint, it's a wonder that any modern, educated woman would want to accept it. The implication is that religious men have to be, at best, sexist, and religious women too blind or naive to know any better.

Jane, and to a lesser extent Antony, focus their critique on what they call reproductive choice. Especially given the abuses of the past, I can understand how important it is that a woman has freedom when it comes to her own body. Contraception is an important piece in that puzzle. I, too, feel that the Catholic Church's resistance to condoms in AIDS-ravaged Africa has been a sorry example of an ideal being held at the cost of putting people in peril. Surely there has to be a way to avoid such a head-in-the-sand dismissal of what's going on in people's lives and the forces they're up against.

When it comes to the question of abortion – which Jane feels especially strongly about – I'm willing to acknowledge that it's an ethically complex issue. Surely, Jane, you can acknowledge the same. I'm not someone who thinks there's never a legitimate case for abortion, but to present this as a simple, cut-and-dried issue of *either* freedom for women *or* oppression for women is highly problematic. I'm especially uncomfortable with the way support for abortion has become a litmus test for authentic feminism, an issue Naomi Wolf addresses in her book *Fire with Fire*.

No matter how hard we might wish to avoid it, the interests, wishes and rights of the mother are inextricably bound up, and sometimes at odds with, the rights of the child. Only one of those two parties has anything like a choice. This means there must at least be a careful, sober conversation had about how to address this issue if we're going to get this right as a society. We all agree that once a baby has been born, the child has certain legitimate expectations of its parents. We just differ as to when those responsibilities begin.

There's no doubt that the way our culture idolises endless freedom and unlimited choice is a critical part of this discussion. But how do those who champion the rights of women feel about the abortion of so many females around the world? It's irrefutable that with ultrasound technologies millions of female babies are now at great risk because of their gender, and that in some parts of the globe the simple message is, if you're a girl, we don't want you. This is just one example of why this is such a complicated issue – though I do recognise that as a man my participation in this discussion is problematic for some.

As a Christian offering my perspective on this question of whether religion oppresses women, I want to look at the sweep of the Bible to sort out the trajectory it takes us on in terms of our understanding of the place of women. Right at the beginning, Genesis poetically describes two archetypal human beings together in a good world created by God. In this relationship, there is 'radical mutuality' – a profound harmony between a man and a woman. It's a beautiful picture of wholeness, with each one needing the other and each being incomplete on their own. In these early chapters we see both the woman *and* the man responsible for caring for the earth and working it to their advancement. This vision of gender and sexuality is one of equality, mutual intimacy and mutual responsibility – a vision of genuine community.[187]

It's not until Genesis 3 with the calamitous effects of the fall that you see an emphasis on the darker aspects of male–female relationships – hierarchy and a struggle for power between the sexes. Fear, distrust, suspicion and accusation are introduced into the mix. 'He will rule over you,' the woman is told. Rather than God-ordained, the struggle between men and women and oppression of women is a function of being 'east of Eden'. Redemption is required.

Antony makes the point that all ancient texts 'contain passages with horrific sexism, racism and violence'. That's true, but the Bible's reports of sexism, racism and violence don't equate to approval of such things. There are plenty of terrible stories in the Old Testament that reveal shocking treatment of women involving polygamy, rape, incest, adultery and girls being taken as concubines. The Bible reports this behaviour, but that's a long way from endorsing it and, in fact, it frequently reveals the people of Israel to be a sorry parody of how they were supposed to live, and clearly shows them to be in need of the renewing action of God to save them from themselves. The Bible is a record of human sin – sometimes involving terrible treatment of women – and of God's redemptive action in history.

In this discussion it's helpful to keep focused on the context in which Christianity first arrived on the scene. It's hard for modern readers to comprehend just how patriarchal the first-century Graeco-Roman world was. It was a man's world in every way. It was broadly the case that women and girls were essentially chattels belonging to their fathers or brothers before being married off at very young ages to men who were usually several years older than them. In many cases women had no legal rights. Apart from the aristocratic classes, women were rarely educated and so had very limited opportunities outside the home and family. We know of some successful businesswomen in this period, but they are notable because they were rare.

Into this environment came Jesus, who rode over the conventions of the time with an extraordinarily high view of women. Jesus was the only rabbi of his day we know of who had women disciples. In Luke 8:1–3 Jesus is on the road with the twelve disciples plus Mary Magdalene, Joanna, Susanna and 'many others' who supported Jesus with their own funds (Mark 15:41). This is thoroughly scandalous for the time. In one famous incident at the house of Martha, we see a woman adopting the place of learning for disciples of prominent teachers, as she listens and is taught by Jesus. In Jesus's famous parables, women often feature as heroines. It would be inaccurate to portray Jesus as some sort of prescient feminist of the 21st-century kind, but every historical Jesus scholar notes the unusually high place given to women in his story.

The Gospels record women as the ones who anointed Jesus, something mostly done by males in Israel's history, as prophets anointed kings.[188] Women are presented as the ones who stayed close to Jesus as he endured crucifixion and as the first witnesses to the resurrection, even though many first-century Jewish men dismissed the testimony of women. It's difficult to overstate the significance of all this in the context in which it all took place. Indeed, the prominence given to women in the Easter story was reason enough for the famous Greek intellectual Celsus to dismiss Christian claims of the resurrection. This was a story of hysterical women, according to him!

The dawning of the Christian age meant a radical shift in the way women were perceived. For women, the new religion provided opportunities to play significant roles in the church, particularly for those from the upper classes. The earliest church building yet found (Megiddo, early third century) honours no fewer than five women on its mosaic floor, but only two men! This flows on from the New Testament singling out significant women such as Lydia, Phoebe, Chloe and Priscilla for special mention as important people in the early church. No wonder so many critics from antiquity heaped scorn on Christianity as a religion of women and slaves.

In early Christian communities girls married later and enjoyed a better quality and longer life than their pagan counterparts. Largely this was due to the high rates of abortion in the Roman world – a decision made by the men, very often with catastrophic implications for the women. Sexual chastity was extended to males as well as females under Christian teaching, with the woman having as much claim to her husband's body as he would expect of hers – another major shift, meaning family life was generally more secure. Infanticide was practised widely on girls in the Graeco-Roman world, and Christianity ruled this out. Christian communities insisted on provision for widows, who were among the most helpless of people in the ancient world. The teachings of the early church prevented Christian husbands from treating their wives with cruelty or abandoning or divorcing them. For these and other reasons, the early centuries of Christianity mark a great leap forward for women.

All these things are true and yet we all know that as Christianity was drawn into the establishment from the fourth century onwards it found itself caught up in struggles for power and wealth and to various degrees was subject to corruption. The Christian church has not exactly covered itself in glory in the matter of the treatment of women – that much must be acknowledged. But you wouldn't judge the strength of a classical composer's work based on the fumbling efforts of an amateurish violinist or pianist. There is no doubt that Jesus and the New Testament writers construct a beautiful composition when it comes to women, even if the church has in some ways botched it. That error has been costly for the church in failing to use the gifts of its people, and painful to many of the women involved.

In my view it is historically naive to claim that an acceptance of women as fully human runs no deeper than the Enlightenment and that it emerges out of thin air. In fact, in the West, the concept of what it is to be a human being, male or female, has a foundation in the Christian story, which provides the vital groundwork for seeing every person as fully human, and deserving of that status and the rights that go with it (see 'What is it to be a human being?'). That vision remains important, even as we recognise the struggle to see it fully realised while millions of women and girls around the world suffer indignities, deprivations and the worst kind of oppression because of their gender.

I have a daughter, and like all parents I have hopes for her as her life unfolds. I love watching her grow and imagining her future. I'm very grateful she has grown up in an era and a place where her gender is (mostly) not an impediment to her using whatever talents and interests she has to take on opportunities and make the most of her life. It's not hard for me to envisage her as a young woman loving music and surfing, reading, painting or some other creative activity. I've no real sense yet of the kind of vocation or career she will be drawn towards, but I'm excited by the idea that she'll be free to pursue her dreams and passions.

I also hope – although this will be entirely up to her – that she'll follow in the ways of the faith of her childhood family; that she'll know God as her strength, comfort and ally through the good times and the difficult episodes; that she'll have a deep sense of belonging to God and, in the times when she messes things up, that she'll experience his grace. It's my desire that, despite the struggles she'll no doubt face, she'll understand God to be a sure and reliable presence in her life and experience the hope that a life of faith can offer.

Obviously, I would find it hard to get excited for her if I thought this meant submitting to an oppressive and life-denying belief system, or that by being Christian she would find herself missing out in life and being anything less than fully human. I would be utterly depressed if she were to marry someone who thought of her as less than his equal or if she were to come to think of herself as subservient to the interests of men. If I feared Jane was right, and that God and women's rights are diametrically opposed, I'd find it hard to drum up enthusiasm for my daughter to follow in my (spiritual) footsteps. I'd like to think I'd be honest enough for her sake, if I feared this were true, to admit such a thing. But instead I believe the opposite to be the case – that if she understands the faith centred on Christ, she'll know what a precious and loved child of God she is and will fully embrace her humanity. It's my strong sense that with such a self-understanding and identity she can be not, as the self-help gurus might want to tell her, 'anything she wants', but rather all that she was made to be.

WHAT HAS RELIGION DONE FOR US ANYWAY?

Rachel Woodlock

There's a moment in the Orthodox Christian church service when the choir, echoing the heavenly angels, sings the Trisagion prayer 'Holy God, holy mighty, holy immortal, have mercy on us'. It's otherworldly in its beauty and symbolism. The whole liturgy is an ancient ritual of sublime grace, invoking all the senses: splendid icons to gaze upon, the sweet smell of burning incense, the bodily movement of standing, bowing, prostrating, the sounds of constant chanting and singing, the taste of the blessed bread.

A world away in Acre, on the coast of northern Israel, is the most holy shrine in the Baha'i world. The founder of the religion died in 1892, and his sepulchre became the direction of prayer and point of pilgrimage for millions. The room in which his remains are entombed is filled with the most glorious Persian carpets, wall hangings, and oriental lamps. Pilgrims, having laid their foreheads on the threshold and whispered words of adoration, come away visibly moved by the opportunity to offer prayers of visitation in this quiet, beautiful and reflective holy space.

In a Sufi *hadra*, worshippers sit in a circle and begin to chant the name of God slowly together, swaying with each heartbeat of sound, losing awareness of the rustling of robes and warmth of others' bodies, as each individual becomes part of a greater whole and the chanting deepens in sound and the ecstasy of union. The worshippers become the breath of life itself, inhaling and exhaling the real.

It's not that such moments of transcendence cannot be found outside formal religion. Some find it in the concert hall, listening to an orchestra perfectly capture the rhythm and crescendo in the opening section of the second movement of Beethoven's seventh symphony. Others in a quiet library, after reading a passage in Ernest Hemingway's *For Whom the Bell Tolls*, in which a flash of insight seems to come from somewhere else, from something more. It's just that religion seems particularly well designed to foster such mystical experiences.

There's no direct equivalent to 'religion' in Qur'anic Arabic. The two words most often translated as such are *din* and *milla*, but they are an ill-fitting match. *Milla* in the Qur'an does appear to refer both to particular religious communities and to the monotheistic 'natural' religion of Abraham. *Din*, which occurs much more frequently, means 'obedience', and is closely related to *dayn*, meaning 'debt'. That is, worshippers are accountable to God for their *din*, the debt of right belief and right living they owe God for bringing them into being and continually and lovingly nourishing their every breath.

We cannot survive as isolated individuals. The water we drink is carried to us through pipes built underground by other people before us. The food we eat is grown and raised by farmers who battle the elements to feed us. Our homes are built by labourers who craft expert shelters to keep us warm. Even our bodies carry other beings, microorganisms, that keep us alive. Every moment of our existence we're indebted to others for our very lives; we live and move in a cosmic embrace of interdependence with God as the constant cause and ground of being. 'To God belongs everything in the heavens and the earth, and the *din* is due to God, constantly' (Q16:52).

But it cannot be forced, for the Qur'an says there must be 'no compulsion in *din*' (Q2:256), a point seemingly lost on heavy-handed religious police in Saudi Arabia and Iran. There's a world of difference between being consciously obedient to God and being blindly obedient to theocrats who claim to speak on his behalf and who seem to think God is a remote sky-cop who needs earthbound deputies to enforce his will. Theocracy, where the state imposes religion, is never a good idea.

The difficulty in translating *din* as 'religion' also explains how people from Muslim cultures sometimes find it difficult to comprehend a Westerner having no religion. Like Antony related, many tourists and visitors simply answer 'Christian' when asked to provide a religious identity travelling across the Muslim world, because the concept of agnosticism or atheism versus belonging to a religion makes no sense in cultures thoroughly infused with Islamic thinking. For Muslims, no one is without a *din* because we all have a view about the nature of reality that informs how we live. So there's good *din* and bad *din*, but not no *din*.

To deny *din* is not some philosophical debate about the non-existence of God, rather it's to be ungrateful and therefore uncaring to others. 'Have you seen the one who denies the *din*? Such is the one who repulses the orphan and feels no urge to feed the poor' (Q107:1–3). Importantly, it's not about labels – the Qur'an censures phoney, hypocritical Muslims and praises those who are moral and upright from among other communities (Q4:145–146, Q2:62, Q5:69).

Din as a concept developed in the Qur'an over the course of the Prophet's ministry. In the early years, it was introduced in connection with the future day of judgement (Q82), to call people to awareness of and accountability for their actions. Then *din* was connected with all the previous revelations given to humanity over the course of history: 'He has ordained the same *din* for you as he enjoined on Noah; that which we have revealed to you and which we enjoined on Abraham, Moses and Jesus' (Q42:13). Although the details of particular religious rites and rules are different from era to era, and people to people, there's an underlying unity in the great religious traditions having come from the same divine source. One tradition states that God has inspired 124,000 emissaries, sent to all the various peoples of the earth over the course of human history, even though only a handful are specifically named in the Qur'an itself.

By the end of the Prophet's mission, *din* in Islam had become the particular religious teachings and commandments of the Qur'an. In one of the last verses to be revealed, God says, 'Today I have perfected your *din* for you and completed my favour upon you and have approved Islam as a *din* for you' (Q5:3). Muslims who understand this in an exclusivist manner take the approach that while older pre-Islamic religions all came from the one divine source, they've been abrogated in favour of the teachings of the Prophet Muhammad, which is now the only true *din*.

Pluralists like myself argue the Qur'an says God has created religious diversity for a reason that's only resolved after death:

> For each we have appointed a law and a way of life. If God had willed, he would have made you a single community, but that he may test you in what he has given you. So race in doing good. To God you will all return and then he will inform you regarding the things over which you differed (Q5:48).

The ostensibly conflicting truth claims between religions really only make sense within each one's particular framework for describing reality, so there's no point arguing about them. It's like trying to say that painting is more truly art than calligraphy, sculpture or drawing. Literalism and factuality, while vital in the objective sciences like biology and physics, aren't very useful in judging whether the music of Mozart or Bach is more beautiful, and neither are they helpful in comprehending the languages of religion, which can only ever be symbolic when pointing to the supernatural.

The usefulness of a scientific explanation is in its ability to convey accurate knowledge of the natural world, whereas the usefulness of a religious explanation is in its ability to elevate human nature beyond that which would otherwise be impossible. Therefore, we need to discern characteristics by which we can know good *din*, good religion – that which is helpful and useful to us.

From my Muslim perspective there are three main aspects to good and useful religion, based on the Qur'anic promise:

Indeed, those who believe, and the Jews, and the Christians, and the Sabians[189] – anyone who believes in God, and the last day, and does righteous deeds – their reward is with their Lord, there will be no fear for them, nor will they grieve (Q2:62).

First, good religion helps a person know and love the source of his or her existence. In a famous Islamic tradition, God says, 'I was a hidden treasure and I desired to be known. Therefore I created creation, that I might be known.' Furthermore, the Qur'an tells us the way to know and love God is to follow the guidance he gives. He instructed the Prophet Muhammad to say, 'If you love God, then follow me. God will love you and forgive your wrongs. God is Ever-Forgiving, Most Merciful' (Q3:31). Through constant self-reflection, we become increasingly aware of the working of God in our lives, as another famous tradition tells us: 'Whoever knows himself, knows his Lord.' Thus, the fullest expression of being human, which good religion fosters, is to be constantly full of awe and wonder at the beauty and magnificence of the totality of existence.

Secondly, useful religion makes us aware of our individual and collective accountability. Whether you call it karma, judgement or just desserts, we're each responsible for how we move about on the earth, and our actions have real consequences. If we continue burning fossil fuels, pouring carbon dioxide into the atmosphere and raising the earth's temperature, the natural consequence will be weather extremes and flooding, decreases in crop yields, huge rises in food prices, poverty and famine, and possibly the breakdown of many societies. If we smoke cigarettes, eat junk food and sit around on our bottoms all day, every day, our lifespan will be decreased and we'll suffer such diseases as diabetes, cancer, heart disease and stroke. These are the natural consequences of our actions. So, too, are there spiritual consequences for how we live and treat each other.

Thirdly, based on our connection with the source of our existence and awareness of our accountability, a life of good deeds refines the human character to the extent where it fully reflects godly attributes. These are qualities such as beauty, mercy, majesty, generosity, might, knowledge – what are called the 'names' of God. As the mystic poet 'Abd al-Rahman Jami (d. 1492) explained:

The entities were all coloured windows,
upon which fell the rays of Being's Sun.
In every window – red, yellow, blue –
the light appeared in the window's colour.[190]

Alternatively, if we backbite and gossip, sow dissent and hatred, are miserly and selfish, our souls wither and our ability to see and reflect the divine attributes lessens progressively. If a mirror becomes dusty, and over time the dirt becomes thickly encrusted, not even the magnificence of the sun can be reflected in it. So the third attribute of good religion is that, in encouraging and instructing in virtues, it rubs and polishes the lamp of the human being to reveal and reflect the divine qualities.

These three characteristics of good religion are indispensable in making us fully and perfectly human. The Qur'an calls such a person: 'God's representative on earth' (Q2:30) and, as Ibn 'Arabi describes it, we become *al-insan al-kamil*, 'the locus for the manifestation of God'.[191]

Antony Loewenstein

The September 2012 headline in the *New York Times* was strong: 'Some religious leaders see a threat as Europe grows more secular.'[192] The article described Jewish, Muslim and Christian spokespeople expressing growing concern that their beliefs and rituals were being shunned and rejected by a secular establishment and population that neither respected nor appreciated their histories. 'It's a secular society,' a Jewish leader in Oslo said. 'People don't have much sense about religion or much knowledge of religion.'

The story was sparked by public unease with Muslims and Jews wanting to continue circumcising their male babies. When a German court found the practice unlawful, there was an outcry in the Jewish community. 'This discussion has shown that we are foreigners in our own country, doing something that Germans are not supposed to do,' said Stephan J. Kramer, secretary-general of the Central Council of Jews in Germany.[193] 'We are accused of torturing our own children.'

It was a strange response. Just because a religious group claims a right to a ritual doesn't make it legal, morally acceptable or just. Although it's undeniably true that male babies have been circumcised for thousands of years in the Jewish religion, it's legitimate for a secular nation to question its safety and ethics. It was hardly a sign, as some Jews claimed, that they were suddenly unwelcome in Germany less than seventy years after the Holocaust.

The issue wasn't Jews being denied the right to live in peace and harmony in Germany but the legitimate health concerns around a controversial practice. Jews should welcome this intervention in a democratic country, and a debate that goes beyond simply respecting religion to the health and wellbeing of a newborn baby.

Religion has given us faux outrage. It's allowed human beings to believe that, because their holy book and rabbis claim something is right and necessary, it shouldn't be questioned. Nothing is that sacred. Or shouldn't be. I've lost count of the number of times an imam, priest, Jewish figure or other religious spokesperson has demanded that somebody stop speaking rudely or offensively about their beliefs.

There's even legislation in some Australian states to stop citizens racially discriminating against others. It's unpopular on the left to argue this, but I feel distinctly uncomfortable being told by the state that we can't offend people.

Surely, a true democracy – and America, with all its faults, has far more evolved views about free speech than most other Western democracies – doesn't need to legislate against thoughts, no matter how derogatory. Incitement to violence is another matter altogether and should be regulated, but the vast bulk of comments deemed inappropriate are often simply ideas that may profoundly upset somebody. I clearly abhor the thought of people being hurt because of their race, but I remain far from convinced that the law should get involved every time. Our challenge is to foster a community that respects and accepts difference and doesn't need to resort to vilification to make a valid point.

Religion has also brought us a moral code that remains largely out of step with the modern world. Although the holy books of the world's major religions may have been in step with their time, today they read like simplistic morality tales that support the demonisation or death of gay people, patriarchy, and extreme violence and death to resolve problems. It is now possible in most Western countries to slander religious beliefs or at least deeply challenge them without facing punishment or death (though undoubtedly some of the most strident opponents of Islam are under physical threat from fundamentalist Muslims). We should encourage the Muslim world to both tolerate and welcome religious debate and diversity.

To think that only a few decades ago the church had such complete power over the state that abortions had to be conducted secretly due to the shame of the act. In many countries, religious authorities still force women to seek out the procedure in the shadows. Even today, the Vatican can dare talk about the supposed evil of condoms, leaving millions of uneducated and vulnerable people, especially in Africa, susceptible to HIV/AIDS. This isn't just irresponsible, it's criminal.

If this is what religion has brought us, any intelligent person shouldn't want any part of it. But that's far too simplistic, and Rachel offers some compelling reasons why. She argues that the Qur'an for her and most

Muslims is a text that provides essential life lessons and ideas she lives with every day. It offers a framework to live by and values to aspire to.

It's hard to disagree with these motherhood statements but I doubt it's enough to convince an increasingly secular West that religion offers anything other than repression, violence, discrimination and guilt. Although religions can't be defined solely through the views expressed by their representatives – equally the new atheists can't be condemned simply because Christopher Hitchens loved American bombs raining down on Muslim cities – in an age of globalised work and play where people's physical location matters less than at any time in history, potential practitioners need to be convinced that their time spent adhering to a prescribed belief is worth it. That it will give them spiritual nourishment. A guide for life. A way to process grief, happiness, or a wedding day or sexuality.

It's to be applauded that more progressive-minded religious figures recognise the stereotype of a rigid hierarchy that offers little to young and busy people, but it may not be enough. I'd love to see ancient religions adapting to the twenty-first century, without removing or diluting their traditions or soul, and understanding that declining interest can be addressed only if the mistakes of the past are addressed and remedied. For example, how can a mature Catholic Church expect to be taken seriously when it still demands celibacy for its priests while cases of paedophilia remain rampant? Despite this, however, I would not argue that an absence of religion would reduce cases of paedophilia in society. Mental sickness may be bred in a religious system, but human beings are prone to such sick behaviour for a range of complex reasons, some of which have nothing to do with ascending to the priesthood.

I remember a moment in Iran in 2007 that moved me to tears and reminded me that religion, even when not fully understood, has an ability to challenge. I was in the city of Yazd, a centre of Zoroastrian culture. Surrounded by desert, the town consists of narrow, windy streets filled with old Persian architecture and mosaics. One evening in my room at the hotel, which was a large restored old home, I turned on the television to find a channel with haunting Islamic prayers being sung while grown men and boys wept uncontrollably. Images crossed the screen of what looked like battle scenes, I presumed from the Iran–Iraq war.

The music was haunting, an unfamiliar Muslim prayer that soared. I started to feel my eyes filling with tears. I wanted to know what was moving me and, although the language was unfamiliar, I couldn't get past the fact that it was perfectly acceptable in the Islamic Republic of Iran to see men crying in complete freedom.

It's a moment I think about fairly often. I can't recall another instance where I was literally moved to tears by a religious ceremony. It proved that I was capable of feeling immense emotion over an Islamic chant. I didn't want to become Muslim or ignore my Jewish background, and perhaps my reaction was partly due to my isolation in Iran when I saw it, but whatever the reason, it reflected a spirituality and feeling I've rarely felt at any other time.

This small, relatively insignificant story is just one example that makes me think religion can't be so easily dismissed as irrelevant or superstitious. It has as much meaning as we want to allow it. It isn't static or dull. It can be oppressive or liberating. Only the small-minded dismiss it entirely.

Simon Smart

There's no doubt that religion has and does provide a great deal that's enormously important to many people around the globe. Religion is about finding meaning and placing our lives within a larger story. It's about community and ritual and symbolism placed within a framework that is coherent and joins us to others. It's really about seeking answers to some of the fundamental questions we've been asking in this book.

And, of course, all religions have something to say about these questions. Rachel and, to some extent, Antony have both touched on the importance of religion in addressing transcendence and the mysteries of life of which we're all aware. I'm glad Antony believes it's only the small-minded who dismiss religion entirely, but I can't help feeling that his understanding of faith is restricted to caricatures of unsophisticated, dated and repressive cultures; that perhaps his legitimate concerns about the way religion sometimes plays out in the world have limited his vision of what might truly be on offer.

And while on this and other questions, Rachel and I have much in common, I can't quite go with Rachel's pluralism, which would have us believe that the conflicting truth claims of different religions are only apparent. I can't see how that can be. She's absolutely right that we can discern among the world religions some expressions of faith that are more positive and useful than others and plenty that are sophisticated and rich in their ability to provide a framework for meaning. But I don't think it's being too literal to say, for example, the Theravada Buddhist claim that there's no God is irreconcilable with the Jewish claim that there's one mighty, all-powerful creator; or to say the Muslim belief that Jesus didn't die on the cross and rise again simply won't match up with the Christian belief that he did.

In this discussion it's left for me to assess what my own faith has given us. I feel the need to speak up when the most vocal critics of religion won't allow even the slightest acknowledgement of the contribution of Christianity to the world. This seems particularly churlish to me. I want to argue that in the West we enjoy, and are beneficiaries of, a vision of understanding the world, ourselves and other people that emerges from the Christian story – that even if we have forgotten the story itself, this world view comes from somewhere and we enjoy its legacy.

The European intellectual Jürgen Habermas, who is not a believer, once famously said that the Judaeo-Christian tradition and nothing else forms the basis of our notions of universalistic egalitarianism, which have spawned the ideals of freedom, conscience, human rights and democracy. The legacy of the Judaic ethic of justice and the Christian ethic of love remains unchanged, he said, and there is no viable alternative to it.[194]

It shouldn't be controversial to say that Christianity has had an enormous, shaping influence on our artistic and cultural pursuits. So many of the masterpieces in galleries around the world explore and imaginatively plumb the depths of the great themes of the Christian story. In his book *Religion for Atheists*, Alain de Botton makes a case for the wonder and beauty of Christian art – think Michelangelo's *Pietà* or Caravaggio's *The Raising of Lazarus*. De Botton says there is precious little in modern art that would tell us anything about what matters in life – what is to be feared, admired, pursued or rejected – whereas Christian art can generate compassion by helping us recognise ourselves in the experiences of others.[195] He says some of the great art of history has been religious in nature and has an educative, therapeutic mission, enhancing our receptiveness to modesty, friendship, courage and self-sacrifice.[196]

Our culture is shot through with the Bible, which has enormously influenced our language and literature – the key stories our culture tells itself. In 2011, on the 400th anniversary of the release of the King James Bible, that great opponent of religion Richard Dawkins acknowledged that 'You can't appreciate English literature unless you are steeped to some extent in the King James Bible ... not to know [it] is to be, in some small way, barbarian.'[197]

Biblical stories and language, along with themes of grace and redemption, darkness and light, forgiveness and hope, are embedded in the works of Shakespeare, Milton, Bunyan, Dostoevsky and Tolkien, and a rich understanding of these works requires some knowledge of Christian faith. The same can be said for the work of such modern writers as John Steinbeck, Tim Winton, Ian McEwan and Marilynne Robinson, regardless of the personal beliefs of these authors.

If I had space I would like to elaborate on the influence of Christianity on music, film and architecture. It would be worthwhile examining how, largely because of Christianity, we came to appreciate the importance of studying history, and to value childhood, and to give education and literacy such a high priority. This is well attested by scholars. Historians now believe that, contrary to popular opinion, the Christian world view provided a critical foundation for the growth of modern science.

But let's move on. The Jesus story has reverberated through our culture in other important ways, in terms of how we see ourselves and each other. Emeritus Professor Edwin Judge from Macquarie University's Ancient History Department has shown how the story of Christianity radically altered what was previously regarded not as a virtue, but as a shameful thing – humility.

In Graeco-Roman culture there was a strong sense that the correct, rational and justified order of things was that the poor people and those limited in ability be at the bottom of the heap, where they should stay. In the early centuries educated people were very critical of Christianity because they thought it 'immoral' to be worrying about those who were simply living in their proper position in life. In the ancient world, honour was thought of as an ethical good. It was right and proper to increase your honour and have the honour that was due to you proclaimed.

But the value of humility, which we have come to see as self-evident, emerges from the Jewish tradition of the poor being the ones God loves. This was then picked up and extended by Christianity and its account of the crucifixion. For educated people in the ancient world, the grotesque execution of Jesus was thought of as the worst kind of humiliation that couldn't possibly have anything to do with divinity. But as the meaning of Jesus's death and resurrection became apparent, this humiliation came to be thought of as profoundly meaningful – salvation itself! The low point became the high point. Jesus urged those who wanted to be great to become the servant, or slave, of all, much like he did, employing his strength in the service of others. Today, everyone in our culture dislikes people who are proud, and see that honour belongs to the truly humble.

Alain de Botton recognises the value of this radical shift:

> Among Christianity's greatest achievements has been its capacity, without the use of any coercion beyond the gentlest of theological arguments, to persuade monarchs and magnates to kneel down and abase themselves before the statue of a carpenter, and to wash the feet of peasants, street sweepers and dispatch drivers.[198]

Closely related to the concept of humility is another massive gift of Christianity to the world – charity. The simple truth is that a world without the Christian gospel would be one where millions more would suffer each day. And while plenty of people are capable of charity without conscious religious commitment, that commitment has been and remains a powerful motivation among believers. Contrary to what some will have us believe, this motivation is not merely the selfish hope of reward in the next life, nor the guilt associated with a failure to act. Many of those who are most heroically involved in works of charity and service do so out of selflessness and love, and do it joyfully for its own sake and because they believe that's how to respond to God's grace towards them.

The early church took from Judaism the important notion of justice for the oppressed and gave its own slant on charity, universal love and forgiveness over condemnation. Jesus's life and teaching showed that love for God and neighbour was right at the heart of his mission – what he called bringing in the Kingdom of God. He expected those who followed him to have a heart for the needy and, in response to God's mercy, to play a role in this work of God for the world. And here's the thing – this was thought of as the doorway into life itself.

Over the centuries, many people took this seriously and saw that in response to God's grace they could get in on this work and make a contribution. The resulting action has and does make a huge difference. This attitude brought about huge and lasting change, from the time of the Roman Emperor Julian complaining about the Christians caring for not only their own poor but 'ours as well', to the establishment of Christian monastic hospitals for the destitute and the dying around the time of Constantine, the Christian noblewomen and scholar St Fabiola (d. AD399) establishing the first public hospital in Western Europe, and preacher John Wesley standing in the snow as an eighty-year-old begging money for the poor.

We could recall someone like the Seventh Earl of Shaftsbury in the nineteenth century working for the reform of factories, mines and mental institutions and developing schools for poor children, or William Wilberforce's twenty-year campaign to end slavery. Today, organisations like Mission Australia or World Vision or TEAR strive to overcome poverty and disadvantage to create flourishing communities. In Australia, of the leading thirty charities, twenty-six are faith-based.[199] Christian notions of charity and the good have made a heck of a difference to our messed-up world.

Christian communities are not a collection of good people. In fact they're quite the opposite. They're more like a 'league of the guilty', as Francis Spufford calls it. There are no laws in Christianity that separate the clean from the unclean, for the simple reason that Christianity doesn't believe anyone is clean, and laws won't be able to solve that problem.[200] Christians believe in God's grace towards flawed and broken people. The more they immerse themselves in that grace and teaching, the more they feel a kind of gravitational pull away from hatred, small-ness, selfishness, pride and violence (our more natural states) and towards costly generosity, kindness, mercy and forgiveness. Plenty of us resist that pull and are not very good at putting those things into practice, but we are better versions of ourselves because of the influence.

Would our world be better off without this influence? Only the most obstinate and biased secularism could say so. The impact of Christian-ity on the world has been enormous. Not all of it has been good. There have been some regrettable chapters in the story of the church and I've tried to acknowledge those in this book. But there is a good story to tell as well, and a sober assessment of the contribution of Christianity reveals a whole lot more to celebrate than to regret, an irreplaceable and unrivalled legacy and force for good.

Jane Caro

Religion is a powerful force, and while I dispute that any one religion has given us our laws or morals – the golden rule, for example, is present in all religions as well as the moral underpinning for those of us who have no religion at all – religious belief has certainly given humanity many great gifts.

In the beginning (to use a resonant phrase), it gave early humans a way to understand and cope emotionally, psychologically and intellectually with a world that would otherwise have seemed vast and terrifying. Religious stories made the world human-scaled and so gave people the courage they needed to both live and prosper. This was probably utterly indispensible if the ape with the oversized brain was to survive as a species. For that alone, religion has my gratitude.

Religion has undoubtedly given us very great art and many technological achievements. From the rock art of Aboriginal Australians, ancient cave paintings in France, the Egyptian pyramids, and Greek and Roman temples, to mosques, cathedrals, sacred music, religious art and literary triumphs such as the King James Bible, the religious impulse has resulted in a deep and rich record of the human story. No one who appreciates the beauty human beings can produce can fail to be grateful to religions – from animist to Abrahamic – for such treasures.

Some people with deep religious faith have used it to inspire them to change the world very much for the better. Anglican William Wilberforce led the fight to abolish the slave trade, Quaker Elizabeth Fry fought for prison reform, and mystical Christian Florence Nightingale created the modern profession of nursing and reformed hygiene and sanitation throughout the British Empire. Even Mary Wollstonecraft, who began the fight for women's rights in 1792, was a devout if unconventional Unitarian.

But religion has also done terrible things. In 2001 the religiously devout Taliban used religion as an excuse to blow up the 1700-year-old Buddhas of Bamiyan in Afghanistan, in the face of worldwide protests. When they invaded the Americas, the all-conquering Catholic Spanish melted down the religious and cultural artefacts of the Aztecs and the

Incas – heathen objects to them – for their gold and shipped them back to Spain as ingots, an act of extraordinary vandalism. The Protestant stormtroopers of Henry VIII burnt illuminated manuscripts, smashed stained-glass windows and stripped churches, convents and monasteries of their decorative religious art in the name of their brand of Christianity.

Religious belief has variously been used to sanctify slavery (particularly of non-believers), rape, torture, forced marriage, child (and adult) sacrifice, sati (the practice of burning widows on their husbands' funeral pyre), female and male circumcision, castration, honour killings, stonings, cannibalism, massacres and war.

Religious faith has inspired human beings to acts of great compassion and heroism but also given others the sense of self-righteousness that allowed them to do the exact opposite. While it has been the engine that has driven people to produce art of great beauty and timelessness, it has also given others the desire and the excuse to obliterate such creations.

Religion causes people to alter history, too. In 2011, the US government finally tracked down and killed Osama Bin Laden. It was one of the biggest stories of the decade. News outlets the world over carried a photograph of the team in the White House Situation Room as they watched the dramatic events unfold. A Brooklyn-based Hasidic newspaper, *Der Zeitung*, also ran the photograph on their front page, but with two changes. All the men in the photograph remained untouched, but Secretary of State Hillary Clinton and director of counterterrorism Audrey Tomason were missing. The two female members of the team directing the operation had been erased because of the religious sensibilities of an Orthodox Jewish newspaper. Apparently, the newspaper never shows pictures of women in case they may cause men to become sexually aroused (what is it about religious men that makes them so uniquely unable to control their own sexual responses?) and because *Der Zeitung* has a religious objection to women in positions of power. There was a storm of protest about the excision of the two powerful women, but I can't help wondering how much greater the response might have been if a white supremacist group had airbrushed Obama out of the picture using a similar rationale about objecting to black people in positions of power. After all, the Orthodox Jews who publish *Der Zeitung* – like many other religious zealots – could justifiably be described as male supremacists.

Indeed, if I were to compare the effect of religion on the health, wealth and happiness of humankind to the effect of – say – feminism, I suspect feminism would win easily. Feminism has never airbrushed men out of the picture – either literally or metaphorically. It has never raised an army, never armed itself and never passed laws restricting the equal rights or opportunities of others. There may have been terrorists who were also feminists – in the IRA or the Baader–Meinhof gang, for example – just as there have been terrorists who were also atheists, but there have been no feminist acts of terror. Feminism has never killed an opponent. Feminists have died, of course, usually at the hands of the religious. The suffragettes certainly smashed a lot of windows and even set a few fires (always in buildings they knew to be empty), but they never actually hurt anyone other than themselves. Suffragette Emily Davison was killed throwing herself under the hooves of the King's racehorse at the Epsom Derby, crying 'Votes for Women!', and many of her colleagues went on hunger strikes when gaoled for their beliefs, and then suffered the indignity and torture of force-feeding.

The evidence for feminism as a force for good is equally unequivocal. We know, for example, that the best protection for women against violence is the presence and activity of independent feminist community organisations (the presence of churches and houses of worship makes no difference at all). Not just that, either – we also know that in countries with the greatest equality between the sexes, the life expectancy of men also goes up, because violence in general falls. We also now know, entirely thanks to feminism, that when you educate a girl and give her opportunities to earn money she would not normally have – often due to religious strictures – the benefits accrue to the whole family and community in a way they do not when you educate only boys. The phenomenon is called 'The Girl Effect'. The lives that feminism has directly saved through agitating for women's reproductive health and rights probably number in the many millions.

Feminism has also encouraged the creation of works of art, from the literature of George Eliot and the Brontës – who, like Eliot, had to publish under male-sounding names to be taken seriously – to that of Virginia Woolf, Margaret Attwood, Hilary Mantel and Toni Morrison. Simply by agitating for women to have access to the same educational and career opportunities as their brothers, feminism has enabled female artists, musicians, novelists, sculptors and filmmakers to express themselves and add to the sum of human creativity. Until relatively recently, religion helped silence their voices and so stifled female creativity for centuries. That alone is a terrible thing to have done, and all humanity is the poorer for it.

Yet, while we're still expected to be deferential around religious belief, including the need to obliterate historical fact so as not to give 'offence', feminism is given no such consideration. Feminism (like its sibling atheism) remains open to derision, scorn and a conspicuous lack of respect. Come to think of it, perhaps that's actually an advantage. Perhaps that's why such secular movements have arguably been a source of more net positive results for humanity than the more cosetted, protected and one-eyed religions. Until very recently, the one eye through which most religions looked at the world was a male eye. Thanks to secular feminism (a movement that also includes believers from many faiths) humanity is just beginning to open its female eye and see the world as a whole.

An example, perhaps, of what can be gained if we take women's different life experiences into account can be seen in the universally applauded Finnish education system. Pasi Sahlberg, director-general of the Centre for International Mobility in Helsinki, believes that one of the reasons Finland takes its school system so seriously and pays its teachers (mostly women) so well is the high level of gender equality in that country. The Finns use no standardised testing, give one-third of school students extra help under their extensive special-needs programs, and place an emphasis in early childhood education not on getting the child ready for school but on ensuring that schools understand how they can be ready to help the child, no matter what level they may be at.

Delegations regularly visit Finland to discover how the Finns have achieved their consistently high educational outcomes as measured through international comparisons such as PISA (the OECD's Programme for International Student Assessment). One of the questions often asked is: 'What are the political influences that enable the Finns to pay so much serious attention to early childhood and student wellbeing?' Sahlberg is unequivocal in his belief that the 40 per cent gender quotas in all public boards, committees and councils – in force in Finland since the 1980s – are the reason. He believes that without that equal representation of women in the legislature and at all levels of decision making, the concentration on student wellbeing and the world-leading maternal and childcare policies that support parents caring for children would not exist. Without them, Sahlberg argues, 'the Finnish education system would never have evolved into today's success story'. According to Sahlberg, it is bringing women to the table that has made the difference.

In humanity's slow journey towards taking the female perspective into account – a journey entirely driven by feminism and almost always in direct opposition to religion – we're seeing that when you do, you also start to take other marginalised groups in society more seriously, too. Children's rights begin to be asserted, so that hopefully the Jimmy Saviles of this world will no longer get away with damaging and exploiting vulnerable children for their own sexual satisfaction. Paedophile priests can no longer expect that the mystique and status conferred on them by their church will offer them a cloak of silence and protection as they do the same. Taking women seriously means taking what they care about seriously, too – like the right of children not to be used sexually. Taking women seriously means taking the feminine in general seriously, so it also means the fight for gay and lesbian rights gaining ground. As the work women do gains status, and as much of that work remains caring work, caring gains status, too.

As I've stated before, while I acknowledge the gifts religions have given humanity, when it comes to the final balance sheet, their universal oppression, control and stifling of one half of the human race remain – for me – their greatest sin.

LAST WORDS

Antony Loewenstein

Believing superstitions is so tempting. I wonder how satisfying it must be for a supposedly rational person to believe that God gave Jews the right to inhabit and occupy a piece of desert in the Middle East. The icing on the cake is that this omnipotent being also crowned the same group as his favourite. As a Jewish atheist, I don't feel part of the chosen club and nor do I want to.

The writing of this book has been an enlightening experience of the earthly kind. The evolution of the debate between a Christian, Muslim, atheist and me has never felt forced but precisely the opposite, with each of us showing a willingness to engage calmly with some of the key issues of our world. I'm thankful that a respectful dialogue is possible between us all, even while still we fundamentally disagree on the sanctity of faith and the ways we live our lives. I readily admit that I'm a little jealous of people who calmly capitulate to the words and deeds of their God. I'm incapable of doing so, obsessed as I am with the known world.

I'm fond of former US Secretary of Defense Donald Rumsfeld's 2002 comment in Washington: 'There are known knowns; there are things we know we know. We also know there are known unknowns; that is to say, we know there are some things we do not know. But there are also unknown unknowns – the ones we don't know we don't know.'

My Jewish atheism has developed organically over the last decade, initially born of rejecting a Judaism that often demanded obedient Zionism and associated abuse of Palestinians. As I've explained throughout this book, I still see my religion as sick at heart, unwilling and incapable of separating itself from a country, Israel, that is today rightly known throughout the world as a brutal, occupying nation. Of course, Judaism should stand completely separate from Zionism but the post-Holocaust decades have rejected this possibility. It's now up to enlightened Jews to reclaim a secular, spiritual and progressive faith that aims for inclusiveness, acceptance, goodness and happiness. I know that I'll be exploring my contested beliefs for the rest of my life.

Before I started this project I wondered if my views would change or if some of my dogmatism would be rightly challenged. In a way, they have. I remain uncomfortable with the so-called new atheist movement: too many of its key spokespeople are enforcers of intolerance, anti-Muslim sentiment and US-backed wars in the Islamic world. But post-9/11, there have undoubtedly been millions of people in the West who want to reject extremism in all its forms. I welcome this and know Jane does, too, as evidenced by her regular public interventions for the rights of women in the face of discrimination or religious bigotry.

Simon and Rachel, passionate about interpreting Christianity and Islam in ways that look and feel modern, are on vital missions that must succeed. I will never share their love of Jesus or Muhammad, but aggressive and misogynist forces within their religions must not be allowed to succeed. It moves me to read their struggles against these groups.

Advocating a world with less religion, as many atheists do, strikes me as a strange preoccupation. Nothing lasts forever and the future isn't written, but the importance of religion to vast swathes of the world, the majority of the globe's population, won't simply be erased or minimised by more education or supposed Western enlightenment. When we advocate tolerance and understanding to Muslims in Pakistan, a nation racked by sectarian chaos, they could rightly question what laws of God are used to justify the murder of civilians by American-fired drones. We should listen far more and preach much less.

Every human being is capable of empathy, intelligence and faith, regardless of their upbringing, religion or atheism. I hope this book proves that improving our communities, whether in the West or East, can be achieved by respecting alternative viewpoints and opening both heart and mind. A world of uniformity is the kind of dystopian nightmare imagined by the passionate neo-liberal writer Ayn Rand.

A diverse society is the only answer to every pertinent question. Religion has its rightful place and atheism will grow. Only if the faithful and the godless better understand themselves and each other can our planet be in far healthier shape.

Jane Caro

Many years ago I realised that I had an unconscious prejudice. My epiphany occurred when I shared a panel with a prominent church leader. Our subject matter was not religion but politics, and I found myself impressed by my fellow panellist's grasp of the issues and his interpretations. I was not just impressed, however, I was surprised, and recognising that emotion gave me pause. I realised that I had unconsciously assumed that the religious were if not stupid exactly, then conventional, predictable and dull. It was a classic prejudice. Exactly the sort of stereotypical assumption I have battled all my life when it comes to women. It was a shock to realise I could also be guilty of the same stupid thinking.

I have worked hard at overcoming my prejudice – a task not always made easier by some of the representatives of the world's major faiths – and I have come a long way. I would like to thank my fellow authors for helping me shed comprehensively the last vestiges of that prejudice.

The process of writing this book and reading the contributions of my fellow authors has been both fascinating and enlightening. I have particularly enjoyed recognising the very real differences between us. Some things both Rachel and Simon have written I find very difficult to grasp. Their deeply held beliefs are something I cannot share. Do I, as Antony has said, envy them their faith? No, I can honestly say that I do not. As I hope I have communicated throughout this book, I am content not to know. But I have gained greater respect for the rich human experiences that their faith, and that of billions of other people, have given us all. It has been a privilege to share ideas and perspectives with three such open, interesting and intelligent human beings. It is also always inspiring to realise you can quite profoundly disagree with people and yet still like and respect them. I don't think it too great a claim to make that it's such generosity of spirit that allows civilisation to prosper.

The rise of the so-called new atheists has also led to a renewed interest in debating the rights and wrongs of religions and their place in the public square. This is a tribute to them, I think. I believe the new, more assertive atheism that many find so alienating has itself arisen out of the shattering of the blue skies over New York on September 11, 2001. Religious fanaticism – like fanaticism of any kind – has always been terrifying to behold. On that day many of the secular decided that enough was enough and began to say as much. Some of their spokespeople – Antony specifically mentions Christopher Hitchens – have a direct and uncompromising way of talking about religion and its failings that many find offensive. Not just believers either; I know many atheists and agnostics who instinctively shy away from such blunt speech. I am not one of them. I do not find plain speaking offensive. All movements that seek to change society – feminism, anti-racism, gay rights, atheism, even, perhaps, the great religions in their early days – have their radical elements. These people often do us all a great service when they decide that it is more important to challenge than to charm, and to disrupt and disturb cherished beliefs rather than play nice.

I have had the experience of a religious opponent (who will remain nameless) refusing to shake my hand after a debate. I had put my views strongly, but I had in no way personally insulted or abused him. I was quite astonished by his behaviour. I was even more astonished some weeks later when his wife sent me an email further criticising me for my 'offensive' contribution. Offensive in what way, I wondered. I disagreed with him, said so and backed up my opinion with evidence. Yes, I was also blunt, uncompromising and got a few laughs, but so what? This very unexpected experience gave me some insight into just how easy it is to offend some people who hold passionate religious beliefs. I am genuinely sorry if my views offend anyone, but no idea is sacred, particularly in a debate. Even more importantly, feeling offended should never be used as a weapon to silence others.

Like Antony, I do not agree with everything the leaders of the new atheism say. Antony despises Hitchens' view of the wars in the Middle East, I find Hitchens' views on women antediluvian, but I can still admire his articulate, passionate and very human expression of his opinions. His crystalline brain, notwithstanding its flaws, will be missed. What others see as arrogance, I see as courage. Hitchens, Dawkins, Hirsi Ali, Nasreen, Harris et al. do not care if you like them. They want to make you think. I admire that.

I saw just how much some of them sacrifice for their outspoken-ness at the 2010 and 2012 Global Atheism conferences in Melbourne. In 2010, Bangladeshi atheist Taslima Nasreen spoke from a stage that was flanked by the security men who follow her everywhere. She is under threat of death because she is an apostate from Islam and speaks out about her lack of belief. In 2012, Ayaan Hirsi Ali was equally well protected, and an undercover policeman confided that they had received credible threats against her life. Say what you like about the new atheists, the worst they will do is offend you. They will not threaten you with physical harm – or refuse to shake your hand.

Some may feel that my defence of the new atheists contradicts my view that you can disagree with people and still like and respect them. On the contrary, I believe it is deeply respectful to be robust and forthright with your views. Protecting your opponents from the full force of your argument is to me both condescending and patronising. I expect you to give as good as you get. I think Simon and Rachel are completely wrong about women and religion, but I like them no less for their strongly held and strongly put views on the subject. In fact, I probably both like and respect them the more for it.

As I said in my preface to this book, I think all four of us are passion-ate believers in something. For Rachel and Simon it is their different faiths, for Antony it is his passionate championing of the rights of the Palestinian people – about which I have learnt a great deal during the writing of this book. For me, of course, the fight for the rights of my own gender is central to my view of the world and how it could be improved. We have all argued our case within these pages as well as we know how. Despite our differences, I think we are all driven by the same basic impulse towards social justice, fairness, a rich and robust market-place of ideas, and the desire for a better life for everyone.

And I hope that in its small way this book and the exchange of ideas within its pages can help advance exactly that.

Simon Smart

When we started planning this book I would sometimes joke with Antony and Jane that the whole concept would be ruined if they were to become religious converts during the writing process.

'Fat chance,' Jane would say with a smile, revealing her incredulity towards any Damascus road experience.

I guess it was equally unlikely that the scales would fall from my eyes, leading me to embrace non-belief (and that was never the point of the book). These days there are some formidable challenges to Christianity, so a robust faith requires careful thought regarding some of the objections voiced here. And that's a good thing. Faith that is anything more than a cultural artefact must be able to be tested in the fires of scepticism.

The questions Rachel, Antony, Jane and I have engaged with in *For God's Sake* relate to our different world views, and I believe are vitally important ones for anyone to ask. To go through life without taking time to reflect on what constitutes a good life, for instance, or what makes us human or what is the nature of the reality we find ourselves in, seems like a tragedy to which, in our age of entertainment and distraction, too many people willingly submit.

It's also a worthy exercise to try to critique our own world view and listen to others as they challenge our assumptions about life. It's been really good to have that opportunity here.

We should all be asking not only what our world view is, but also whether it is coherent, whether it takes account of all of life or leaves chunks of it out, and whether we have thought about and can live with the implications of our beliefs. Inasmuch as this book goes some way to encourage people to do that, it will be worthwhile.

I've enjoyed being able to write a book with people who, in various ways, see the world so differently from me. In light of the pretty nasty debates between atheists and the faithful in recent years, it's been good to be involved with people who could maintain a sense of humour even while dealing with weighty questions and disagreements.

I agree with Jane that, if we are going to be able to exist well together, we need to spend time understanding not only the things we have in common (and there are plenty of those) but also our differences and, vitally, *why* we hold certain positions on contested issues.

In taking on this project I always envisaged an extended dinner-party conversation where we each took turns to say what we think. As we wind up that conversation it's clear there's more to be said. We need more opportunities for meals and glasses of wine to clarify things we thought we heard others say, or press further and ask, 'Did you really mean that?' I know I'd like to keep discussing the importance of history and where historical errors, by both supporters and opponents of religion, have marred judgements about religion's past and likely future.

I still feel that among my co-authors there is a degree of misunderstanding about what Christianity, at its heart, is all about, and can't help feeling that to some extent cartoonish images of Christian faith still prevail in especially Antony and Jane's thinking. I have to acknowledge, though, that Christians sometimes behave in ways that contribute to this problem. I imagine Rachel would share with me huge reservations about a way of understanding life that either has no room for the non-material, or is inadequate to explain it. No doubt Antony and Jane would want to challenge my thoughts on this and other matters, and fair enough.

Humans of all stripes tend to be tribal and stick with 'their people'. That's understandable, but if that's all we do it's a recipe for disaster as our society becomes increasingly complex. It's easy and tempting to read only those we agree with, to seek only a perspective that will affirm our positions and prejudices. We can 'de-friend' or block those whose views don't gel with our own, but when we do so we run the risk of effectively living in a gated community. Religious people are guilty of this. When I lived in North America I came across the 'Christian Yellow Pages', which allowed you to deal with only Christian plumbers, mechanics or architects. Match that with your Christian school and university and you could go through life without having to engage with anyone substantially different from you. The idea is deeply unappealing to me.

Equally, non-believers can find it easy to ignore, mock and dismiss those who have a strong faith. And of course getting people from different religions to play nicely together is far from straightforward. But engage we must. Religion or spirituality isn't going anywhere. It remains a powerful part of the lives of the majority of people on this planet. That doesn't mean we all have to hold hands and sing 'Kumbaya' (or even John Lennon's 'Imagine') together, but we do need real interaction, thorough and respectful engagement – and friendship. The process of writing this book has affirmed my belief that this is not too much to hope for.

Rachel Woodlock

I've surprised myself writing this book. Having shifted from one religion to another, I can still see the beliefs and attitudes from my upbringing resonating like an ancient cosmic microwave in the background. As a young woman in my early twenties I left the Baha'i Faith for Islam because I fell in love with one of the world's greatest spiritual traditions, but also because of a mixture of frustration with the oh-so-human failings of Baha'i organisations, a need to assert my adult independence, and my search for a solution to the terrible mental depression I suffered in my twenties. I'm older now and, if not wiser, then certainly more mellow. I can look back and view my battles with kinder eyes.

I accept Simon's criticism that religious pluralism fails to resolve the problem of conflicting truth claims. I don't have an easy answer to that, except to say I think there's a difference between factuality and truth. No one thinks the phrase 'my heart is broken' is literally true, but we all instantly understand the reality of the rejected lover's pain. Poetry and literature reveal some of the deepest truths about the human condition, but we do not insist they be factually accurate to be worthy of our esteem. Likewise, profound religious truths are often expressed in metaphor and myth.

Did Jesus literally, physically, die on the cross and then return to life? Whatever happened to the first-century Palestinian rabbi, the story of his death and resurrection profoundly altered the course of human history, inspired acts of sacrificial love in countless numbers of his followers, and formed the basis for an unparalleled theology of forgiveness.

But the story also generated schism and persecution as Christians fought each other from earliest times, attempting to enforce this or that interpretation of the narrative as orthodoxy. In late antiquity, thousands of heretics were killed, and those remaining fled to the margins of Christendom, including Arabia, the birthplace of Islam. A different story was needed and it came in the form of the Qur'an.

I have learnt so much reading Jane, Antony and Simon's perspectives. They have been worthy interlocutors and I have come away with a new respect for their commitment to truth, justice and personal integrity.

They hold their beliefs and opinions with deep thought and consideration, as Socrates might commend.

As for me, I am still a seeker of truth and all I can offer is what partial mite I think to be true, knowing that final certainty is unachievable for any of us, at least in this life:

> My heart has become receptive for every form.
> It is a lush pasture for gazelles and a monastery for monks,
> A sanctuary for idols and the Ka'ba for circling pilgrims,
> The tablets of the Torah, and the script of the Qur'an,
> I serve the religion of love.
> Wherever love's caravan has borne me aloft,
> Such is my religion and my faith.[201]

Notes

First Words

1 The list of questions are influenced by the work of James W. Sire in *Naming the Elephant: Worldview as a Concept*, InterVarsity Press, Downers Grove, Illinois, 2004, p. 2.

Why I believe what I believe

2 'Defend the right to be offended', *openDemocracy*, 7 February 2005, http://www.opendemocracy.net/faith-europe_islam/article_2331.jsp.

3 All quotes from the Qur'an follow the pattern Q then chapter number, followed by verse number. So Q1:1 would be the first verse of the first chapter of the Qur'an. Unless otherwise indicated, all translations of the Qur'an are mine.

4 Alvin J. Fine, 'Birth is a Beginning', in *Gates of Repentance: The New Union Prayerbook for the Days of Awe*, Central Conference of American Rabbis, New York, 1978, pp. 283–4.

5 City Congregation website: http://www.citycongregation.org/about/what-we-believe/.

6 ABC TV, *Q&A*, broadcast 9 April 2012, http://www.abc.net.au/tv/qanda/txt/s3469101.htm.

What is the nature of the universe?

7 Abu Hamid Muhammad b. Muhammad al-Ghazali, *Tahafut al-Falasifah* [*The Incoherence of the Philosophers*], from the seventeenth section, on causality, my translation.

8 Ibid.

9 Ebrahim Schuitema, 'Atheism and the Modern World', *Zawia Ebrahim Media*, 22 May 2009, https://sites.google.com/site/zawiaebrahimmedia/audiodars2009.

10 Apart from the works already cited, for this chapter I drew on: William C. Chittick, *The Self-Disclosure of God: Principles of Ibn al-'Arabī's Cosmology*, State University of New York Press, Albany, 1998; and Majid Fakhry, *A History of Islamic Philosophy*, Columbia University Press, New York, 2004.

11 Alain de Botton, *Religion for Atheists: A Non-Believer's Guide to the Uses of Religion*, Hamish Hamilton, London, 2012, p. 12.

12 Ibid., p. 17.

13 Richard Dawkins, *River Out of Eden: A Darwinian View of Life*, Basic Books, New York, 1995, pp. 131–2.

14 Peter Hitchens, *The Rage Against God: How Atheism Led Me to Faith*, Zondervan, Grand Rapids, Michigan, 2010, pp. 205–6.

15 Timothy Keller, *The Reason for God: Belief in an Age of Skepticism*, Dutton, New York, 2008, p. 127.

16 Paul Davies, 'What Happened Before the Big Bang?', in Russell Stannard (ed.), *God for the 21st Century*, Templeton Press, West Conshohocken, Pennsylvania, 2000, p. 12.

17 Antony Flew, quoted in William Grimes, 'Antony Flew, Philosopher and Ex-atheist, Dies at 87', *New York Times*, 16 April 2010.

18 Francis Collins, quoted in Timothy Keller, *The Reason for God: Conversations on Faith and Life*, Dutton, New York, 2008, p. 129.

19 Hitchens, *The Rage Against God: How Atheism Led Me to Faith*, p. 11.

What is it to be a human being?

20 William Shakespeare, *Hamlet*, 2.2.293–97, Norton Shakespeare, New York, 1997, p. 1697.

21 Maxine Hancock, 'To Be Fully Human', *Crux*, vol. XXXVI, no. 4, December 2000, p. 34.

22 James W. Sire, *The Universe Next Door: A Basic Worldview Catalog*, 4th edition, InterVarsity Press, Downers Grove, Illinois, p. 66.

23 Hancock, 'To Be Fully Human', p. 35.

24 Tony Golsby-Smith, 'The Bible and Design', (unpublished article).

25 David Bentley Hart, *Atheist Delusions*, Yale University Press, New Haven, 2009, p. 163.

26 Ibid., p. 214.

27 Abu Hamid Muhammad b. Muhammad al-Ghazali, *The Alchemy of Happiness*, trans. Claud Field, J. Murray, London, 1909, p. 18, available at http://ghazali.org/books/alchemy.

28 Viktor Frankl, *Man's Search for Meaning: The Classic Tribute to Hope from the Holocaust*, Rider Books, UK, 2004, p. 49. Reprinted by permission of the Random House Group Limited.

29 Traditions relating Prophet Muhammad's sayings were collated into a number of different canons in the centuries after the Prophet's passing, the most famous of which are Sahih Bukhari and Sahih Muslim for Sunni Muslims and al-Kafi for Shi'i Muslims.

30 al-Ghazali, *The Alchemy of Happiness*, p. 120.

31 Bediuzzaman Said Nursi, *The Words: The Reconstruction of Islamic Belief and Thought*, The Risale-i Nur Collection, trans. Huseyin Akarsu, The Light, Inc., Somerset, New Jersey, 2005, p. 637.

32 'Abbas Effendi 'Abd al-Baha, *Selections from the Writings of 'Abdu'l-Baha*, Bahá'í World Centre, Haifa, 1982, p. 27.

33 William C. Chittick, *Fall of Adam*, lecture, available at https://itunes.apple.com/ie/podcast/islam-from-inside-podcast/id80620249. See also, William C. Chittick, 'The Fall of Adam', *Sufism: A Beginner's Guide*, Oneworld, Oxford, 2008, pp. 141–77.

34 Muhammad Iqbal, *Baal-i-Jibreel* [*Gabriel's Wing*], trans. Mustansir Mir, available at http://allamaiqbal.com/works/poetry/urdu/bal/translation/06gabriel.pdf. Note: Mir translates the first line as 'I am at fault, and in a foreign land' but here I have given the wording provided by Naeem Siddiqui available at http://www.allamaiqbal.com/works/poetry/urdu/bal/translation/part01/04.htm.

35 Apart from the works already cited, for this chapter I drew on: Fadhlalla Haeri, *Cosmology of the Self*, Zahra Publications, Cape Town, 1987; Athanasios N. Papathanasiou, 'Some Key Themes and Figures in Greek Theological Thought', in *The Cambridge Companion to*

Orthodox Christian Theology, Mary B. Cunningham and Elizabeth Theokritoff (eds), Cambridge University Press, Cambridge, 2008, pp. 218–31; Fazlur Rahman, *Major Themes of the Qur'ān*, Bibliotheca Islamica, Minneapolis, Minnesota, 1989; Sa'di, *The Gulistān* [*The Rose-Garden*], trans. Edward B. Eastwick, Stephen Austin, Hertford, UK, 1852; Ebrahim Schuitema, *Intent: Exploring the Core of Being Human*, Ampersand Press, Cape Town, South Africa, 2004; Ebrahim Schuitema, 'The Transformation of Our Terror to Awe', *Zawia Ebrahim Media*, 15 October 2011, https://sites.google.com/site/zawiaebrahimmedia/audiodars2011; and Frithjof Schuon, *Roots of the Human Condition*, Library of Traditional Wisdom, World Wisdom Books, Bloomington, Indiana, 1991.

36 Noam Chomsky in conversation with Mary Kostakidis, 'Problems of Knowledge and Freedom', Sydney Opera House, 3 November 2011, http://play.sydneyoperahouse.com/index.php/media/1502-Noam-Chomsky-Problems-Knowledge-Freedom.html.

37 Christopher R. Beha, 'The Literary Response to Radical Atheism', The Stream, *Harper's Magazine*, 9 July 2012.

38 Harry Ostrer, *Legacy: A Genetic History of the Jewish People*, Oxford University Press, New York, 2012, pp. xiii, xvi.

39 Radiohead, 'Fitter Happier', *OK Computer*, Parlophone, London, 1997.

What is a good life?

40 Frankl, *Man's Search for Meaning: The Classic Tribute to Hope from the Holocaust*, p. 105. Reprinted by permission of the Random House Group Limited.

41 Quoted in Pete Lowman, *A Long Way East of Eden: Could God Explain the Mess We're In?*, Paternoster Press, Carlisle, 2002, p. 48.

42 Quoted in Frederick Buechner, *Now and Then: A Memoir of Vocation*, HarperOne, New York, 1983, p. 50.

43 Quoted in Buechner, *Now and Then*, p. 50.

44 Hart, *Atheist Delusions*, 2009, p. 21.

45 Ibid., p. 22.

46 Christopher Hitchens, *Hitch-22: A Memoir*, Atlantic Books, London, 2010, p. 331.

47 Stott, *Why I Am a Christian*, p. 113.

48 Lowman, *A Long Way East of Eden*, p. 55.

49 Frederick Buechner, *Secrets in the Dark: A Life in Sermons*, HarperOne, New York, 2006, p. 157.

50 Bruce K. Waltke, *An Old Testament Theology: An Exegetical, Canonical, and Thematic Approach*, Zondervan, Grand Rapids, Michigan, 2007, p. 13.

51 Leon R. Kass, *The Hungry Soul: Eating and the Perfecting of Our Nature*, University of Chicago Press, Chicago and London, 1999, p. xx.

52 Hugh Mackay, *What Makes Us Tick: The Ten Desires that Drive Us*, Hachette, Sydney, 2010.

53 George F. Hourani, *Reason and Tradition in Islamic Ethics*, Cambridge University Press, Cambridge, 1985, p. 27.

54 Amira Sonbol, 'Women in Shari'ah Courts: A Historical and Methodological Discussion', *Fordham International Law Journal*, vol. 27, no. 1, 2003, http://ir.lawnet.fordham.edu/cgi/viewcontent.cgi?article=1918&context=ilj, pp. 232–33.

How do we know right from wrong?

55 More details can be found at https://en.wikipedia.org/wiki/Aramoana_massacre, retrieved 29 August 2012.

56 A mufti is a specialist in Islamic religious law.

57 Interview published at http://berkleycenter.georgetown.edu/interviews/a-discussion-with-sheikh-saleh-habimana-head-mufti-of-the-islamic-community-of-rwanda, retrieved 7 August 2012.

58 Margaret Smith, 'Rabi'a al-'Adawiyya al-Kaysiyya', in *Encyclopaedia of Islam*, new edition, C.E. Bosworth, E. Van Donzel, W.P. Heinrichs, and G. Lecomte (eds), Brill, Leiden, 1986–1993.

59 For this chapter I drew on: Majid Fakhry, *Ethical Theories in Islam*, Brill, Leiden, 1994; George Hourani, *Reason and Tradition in Islamic Ethics*, Cambridge University Press, Cambridge, 2007; Ayman

Shihadeh, *Teleological Ethics of Fakhr al-Din al-Razi*, Brill, Leiden, 2006; and podcasts available to download from *Zawia Ebrahim Media,* https://sites.google.com/site/zawiaebrahimmedia.

60 David Samuels, 'Q&A: Sam Harris', *Tablet*, 29 May 2012, http://www.tablemag.com/jewish-life-and-religion/100757/qa-sam-harris?all=1.

61 Dale S. Kuehne, *Sex and the iWorld: Rethinking Relationship beyond an Age of Individualism*, Baker Academic, Grand Rapids, Michigan, 2009, p. 71.

62 Dallas Willard, *Knowing Christ Today: Why We Can Trust Spiritual Knowledge*, HarperOne, New York, 2009, p. 82.

63 Sire, *The Universe Next Door*, p. 102.

64 Ibid., p. 227.

65 Nicholas Wolterstorff, *Justice: Rights and Wrongs*, Princeton University Press, Princeton New Jersey, 2008, p. 393.

66 Peter Hitchens, 'Without God There Can Be No Good', ABC Religion and Ethics webpage, 12 April 2012, http://www.abc.net.au/religion/articles/2012/04/12/3475545.htm.

67 Willard, *Knowing Christ Today*, p. 92.

How do we account for conscience, beauty, love?

68 Nick Cave, *The Secret Life of the Love Song/The Flesh Made Word: Two Lectures*, Mute Records, London, 2000.

69 Ibid.

70 Plantinga, *Where the Conflict Really Lies*, pp. 131–2.

71 Ibid., p. 132.

72 Kass, *The Hungry Soul: Eating and the Perfecting of Our Nature*, p. xi.

73 Ibid., pp. 9–10.

74 A. C. Grayling, 'Grayling's Question', *Prospect*, 26 July 2008, http://www.prospectmagazine.co.uk/magazine/10240-graylingsquestion.

75 Ibid., p. 205.

76 Ibid., pp. 205–6.

77 Quoted in Peter Vardy, *Being Human: Fulfilling Genetic and Spiritual Potential*, (Harper Collins) Darton, Longman & Todd, London, 2003, p. 191.

78 Ibid.

79 Lizette Alvarez, 'For Young Jews, a Service Says, "Please, Do Text"', *New York Times*, 17 September 2012, http://www.nytimes.com/2012/09/18/us/for-young-jews-a-service-says-please-do-text.html?_r=0.

80 Martin E. Marty and R. Scott Appleby (eds), *The Fundamentalism Project*, University of Chicago Press, Chicago, 1993–2004.

81 Kerim Fenari, *The Wahhabi who Loved Beauty*, http://www.masud.co.uk/ISLAM/misc/wobb.htm.

Where do we find hope?

82 David Marr, 'Stonewalled', *Good Weekend*, 13 April 2012, http://www.smh.com.au/lifestyle/stonewalled-20120413-1wyec.html.

83 Susannah Moran, 'Islam Defies the Slow Loss of Faith', *The Australian*, 22 June 2012, http://www.theaustralian.com.au/national-affairs/islam-defies-the-slow-loss-of-faith/story-fn59niix-1226404867350.

84 Miroslav Volf, *A Public Faith: How Followers of Christ Should Serve the Common Good*, Brazos Press, Grand Rapids, Michigan, 2011, p. 58.

85 Ibid., p. 60.

86 Ibid., p. 61.

87 Alasdair MacIntyre, *After Virtue: A Study in Moral Theory*, 2nd edn, University of Notre Dame Press, 2007, Notre Dame, Indiana, p. 216.

88 Frederick Buechner, *The Longing for Home: Recollections and Reflections*, HarperSanFrancisco, San Francisco, 1996, p. 110.

89 Volf, *A Public Faith*, p. 56.

90 Ibid.

91 Ibid.

92 Quoted in Frederick Buechner, *Telling the Truth: The Gospel as Tragedy, Comedy, and Fairy Tale*, HarperOne, New York, 1977, p. 81.

93 Fazlur Rahman, *Major Themes of the Qur'ān*, 2nd edn, University of Chicago Press, Chicago and London, 2009, p. 30.

94 Issues Deliberation Australia/America, *Australia Deliberates: Muslims and Non-Muslims in Australia*, Final Report available at: http://ida.org.au/content.php?p=dpprelease.

95 Australian Bureau of Statistics, *Reflecting a Nation: Stories from the 2011 Census, 2012–2013*, available at: http://www.abs.gov.au/ausstats/abs@.nsf/Lookup/2071.0main+features902012-2013.

Doesn't religion cause most of the conflict in the world?

96 'Persecution of Christians in the Soviet Union', *Wikipedia* available at: http://en.wikipedia.org/wiki/Persecution_of_Christians_in_the_Soviet_Union.

97 I have changed their names to protect their privacy, particularly as many Baha'is who fled to Australia still have relatives living in Iran.

98 See Mark Perry, *A New Dress for Mona: A Play*, 2010, http://www.adressformona.org/play/ANewDressForMona2010.pdf, retrieved 20 August 2012.

99 Charles Kimball, *When Religion Becomes Evil: Five Warning Signs*, HarperCollins, San Francisco, 2008, p. 47.

100 It's worth noting the Qur'an doesn't use the term 'holy war' to describe the defensive measure the early Muslims were forced to employ, even though the word jihad – 'struggle' – is often mistranslated into English as such.

101 Kimball, *When Religion Becomes Evil*, p. 31.

102 Apart from the works already cited, for this chapter I drew on: Luc Reychler, 'Religion and Conflict', *International Journal of Peace Studies*, vol. 2, no. 1, 1997, pp. 19–38; Mark Sedgwick, 'Inspiration and the Origins of Global Waves of Terrorism', *Studies in Conflict & Terrorism*, vol. 30, no. 2, 2007, pp. 97–112; Asma Afsaruddin, *The First Muslims: History and Memory*, Oneworld, Oxford, 2007; and *Tafsir al-Jalalayn*, available at http://www.altafsir.com/Al-Jalalayn.asp.

103 Bryan Appleyard, 'The God Wars', *New Statesman*, 28 February 2012, http://www.newstatesman.com/religion/2012/02/neo-atheism-atheists-dawkins.

104 Ibid.

105 Robert Winnett, 'Britain being overtaken by "militant secularists", says Baroness Warsi', *The Telegraph*, 13 February 2012.

106 Jonathan Wynne-Jones, 'Tony Blair Believed God Wanted Him to Go to War to Fight Evil, Claims His Mentor', *The Telegraph*, London, 23 May 2009, http://www.telegraph.co.uk/news/religion/5373525/Tony-Blair-believed-God-wanted-him-to-go-to-war-to-fight-evil-claims-his-mentor.html.

107 Christopher Hitchens, *God Is Not Great: How Religion Poisons Everything*, Twelve, New York, 2007, p. 6. By permission of Grand Central Publishing. All rights reserved.

108 Ibid., p. 56.

109 Quoted in Miroslav Volf, 'Christianity and Violence', Boardman Lectureship in Christian Ethics, XXXVIII, Paper 2, 3 January 2002, http://repository.upenn.edu/boardman/2, p. 7.

110 Hart, *Atheist Delusions*, p. 45.

111 Ibid.

112 Greg Austin, Todd Kranock and Thom Oommen, 'God and War: An Audit and an Exploration', http://news.bbc.co.uk/2/shared/spl/hi/world/04/war_audit_pdf/pdf/war_audit.pdf, p. 2.

113 Hart, *Atheist Delusions*, p. 13.

114 Volf, 'Christianity and Violence', p. 8.

115 Ibid., p. 5.

116 Tomas Halik, *Night of the Confessor: Christian Faith in an Age of Uncertainty*, Doubleday Religion, New York, 2012, p. 160.

117 Ibid.

How can we believe in the supernatural in an age of science?

118 Leesha McKenny, 'Churchgoers Keen to Take a Pew Despite Their Disbelief', *Sydney Morning Herald*, 7 January 2012, http://www.smh.com.au/nsw/churchgoers-keen-to-take-a-pew-despite-their-disbelief-20120106-1posf.html.

119 Damon Young, 'If God is Dead or Dying, Why Criticise Religion?' The Drum Opinion, 4 May 2012, http://www.abc.net.au/unleashed/3990158.html.

120 Mike Lofgren, *The Party Is Over: How the Republicans Went Crazy, Democrats Became Useless, and the Middle Class Got Shafted*, Viking, New York, 2012, p. 129.

121 Laurence R. Iannaccone and Eli Berman, 'Religious Extremism: The Good, the Bad, and the Deadly', *Public Choice*, vol. 128, no. 1, 2006, p. 113.

122 Rodney Stark, 'Secularization, R.I.P.', *Sociology of Religion*, vol. 60, no. 3, 1999, pp. 249–73.

123 Gary Bouma, *Australian Soul: Religion and Spirituality in the Twenty-first Century*, Cambridge University Press, Melbourne, 2006, p. 5.

124 Robert Putnam, interview by Andrew West, 'Busting the Myths About American Religion,' *Religion and Ethics Report*, ABC Radio National, 13 June 2012, http://www.abc.net.au/radionational/programs/religionandethicsreport/busting-the-myths-about-american-religion/4068710#transcript.

125 David Martin, *On Secularization: Towards a Revised General Theory*, Ashgate, Aldershot, 2005, pp. 17–25.

126 Rodney Stark, Laurence R. Iannaccone and Roger Finke, 'Religion, Science, and Rationality', *American Economic Review*, vol. 86, no. 2, 1996, p. 435.

127 Ibid.

128 M. Shoja Mohammadali and R. Shane Tubbs, 'The History of Anatomy in Persia', *Journal of Anatomy*, vol. 210, no. 4, 2007, p. 369.

129 Huston Smith, *Why Religion Matters: The Fate of the Human Spirit in an Age of Disbelief*, HarperCollins, New York, 2001, p. 196.

130 Derren Brown, 'Fear and Faith', *Derren Brown: The Specials*, television broadcast, Channel 4, UK, broadcast 16 November 2012, http://www.channel4.com/programmes/derren-brown-the-specials/episode-guide/series-14/episode-4.

131 Apart from the works already cited, for this chapter I drew on: Salim T. S. al-Hassani, Elizabeth Woodcock and Rabah Saoud (eds), *1001 Inventions: Muslim Heritage in Our World*, 2nd edn, Foundation for Science, Technology and Civilization, Manchester, 2007; Jonathan Lyons, *The House of Wisdom: How the Arabs Transformed Western Civilization*, Bloomsbury, London, 2010; and W. Jay Wood, *Epistemology: Becoming Intellectually Virtuous: Contours of Christian Philosophy*, InterVarsity Press, Downers Grove, Illinois, 1998.

132 Robert Banks, *And Man Created God: Is God a Human Invention?*, Lion Hudson, Oxford, 2011.

133 Alvin Plantinga points out that many of these theories contradict each other. Religion is adaptive according to some, and non-adaptive or even maladaptive according to others. Some will say that religion emerges from group selection while others say group selection is impossible. (Plantinga, *Where the Conflict Really Lies*, p. 137.)

134 Ibid., p. 140.

135 Ibid., p. 149.

136 John Gray, 'Joseph Conrad, Our Contemporary', in John Gray, *Heresies: Against Progress and Other Illusions*, Granta, London, 2004, pp. 106–7.

137 Quoted in Brian Rosner, 'Reason Has its Place, but the Human Heart Yearns for Awe', *The Australian*, 13 September 2012, http://www.theaustralian.com.au/national-affairs/opinion/reason-has-its-place-but-the-human-heart-yearns-for-awe/story-e6frgd0x-1226472936686.

138 Ibid.

139 Peter Popham, 'No Secularism Please, We're British', *The Independent*, 15 February 2012, http://www.independent.co.uk/news/uk/home-news/no-secularism-please-were-british-6917549.html.

140 Kelefa Sanneh, 'The Hell-raiser: A Megachurch Pastor's Search for a More Forgiving Faith', *New Yorker*, 26 November 2012, pp. 56–65.

141 Julian Baggani, 'Is Religion Really Under Threat?', *The Guardian*, 14 February 2012, http://www.guardian.co.uk/world/2012/feb/14/is-religion-really-under-threat.

142 Ibid.

How can we believe in a good God when there is so much suffering in the world?

143 Simon Smart, *Bright Lights Dark Nights: The Enduring Faith of 13 Remarkable Australians*, Blue Bottle Books, 2008, p. 22.

144 John Dickson, *A Spectator's Guide to World Religions: An Introduction to the Big Five*, Blue Bottle Books, Sydney, 2004, p. 60.

145 Christopher Hitchens, *Mortality*, Allen & Unwin, Sydney, 2012, pp. 4, 6.

146 Hart, *The Doors of the Sea: Where Was God in the Tsunami?*, Eerdmanns, Grand Rapids, Michigan, 2005, p. 22.

147 Romans 8:22 (New International Version).

148 John Lennox, interviewed by John Dickson, 'Hope for a Mucked-up World', Centre for Public Christianity, 8 August 2008, https://publicchristianity.org/library/lennoxvids#.UCxZDURhg7A.

149 For this chapter I drew on: Muhiyyi'd-din Ibn al-'Arabi, *The Seals of Wisdom (Fusus al-Hikam)*, trans. Aisha Bewley, 17 November 2012, available at http://bewley.virtualave.net/fusus.html; and Irfan Omar, 'Khiḍr in the Islamic Tradition', *The Muslim World*, vol. 83, nos 3–4, 1993, pp. 279–94.

150 Benjamin Kerstein, 'Yes, All Criticism of Israel is Anti-Semitic!', *Jerusalem Post*, 20 May 2012, http://www.jpost.com/Opinion/Op-EdContributors/Article.aspx?id=270755.

How do we account for evil?

151 Alice Miller, 'Adolf-Hitler, How Could a Monster Succeed in Blinding a Nation?', trans. Hildegarde and Hunter Hannum, originally published in *Spiegel Special*, 2/1998, p. 92, http://www.naturalchild.org/alice_miller/adolf_hitler.html.

152 Quoted in Jonathan Glover, *Humanity: A Moral History of the Twentieth Century*, Pimlico, London, 1999, p. 61.

153 Henri Blocher, *Evil and the Cross: An Analytical Look at the Problem of Pain*, InterVarsity Press, Downers Grove, Illinois, 1990, p. 11.

154 Margaret Somerville, *The Ethical Canary: Science, Society and the Human Spirit*, McGill-Queen's University Press, Montreal, 2004, p. 296.

155 Alexander Solzhenitsyn, *The Gulag Archipelago*, Vol. I, Part I, Chapter 4, trans. Thomas P. Whitney, Harper and Row, New York, 1974, p. 168.

156 Aleksandr Solzhenitsyn, *The Gulag Archipelago*, Vol. II, Part IV, Chapter I, trans. Thomas P. Whitney, Harper and Row, New York, 1974, p. 615.

157 Blocher, *Evil and the Cross*, p 13.

158 Ibid., p. 14.

159 Tom Wright, *Simply Christian*, SPCK, London, 2006, p. 4.

160 Blocher, *Evil and the Cross*, p. 84.

161 Unicef, *Committing to Child Survival: A Promise Renewed*, Progress Report 2012, http://www.unicef.org/videoaudio/PDFs/APR_Progress_Report_2012_final.pdf.

162 Blocher, *Evil and the Cross*, p. 130.

163 Ibid.

164 Erik Larson, *In the Garden of Beasts: Love, Terror, and an American Family in Hitler's Berlin*, Crown, New York, 2011.

165 Ibid., p. 33.

166 Gregory S. Paul, 'Cross-national Correlations of Quantifiable Societal Health with Popular Religiosity and Secularism in the Prosperous Democracies', *Journal of Religion & Societies*, vol. 7, 2005, http://moses.creighton.edu/JRS/2005/2005-11.pdf.

167 M. Scott Peck, *People of the Lie: The Hope for Healing Human Evil*, 2nd ed., Simon & Schuster, New York, 1998, p. 75.

168 Frithjof Schuon, *Roots of the Human Condition*, The Library of Traditional Wisdom, World Wisdom Books, Bloomington, Indiana, 1991, p. 112.

Doesn't religion oppress women?

169 Quoted in Sharon Otterman and Ray Rivera, 'Ultra-Orthodox Shun Their Own for Reporting Child Sexual Abuse', *New York Times*, 9 May 2012, http://www.nytimes.com/2012/05/10/nyregion/ultra-orthodox-jews-shun-their-own-for-reporting-child-sexual-abuse.html?pagewanted=all.

170 Michael M. Grynbaum, 'Ultra-Orthodox Jews Rally to Discuss Risks of Internet', *New York Times*, 20 May 2012, http://www.nytimes.com/2012/05/21/nyregion/ultra-orthodox-jews-hold-rally-on-internet-at-citi-field.html.

171 Christopher Hope, 'We Will Legalise Gay Marriage by 2015, Says David Cameron', *The Telegraph*, 24 July 2012, http://www.telegraph.co.uk/news/politics/9425174/We-will-legalise-gay-marriage-by-2015-says-David-Cameron.html.

172 Christopher Hitchens, *God Is Not Great: How Religion Poisons Everything*, Allen and Unwin, Sydney, 2007, p. 10.

173 Christopher Hitchens, 'Images in a Rearview Mirror', 15 November 2001, *The Nation*, http://www.thenation.com/article/images-rearview-mirror.

174 Quoted in Lila Abu-Lughod, 'Do Muslim Women Really Need Saving? Anthropological Reflections on Cultural Relativism and Its Others', *American Anthropologist*, vol. 104, no. 3, 2002, p. 784.

175 Annie Van Sommer and Samuel Marinus Zwemer (eds), *Our Moslem Sisters: A Cry of Need from Lands of Darkness Interpreted by Those Who Heard It*, Fleming H. Revell Company, New York, 1907, p. 9, available at http://www.gutenberg.org/files/30178/30178-h/30178-h.htm.

176 Abu-Lughod, 'Do Muslim Women Really Need Saving?', p. 789.

177 Christina Ho, 'Muslim Women's New Defenders: Women's Rights, Nationalism and Islamophobia in Contemporary Australia', *Women's Studies International Forum*, vol. 30, 2007, p. 295.

178 Beverly Mack and Jean Boyd, *One Woman's Jihad: Nana Asma'u, Scholar and Scribe*, Indiana University Press, Bloomington, Indiana, 2000, p. 91.

179 Negar Mottahedeh, 'Ruptured Spaces and Effective Histories: The Unveiling of the Bábí Poetess Qurrat al-'Ayn-Táhirih in the Gardens of Badasht', in Sabir Afaqi (ed.), *Táhirih in History: Perspectives on Qurrat'l-'Ayn from East and West*, Studies in the Bábí and Bahá'í Religions 16, pp. 203–30, Kalimát Press, Los Angeles, 2004, p. 204.

180 Fadwa El Guindi, *Veil: Modesty, Privacy, Resistance*, Oxford, Berg, 1999; see also Rachel Woodlock, 'Many Hijabs: Interpretative Approaches to the Questions of Islamic Female Dress', in Tugrul Keskin (ed.), *The Sociology of Islam: Secularism, Economy and Politics*, pp. 395–417, Reading, Ithaca Press, 2011.

181 Yedida Kalfon Stillman, *Arab Dress: A Short History: From the Dawn of Islam to Modern Times*, Norman A. Stillman (ed.), 2nd edn, Brill, Leiden, 2000, p. 139.

182 Sarah J. Gervais, Theresa K. Vescio, Jens Förster, Anne Maass and Caterina Suitner, 'Seeing Women as Objects: The Sexual Body Part Recognition Bias', *European Journal of Social Psychology*, vol. 42, no. 6, 2012, pp. 743–53.

183 Khaled Abou El Fadl, 'Terrorism Is at Odds with Islamic Tradition', *Los Angeles Times*, 22 August 2001, available at http://www.scholarofthehouse.org/terisatodwit.html.

184 Al-Haqq, 'the Real', is one of God's names frequently used by Ibn 'Arabi.

185 Ibn 'Arabi, *Fusus al-Hikam*, Dar al-Kitab al-'Arabi, Beirut, n.d., p. 217.

186 Apart from the works already cited, for this chapter I drew on: Asma Afsaruddin, *The First Muslims: History and Memory*, Oneworld, Oxford, 2007; Camille Adams Helminski, *Women of Sufism: A*

Hidden Treasure; Writings and Stories of Mystic Poets, Scholars and Saints, Shambhala, Boston, Massachusetts, 2003; Chandra Talpade Mohanty, 'Under Western Eyes: Feminist Scholarship and Colonial Discourses', *Feminist Review*, vol. 30, 1988, pp. 61–88; Sachiko Murata, *The Tao of Islam: A Sourcebook on Gender Relationships in Islamic Thought*, State University of New York Press, Albany, 1992; Basim Musallam, *Sex and Society in Islam: Birth Control Before the Nineteenth Century*, Cambridge University Press, Cambridge, 1983; 'Muslim Women: Past and Present', WISE, http://www.wisemuslimwomen.org/muslimwomen; Annemarie Schimmel, *My Soul Is a Woman: The Feminine in Islam*, Continuum, New York, 1997; Elora Shehabuddin, 'Gender and the Figure of the "Moderate Muslim": Feminism in the Twenty-first Century', in Judith Butler and Elizabeth Weed (eds), *The Question of Gender: Joan W. Scott's Critical Feminism*, 21st Century Studies 4, pp. 102–42, Indiana University Press, Bloomington, 2011; and Amina Wadud, *Qur'ān and Woman: Rereading the Sacred Text from a Woman's Perspective*, Oxford University Press, New York, 1999.

187 Iain Provan, 'Why Bother with the Old Testament Regarding Gender and Sexuality?', in Maxine Hancock (ed.), *Christian Perspectives on Gender, Sexuality and Community*, Regent College Publishing, Vancouver, 2003, p. 41.

188 Lynn H. Cohick, 'Why Women Followed Jesus: A Discussion of Female Piety', *Scottish Bulletin of Evangelical Theology*, vol. 25, no. 2, 2007, p. 191.

What has religion done for us anyway?

189 A pre-Islamic Middle Eastern religious group.

190 Quoted in Sachiko Murata, *The Tao of Islam: A Sourcebook on Gender Relationships in Islamic Thought*, State University of New York Press, Albany, 1992, p. 33.

191 Apart from the works already cited, for this chapter I drew on: Sachiko Murata and William C. Chittick, *Vision of Islam*, I. B. Tauris, London, 2006; and Patrice C. Brodeur, 'Religion', in Jane Dammen

McAulliffe (ed.), *Encyclopaedia of the Qur'ān*, vol. 4 P–Sh, Brill, Leiden, 2004, pp. 395–8.

192 Jack Ewing, 'Some Religious Leaders See a Threat as Europe Grows More Secular', *New York Times*, 19 September 2012, http://www. nytimes.com/2012/09/20/world/europe/circumcision-debate-in-europe-reflects-deeper-tensions.html?pagewanted=all&_r=0.

193 Ibid.

194 Jürgen Habermas, *Religion and Rationality: Essays on Reason, God, and Modernity*, MIT Press, Cambridge, Massachusetts, 2002, p. 149.

195 Alain de Botton, *Religion for Atheists*, p. 224.

196 Ibid., p. 219.

197 'Richard Dawkins Lends his Support to the King James Bible Trust', King James Bible Trust, 19 February 2010, http://www. kingjamesbibletrust.org/news/2010/02/19/richard-dawkins-lends-his-support-to-the-king-james-bible-trust.

198 Alain de Botton, *Religion for Atheists*, pp. 32–3.

199 *BRW Magazine*, June 29 – July 5, 2006, p 56. (These were ranked according to gross annual revenue.)

200 Francis Spufford, *Unapologetic: Why, Despite Everything, Christianity Still Makes Surprising Emotional Sense*, Faber, London, 2012, pp. 46–7.

Last Words

201 Ibn 'Arabi, *Tarjuman al-Ashwaq*, my translation.

Acknowledgements

Heartfelt thanks to our publisher Ingrid Ohlsson, for her enthusiastic response to the original idea and her skill in making it happen; to our editors Vanessa Pellatt and Nicola Young, and to the Pan Macmillan team for bringing this project to completion with professionalism and style.

Jane

It has been an absolute pleasure writing this book with Antony, Simon and Rachel, and I thank them all for their skill, thoughtfulness and natural good manners. Thanks also to my family Ralph, Polly and Charlotte, for being so patient with all the 'stuff' I do, and my parents Kate and Andy for bringing me up to think for myself.

Antony

Thanks to my parents Violet and Jeffrey for providing love and endless support. I have no atheist deities to thank but countless friends, colleagues and opponents in the last decades, in Australia and overseas, have engaged me on vital issues of the day, making me the person I am today – curious but rarely settled. Finally, and not least, thank you to Jane, Simon and Rachel for believing in the power of argument to challenge and provoke.

Simon

Thanks to Jane, Antony and Rachel for their willingness to tackle important and difficult questions with grace, respect and humour. I thank my dad and mum, Peter and Elizabeth, for introducing me to authentic Christian belief and practice. Thanks to my fabulous wife Michele for invaluable and much-needed editing advice. Thanks to my colleagues at the Centre for Public Christianity: Al, Justine, John, Hugh, Vaughan, Kerryn and Richard. And thanks to my non-believing mates for friendships that span years and for never allowing me a faith that could be unthinking or complacent.

Rachel

I would like to thank my fellow authors Jane, Antony and Simon – three of the finest minds and debating partners one could ask for – as well as Professors Abdullah Saeed, Gary Bouma, and Greg Barton, and Dr Pete Lentini; all my wonderful Muslim friends, most especially Waleed Aly and Susan Carland, along with Waleed's mum Salwa; and the quirky assortment of family members that Allah most holy placed in my life: my mum Gail; my dad Noel; my brothers Evan and Michael; my parents-in-law Pat and Mary; and finally my patient, kind and wise husband John and the light of our life, our beloved daughter Yasmin Rabia.

Index

9/11 *attacks, see* September 11 attacks

'A'isha, 240
ABC Religion & Ethics website, 3
'Abd al-Baha', 56
Aboriginal Dreaming, 167
abortion, 54, 100, 214–15, 231–2, 234, 235, 246, 260
Abou El Fadl, Khaled, 243
Abu-Lughod, Lila, 238
accountability, 257
Adam and Eve, 57–8, 136, 247
al-'Adawiyya, Rabi'a, 91, 240
adultery, 96
  stoning for, 97, 203, 208, 228
Afsaruddin, Asma, 241
Ahmed, Leila, 238, 241
AIDS, 191–2, 228, 236, 245, 260
Al-Ghazzali Centre
  Mizaan project, 143
Ali, Ayaan Hirsi, 153, 238, 278, 279
Al-Qaeda
  suicide bombers, 88, 119
American Atheists Convention 2012, 130
anti-Semitism, 16
Antony, Professor Louise, 134
Anwar, Zainah, 241
Apollo space missions, 38
Appleyard, Bryan, 153
Arab Spring, 36, 228
Aramoana massacre (NZ), 89
al-Arefe, Mohamed, 129
art
  pleasure and, 118
  transcendence of, 115
Asian tsunami, 187
Asma'u, Nana, 239
atheism, 7–10, 27–31
  concern with questions, 28
  on evil, 203–6
  on hope, 139–41

materialist atheism, 33
militant atheism, 36, 71, 178
new atheism, 153, 160, 276, 277–8, 279
on oppression of women, 230–6
on right vs wrong, 98–101
significance of beliefs, 268–72
state-imposed 147
on suffering, 188–9, 193–4
on supernatural beliefs, 165–9
view of beauty, 116–21
view of conflict, 157–9, 162–3
view of good life, 78–81
atonement, 215
Attwood, Margaret, 271
Austin, Greg, 162
Australia Deliberates: Muslims and
  Non-Muslims in Australia conference,
  143

Babi movement, 149, 239
Babism, 150, 239
  female martyrs, 150
  see also Babi movement; Baha'i Faith
Bach, Johann Sebastian, 112
Baggani, Julian, 183
Baha'i Faith, 11–12, 149–50, 239, 253, 283
Bali bombings, 158
Banks, Robert, 176
Baraghani, Fatimih
  see Tahirih
Barlas, Asma, 241
Barry, Sebastian, 210
Basra, Rabi'a of,
  see al-'Adawiyya, Rabi'a
beauty
  atheist Jewish view of, 121–4
  atheist view of, 116–21
  Christian view of, 111–15
  holy places and, 121–2
  reproduction and, 116–18

Index

Index

Global Atheist Convention
  2010 convention, 279
  2012 convention, 30, 98, 153, 279
globalisation, 148
God
  demise of, 39
  as father, 106
  fingerprints of, 39
  personal nature of, 41, 106, 175, 181
  and suffering, 187–92
golden ratio, 116–17
golden rule, 56, 99, 118, 268
good life
  atheist Jewish view of, 67–71
  atheist view of, 78–81
  Christian view of, 72–7
  Muslim view of, 82–4
gratitude impulse, 8
Gray, David, 89
Gray, John, 178–9
Grayling, A. C., 114
Green Menace, 143
Guthrie, Sergeant Stewart, 89

Habermas, Jürgen, 264
Habimana, Sheikh Saleh, 89–90
Haddad, Yvonne, 238
Hagar, 240
Haiti earthquake, 94
Halappanavar, Savita, 234, 235
Hanson, Pauline, 143
happiness, 76, 193
Happiness and Its Causes conference, 76
Harris, Sam, 95–6, 153, 278
Hart, David Bentley, 49–50, 73–4, 162
al-Haruriyya, Ghazala, 240
Hazrat Babajan, Gulrukh, 241
Heaven, 54
Heilman, Samuel, 225
Hemingway, Ernest, 253
Henry VIII, 269
Henson, Jim, 219–20
Hepburn, Audrey, 11
al-Hibri, Azizah, 241
Hijau, Raju, 241
Hindu faith, 68
Hitchens, Christopher, 39, 43, 71, 74, 98, 153, 154, 164, 183, 189, 227, 278
  opposition to Islam, 227–8, 261

Hitchens, Peter, 39, 43, 106
Hitler, Adolf, 57, 158, 212
  see also Holocaust
HIV, 119
Ho, Christina, 238
Holocaust, 14, 57, 72, 88
  survivors, 16, 55, 212–14
  see also Hitler, Adolf; National Socialism (Nazis)
holy places, 121–2
holy war, 151
homosexuality
  in Catholic Church, 154–5
  gay marriage, 226
  gay rights, 272, 278
  gay spring, 131
  in Muslim world, 130–1
  honour killings, 155, 237
hope, 127–43
  atheist Jewish view of, 129–33
  atheist view of, 139–41
  Christian view of, 21, 134–8
  Muslim view of, 142–3
Hourani, George, 83
Human Genome Project, 40
human rights, 104
  see also humanity
humanism
  shift to, 135
Humanistic Judaism, 15
humanity
  as advanced machines, 48
  atheist Jewish view of, 61–4
  atheist view of, 51–4
  Christian view of, 47–50
  faith in goodness of, 78
  in God's image, 49, 74, 76, 104
  humans as simply animals, 51
  Muslim view of, 55–60
  as tribal species, 61
  universality of, 62
  see also desires; ethnic communities
humility, 81, 265
Hussein, Saddam, 151–2, 217

Iannoccone, Laurence, 171
ibn 'Abd al-Wahhab, Muhammad, 125
ibn Shariq, al-Akhnas, 151
Ihram, Silma, 241

Index